The Puddin Hill Cookbook

RECOLLECTIONS & RECIPES

by Mary "Pud" Lauderdale Kearns

Copyright © 1988
by Mary of Puddin Hill, Inc., Greenville, Texas

Illustrations copyright © 1988
by Mary of Puddin Hill, Inc., Greenville, Texas

All rights reserved.

No part of this publication may be reproduced, stored in a retrieval system or transmitted in any form or by any means, electronic, mechanical, photocopying or otherwise without the prior written permission of the publisher.

Library of Congress Number 88-90762

Printed by Hart Graphics, Inc.
8000 Shoal Creek Blvd.
Austin, Texas 78758

Table of Contents

FOREWORD
    By Mary Faulk Koock i

INTRODUCTION
    By Mary Horton Lauderdale ii

AUTHOR'S NOTE & ACKNOWLEDGEMENTS iii

CHAPTER ONE
    Grandmother's Legacy 1

CHAPTER TWO
    Gertrude and Hal 19

CHAPTER THREE
    The Rest of the Horton Crowd 57

CHAPTER FOUR
    Sam and Mary 79

CHAPTER FIVE
    The Puddin Hill Store 115

CHAPTER SIX
    Pud and Mike 145

CHAPTER SEVEN
    Weddings to Wakes 167

CHAPTER EIGHT
    Good Times at Club Lake 203

CHAPTER NINE
    A Puddin Hill Christmas 223

CHAPTER TEN
    When Company Comes 249

CHAPTER ELEVEN
    Something Extra 275

To my husband Mike . . .
who washed the dishes.

Foreword

In this wonderful book Pud Kearns takes us on a delightful culinary journey back through five generations to the time when her great-great-grandparents came from Tennessee to Texas and built their log homes on Puddin Hill. The author gives us a colorful account of this event and tells why Puddin Hill was so named. Incredible as it seems, the Horton family has lived all these years on this very same land. Today Puddin Hill is identified around the world with Mary of Puddin Hill Fruitcakes, one of the largest mail-order food businesses.

True to the Horton legacy, each generation has passed on to the next not only their recipes, but their sense of values; close family ties, marvelous stories, a real caring for their family, friends, and their community. We must concede the real Horton hallmark is that of genuine Texas hospitality and the fine food it has generated. That is really what this book is all about.

This is a perfect time for Pud to "go public" with this rare collection of down-to-earth recipes as the food trends nowadays are definitely back to the basics.

Great-great-grandmother Horton's Ham Baked in Milk, Fried Roastin Ears, and Drunk Fruit Chess Pie are just the beginning. There's Forest, a long time family friend, who concocts a fantastic dessert that inspires the guest to burst forth in singing Glory Glory Hallelujah and a taste of sophistication in well known cooking expert Nancy Parker's Grapefruit Sorbet that is superior. The pages are filled with one tantalizing recipe after the other and are laced together with fascinating anecdotes and bits of history.

But just a word of warning to those who say they only like to read cookbooks but not use them; The Puddin Hill Cookbook-Recollections and Recipes may compel you into the kitchen. The recipes are too irresistible and easy to follow. Pud shares her thoughts on relaxed expressive entertaining, whether it's having a few friends over for herbal tea and Mama Carlisle's Tea Cakes or something exotic like Mary and Pud's Chocolate and Champagne Celebration. It should be personal. It's not the elaborate techniques, but the warmth, friendship, and individual style that makes for a memorable occasion and it's in this book.

              Mary Faulk Koock
              June, 1988
              Austin, Texas

Introduction

By Mary Horton Lauderdale

The phrase "proud as a peacock" certainly applies to my feelings about my daughter and about this cookbook. Pud has done a fine job, and now the dream of three generations has finally been realized.

My husband Sam and I have watched her work through all the long hours of recipe testing, writing and rewriting, and proofreading time and time again. The deadlines have been close and the frustrations too many to count, but it has been worth it all to see the outcome. We always knew she had the determination to do it. An added plus has been the delight we have taken in seeing her writing style develop — she has really brought the family stories to life.

We have all enjoyed the research into the heritage of Puddin Hill that has been required for this book. "Pud's Project" has included my entire family — brothers, sister, in-laws, nieces and nephews. In fact, we have promised ourselves to continue learning more. There are lots of little "mysteries" and unanswered questions that have been raised, and now we are all curious about them.

My mother, Gertrude Horton, would have been so pleased to know her dream of compiling all those family recipes into a cookbook has been fulfilled. I know she would say that she could not have done nearly as good a job as Pud has done.

Lastly, Sam and I know that some day we will be leaving Mary of Puddin Hill in good hands. Pud and her husband Mike will carry on the principles of quality and customer care that we have believed in for the 40 years we have been in business.

To a wonderful daughter . . . you have done a magnificent job. I love you.

Mother

Author's Note

This book is the culmination of ten years of work. It began as a promise I made to myself and my grandmother, Gertrude Horton, after her death in 1977. When the family was going through her papers, twenty-one recipe boxes were found! Grandmother was well-known throughout the area for her skills in the kitchen and as a hostess. Mother sadly mentioned that Grandmother had dreamed of writing her own cookbook one day, and now it would never be done. I guess I felt a need to let the world know what an extraordinary woman Grandmother was, so I said I'd like to try and put that cookbook together.

What a project it turned out to be! Just sorting through the masses of recipes was a monumental task. Plus, there were lots of recipes that my mother, Mary Horton Lauderdale, and the rest of the family added to my ever-growing collection. Soon, the recipe boxes turned into shoe boxes, then into large storage boxes that took over my kitchen.

As I looked at the recipes, I realized that I was discovering my heritage, for there, in Grandmother's boxes, were recipes written down by several generations. All the misty characters in the stories I had heard during my childhood became real people through the bits of paper. These were women who, like me, took pride in their families and their homes. They wrote down their recipes to share with others in order to pass something of themselves on to the next generation. I also learned that both the women and the men were strong, independent folks who were capable of making the best out of whatever life offered.

I gained a new appreciation for the accomplishments of my mother and father as they built Mary of Puddin Hill into the mail-order fruit cake and candy company now in its fortieth year. It took many years of hard work and belief in themselves to turn their dreams into realities. I'm not sure I could have done it. This book is in part a tribute to them. Although none of the recipes for the famous Mary of Puddin Hill products are included in this collection, many of the recipes from the Puddin Hill Store and Mother's own kitchen are found in these pages.

This cookbook has become a medley of both recipes and recollections as I share the heritage this remarkable family has left to me.

Grandmother, I think you would be proud.

Acknowledgements

This project has taken a good part of my life for the past few years, and I must thank the many people who have endured it all and given me lots of support.

Mother spent many hours going through all the old family papers to help me find letters, recollections of events and documents that might help me put the story of Puddin Hill and the Horton family together. She also waded through mountains of recipes with me to pull out those that were the family "jewels," and read and re-read others to make sure that all the ingredients looked right before testing. And Dad was enthusiastic about seeing the book become a reality, believing enough in the idea to allow me to go forward.

Mother's brothers, Hal and Jack Horton, and sister, Sarah Plunket, were most willing to add details to many of the old family stories. Sarah also helped with some of the older recipes by filling in the gaps or helping me get the tastes right. Hal provided information on the Horton family, especially James and Mary Horton. Jack was a wealth of information about the early days of Greenville and Hunt County. Hal's son, Hal R. Horton of Anchorage, Alaska, graciously loaned me his copy of the abstract on Puddin Hill, as well as other old family papers. Lelloine Horton, Joyce Horton and Paul Plunket shared their recollections of Hal and Gertrude Horton as well as their own lives.

Just getting all the recipes into legible form was a real task! My earliest efforts were helped along by Nola Proctor, a dear friend who loves to cook and saw the chance to go through the recipes as a dream come true. I had lots of help from Linda Evans and the Mary of Puddin Hill Office Staff, Linda Ellis, Arlene Mann and the Mary of Puddin Hill Store Staff, Laura Waits and Angie Hemby. Liz Thompson patiently entered recipes on the computer.

Getting volunteers to taste everything was no problem, but there needs to be a special thanks to everyone who tasted and offered their opinions . . . and apologies to those who suffered through the meals when we served disasters. After all, even the best-reading recipe doesn't always work.

I had lots of help from friends who were willing to read the manuscript or the recipes to help me make everything clear. Bobbie Lake, Donna Plunket and Hazel Coley patiently read recipes. Fred Allen, Marie Heidmann, Polly Hitt, Jo and Bob Kearns, Susan Mouser and John and Bette Price read the narrative, and offered lots of suggestions. And a special thanks to Marilyn Hillyer, who searched the manuscript for punctuation and grammatical errors. Or as she so aptly phrased it, she "garnished my words with her work, just as Grandmother garnished her cooking."

Encouragement on this project came from many sources. Besides all the folks listed above, Ted Davidson never doubted for a moment that I could do it, and often was the reassuring voice I needed. Mary Faulk Koock's encouragement also kept me plugging along. She was the one who said, "Pud, you have the chance to tell the world about all those wonderful Hortons, so go do it!" Chuck Stovall kept the production of the book going smoothly, adjusting deadlines as necessary, running interference, or just making me laugh on occasions . . . and Scott Millburn who saw to those deadlines were met when it seemed I would never make it. The talented team at Hart Graphics did a great job, especially Nan Mulvaney, Jennifer Burgette and Stacy Buntrock. Even Mary of Puddin Hill customers and people around Greenville have been enthusiastic about the book, asking me regularly how it was coming along. And Bill Carr brought my words to life with his wonderful illustrations. What a thrill it was to see Mary Horton standing on Puddin Hill in the mud!

Although I've dedicated the book to him, I must say more to thank my dear husband, Mike Kearns, who washed many dishes and gulped down many meals that ventured into uncharted culinary territory. My sons Robert and Richard were as patient as two young boys could be. Every evening, when supper was put on the table, they asked, "Mom, is this Yuk or Yum?"

And finally, a special thanks to Carol Taylor who has given herself wholeheartedly to this project. Her knowledge of Hunt County and Texas history, her willingness to plunge into anything that needed to be done, her hours testing recipes and her spirit have made this book as much hers as it is mine. Her husband Michael and son Matthew also deserve a thank-you for their patience with "Mother and Pud's Project," as they called it.

No recipe box is ever filled with original recipes. Whether someone actually hands over a recipe or simply describes something they've tasted, the inspiration is there. For both the recipes... and the inspiration, the following people must be thanked.

Dee Arledge
Gwen Barclay
Cynthia Beacom
Marge Blosser
Alice Boaz
Velma L. Buckman
Malcolm Campbell
Mrs. J.B. Clark
Vella Mae Clayton
Aline Covington
Mrs. Wendell Cox
Betty Curtis
Lallie Carlisle Davis
Lucille Davis
Patricia DeVeny
Lindsey Godfrey
Annie Lee Gordy
Roberta Gustafson
Vernon "Sally" Hart
Marie Heidmann
Laura Henson
Madalene Hill
Mariann Hilton
Mary Jean Hilton
Polly Hitt
Beth Horton
Hal C. Horton, Jr.
Joyce Horton
Lelloine Horton
Terry Horton
Trudy Plunket Hutton
Laura Imhoff

Mamie Jones
Bob Kearns
Jo Kearns
Barbara Kendall
Arvella Kirk
Mary Faulk Koock
Bobbie Lake
Forest K. Lake
Mrs. Dale Miller
Billie Morgan
Novelle (Jackie) Murphy
Judy Horton Newton
Nancy Parker
Phil Peterlin
Mary Frances Pizareff
Delores Plunket
Sarah Plunket
Frank Proctor
Nola Proctor
Alicia Smith
Ann Smith
Roberta Smith
Jacqueline Smyers
Mitzi Thomas
Bette Vallancey
Laura Waits
Lelloine Horton Waits
Sue Wallace
Crede Warren
Wilhelmina Warren
Oweta Watson

And these contributors, now deceased, must also be acknowledged.

Mrs. A.E. Ball
Mary Callahan
Lallie Briscoe Carlisle
Mrs. Harold Clayton
Stella Denney
Mrs. Ellis Hardie
Toddie Holloway
Gertrude Horton
Hal C. Horton, Sr.
Mary Horton
Pearl Jordan

Kate Lauderdale
Marie Lewis
Mrs. H.L. McLow
Mrs. R.R. Neyland
Bernice Roland
Helen Rosenberg
Bess Shrum
Mrs. T.A. Smith
Mrs. T.C. Strickland
Mrs. R.V. Sullenger
Mrs. Lem Tittsworth

"As Mary struggled through the ankle-deep mud, she remarked that it was like trying to 'walk through puddin.' James proclaimed, 'Welcome to Puddin Hill.'"

Chapter One

Grandmother's Legacy
We commence to begin

The heritage of good cooking at Puddin Hill goes back many generations to the days of the early settlers in what is now Hunt County in northeast Texas. All the family stories have it that Great-great grandfather James R. Horton and his young bride Mary Merrill Horton arrived on their land in the waning months of the Republic of Texas. James had received the patent rights to 620 acres of land as payment for his service in the Army of the Republic of Texas during the War of Independence in 1835-36. Information on whatever he did to earn the land has been lost to succeeding generations . . . which has always led to a few raised eyebrows.

Great-great grandmother Mary Merrill Horton lived to be ninety-one. She raised twelve children and lived most of her life on the farm she and James settled when they first came to Texas. All her life Mary was known for her lively tales of life on the frontier, and fortunately, many of those stories were recorded by historians at the turn of the century. My grandfather, Hal C. Horton, Sr., used to entertain all of us grandchildren with many of the old family stories, too. He must have inherited Grandmother Mary's gift for story-telling, because I can still remember how I would be fascinated as he spun tale after tale . . . or was it yarn after yarn? It is these narratives, handed down from generation to generation, that are the heart of the Puddin Hill legend.

James Horton's land gently sloped down to the pecan and walnut trees that flourished on the banks of the Sabine River. It was in the heart of the Blackland Prairie, a stretch of fertile coal-black soil that runs through East Texas. And it was this black earth that inspired the name that the young couple would bestow upon their farm. For the day before they arrived, a fierce spring storm had drenched the land, turning the hill into a black quagmire that clung to boots, hooves, wagon wheels and anything else trying to reach the top. As Mary struggled through the ankle-deep mud, she remarked that it was like trying to "walk through puddin." Family legend has it that James spread his arms wide, looked all about him and proclaimed, "Welcome to Puddin Hill!"

The young family immediately set to work to build their home, a one-room cabin built of logs from the nearby grove of oak trees. The cabin sat on the top of a slight rise, giving it the benefit of southerly breezes in the summer and away from any "varmits" that might come out of the river bottom in the evenings. Later the cabin was expanded to become a dogtrot cabin. Actually, James built another cabin and combined the two with a roofed porch. The new cabin served as a bedroom and parlor to the growing family. But the first cabin was still the place where everyone gathered, because that was where Mary had her kitchen. A large fireplace served as her cookstove and as the main source of heat when a "Texas Blue Norther" would come roaring in. From the rafters hung dried herbs grown in the family garden. A long table was used for both fixing and eating the food.

Because the Hortons were fairly affluent settlers (it seems that James was as good a gambler as he was a farmer), their home had a floor made of split logs. In her memoirs, Mary told a story about the Riley brothers who came to their home to collect for some hogs that James had bought. The young men lived in a dugout some distance away and had never seen wooden floors or braided rugs. One of the young men tied up the horses while his older brother went on inside. When he got to the doorway and saw his brother standing across the room in front of the fireplace, he was amazed! How could anyone get over that "thing," as he called the rug? The older brother boasted that he had cleared it in two jumps. Naturally the younger brother was not to be bested. Over he leaped, joining his brother at the fireplace, much to the delight of Mary and James, who invited the young men to sit a spell and have supper with them.

Mary Horton enjoyed a reputation throughout the area for being a good cook. Many of the recollections that she shared about her early days on Puddin Hill included accounts of what was eaten or what she cooked. Her cooking skill was a real source of pride to her throughout her life, and she enjoyed the challenge of putting together the few ingredients that were available to her in as many combinations as possible. By using the native pecans that were abundant on Puddin Hill, Mary created the original pecan fruit cake that would pass down through the generations to become the recipe which brings Mary of Puddin Hill fame today... and which, as it was in Mary's day, is still a carefully guarded secret.

Mary loved nothing better than cooking for a crowd, and shortly after their arrival in Hunt County, she had the pleasure of showing off her talent. James joined the handful of men who got together to raise the first courthouse, a simple log structure in nearby Greenville, and Mary cooked a big dinner for the group. But the biggest crowd Mary recalled cooking for was the bunch that came to the barbecue her family hosted to celebrate the new state of Texas' first Fourth of July in 1846. Over one hundred guests came from far and wide, many in wagons to camp out on the Horton farm for several days. All of the food was cooked by Mary herself, and she remembered serving ham, baked sweet potatoes, corn and salt rising bread.

Soon after settling in Hunt County, James Horton realized the advantage of raising hogs. Forage was readily available and pork could be smoked and preserved for a good length of time. Mary's recollections were that within a year of their arrival on Puddin Hill, James was raising over 250 head of hogs. Naturally pork was served often. Although I suspect that this recipe was written down in her later years, Mary's recipe for ham baked in milk seems to have been a well-tested recipe. The comments in parentheses are my attempts to make her words a bit clearer.

Ham Baked In Milk

Place a thick slice (½ – ¾ inch) of center cut ham in an iron skillet. Cover with cold sweet milk, preferably skimmed (*she means fresh cows' milk with the cream skimmed off – whole or 2% milk in today's terms. Use about 2 cups, depending on your skillet size.*) Place in a moderate (*350°*) oven and bake uncovered until the meat is extremely tender, about 2 hours. As skin forms on milk and browns, stir back into pan juices, repeating until all liquid has disappeared and drippings accumulated in pan are well-browned. It may be necessary if meat is not tender to add (*from ½ to 1 cup*) boiling water. Remove meat when tender and drain off all but 2 tablespoons of drippings. (*Place skillet on stove over medium heat.*) Stir in 1 tablespoon plus 1 teaspoon flour, then add 1 cup milk, stirring constantly. Simmer until thickened, and add salt if necessary. Be sure and serve biscuits to soak up all that good gravy. SERVES: 4

James and Mary had plenty of fresh corn, too. They grew it for the hogs, only to discover the hogs preferred the pecans found in the river bottom. But the twelve Horton kids could eat their weight in corn, especially Fried Roastin' Ears. I know this recipe has been served for many, many years to the descendants of James and Mary, because, when I asked my mother's sister and brothers to name dishes they remember from their childhood, this was one of the first mentioned.

Fried Roastin' Ears

6 large roasting ears (corn on the cob)
½ cup (1 stick) butter or margarine
2 cups milk
2 tablespoons sugar
¼ teaspoon salt

Shuck corn and remove all silks. With a very sharp knife, cut the tip from each ear. Use a dull knife to scrape all corn from the cob leaving as little as possible. Melt butter in a large skillet and add corn, milk, sugar and salt. Cook about 30 minutes, stirring constantly with a spoon or spatula to prevent sticking. If corn becomes too thick, add more milk or water. SERVES: 4 – 6

There was a patch of sandy soil in the river bottom that was ideal for growing sweet potatoes, and my grandfather, whom I always called "Pop", used to tell about eating sweet potatoes cooked in the fireplace. Although he was willing to eat sweet potatoes baked in an oven, he claimed that the fireplace was the only place to "cook 'em proper", and he continued to prepare them that way whenever he had the chance.

Sweet Potatoes Baked in the Fireplace

Use an old-fashioned cast-iron Dutch oven lined with aluminum foil. Put coals under and on top of the oven until it is hot. Wash and trim ends, then smear each potato with bacon drippings or oil. Put potatoes in hot Dutch oven, add 1 tablespoon of water and cover. Place more coals on top. Cook until soft, about 1 hour. Serve with plenty of butter.

According to Pop, if your cast iron Dutch oven wasn't particularly fit to cook in, you needed to build a good bed of hot coals and use them to cover the Dutch oven (or your iron skillet). Leave it in the coals overnight and, in the morning, your pot would look like new! If it didn't, you hadn't gotten your coals hot enough. After the Dutch oven was cleaned, you had to season it again, of course, so this method of cleaning was only used when you had a big mess.

Almost all the food was grown on the farms in those days, and if an ingredient was not readily available, something was found to take its place. Mary said that anything not homemade or homegrown had to come by boat to Jefferson, the nearest port on the Sabine River. Goods were then hauled the hundred or so miles by ox teams on heavy freight wagons. The trip from Jefferson took at least three weeks and could not be made in winter or spring because of muddy roads. Therefore, yeast as we know it was impossible to get. Salt-rising bread became one of the most common breads baked in Mary's kitchen and in the kitchens of her neighbors.

Mary's recipe for salt-rising bread is fun to make, especially when you have plenty of time. It will take the better part of two days from start to finish — although you won't be working on it all that much. As Mary wrote when she set her recipe down, "While there is nothing especially difficult about the making of this bread, it does require care in the temperature in which it rises. Don't be discouraged because the process seems very slow to those of us who now use modern yeast. Never allow the sponge, as the dough is called, to become cool after it is started." I have found that making this bread is a wonderful way for children to learn food preparation methods used in the 19th century.

Mary wrote her recipe in simple, straightforward terms, as if she was writing it for an inexperienced cook, or for future generations used to quick-rising yeast. However, I felt some of her words needed a little clarification, so those comments in parentheses are mine.

Salt Rising Bread

Break one egg into a teacup (*small mixing bowl*), and beat with a rotary beater (*or wire whisk*) until light. Add 1 rounded tablespoon cornmeal and 1 even tablespoon of sugar and beat again. Fill cup with boiling water (*about ¾ cup*) and stir well. Set in a pan of warm water, cover and place in a warm place until morning (*try oven set just to the point where the thermostat comes on — about 95°*.) This needs to work for at least 10 hours. In the morning, to one cup warm milk and 1 cup lukewarm water (*neither should be hot*), add enough flour to make a stiff batter (*about 3 cups*). Stir into this the cornmeal and egg mixture to which you have just added ½ teaspoon salt — no more. Set in a warm place and let rise again. When light and bubbly (*6 – 8 hours*) add more flour (*3 – 3½ cups*) and knead to make a smooth dough. Make into loaves. (*Put into two 8½ × 4½ × 2¾-inch well-greased loaf pans.*) Brush with butter and let rise again (*about 3 hours*). Bake in a moderate (*350°*) oven for 40 – 45 minutes. *MAKES: 2 loaves*

NOTE: Salt rising bread is good toasted for breakfast.

James Horton died on the eve of the Civil War, and Mary was left alone on the Puddin Hill farm with three young children. By the time of his death, James and Mary Horton had plenty of money and livestock, and Mary managed the farm quite efficiently. But being a widow and being alone meant that she had to have an extra measure of courage. Once, during the war years, Mary and a neighbor were discussing some steers she had sold and some sheep she was having sheared. A stranger overheard the conversation and decided to pay an unannounced visit on Mrs. Horton a few nights later. When Mary looked out the window and saw the intruder, she shot at him with her rifle and wounded the fellow slightly. Then Mary took her children out the back door to hide in the grass. One of the children had the measles and Mary was fearful that the damp grass would complicate the disease, but decided that the other alternative was worse. The would-be robber fled, only to be captured by a neighbor who had heard the shot. The offender was "sentenced" to join the Confederate Army — he later deserted and joined the Union forces.

In the 1870's Mary divided the farm among her children and moved into town to live with her daughter, Alpha Kimbrough. She remained the family matriarch until her death in 1910 at the age of ninety-one. Her love of Texas and the South never diminished, and neither did her interest in cooking. A recipe combining those interests was her fruit chess pie, a very Southern recipe if ever there was one. When I make this pie, I modernize the recipe a bit to take advantage of some of today's dried fruits, but the taste is still distinctively Southern... and delicious. Soaking the fruit in whiskey inspired the name which her descendants bestowed upon it.

Drunk Fruit Chess Pie

1 cup mixed dried fruit (I like Sunkist Fruit Bits), chopped
⅓ cup bourbon whiskey or Southern Comfort
½ cup (1 stick) butter or margarine, softened
1 cup sugar
3 eggs
1 9-inch pie crust (deep-dish type if using a commercial crust)

Soak fruit in liquor for at least 2 hours (it may soak overnight). Preheat oven to 325°. In a mixing bowl, cream butter, then gradually add sugar and beat until mixture is light. Add eggs, beating until well-blended, then stir in undrained fruit. Bake unfilled pie shell for 2 minutes, then pour in filling. Bake at 325° for 45 – 50 minutes, until filling is browned and set. Cover top of pie loosely with foil if it seems to be browning too much. Cool. *SERVES: 6 – 8*

Mary Horton wasn't the only great cook and lively story teller in my heritage. My grandmother, Gertrude Briscoe Horton, also came from an early Hunt County family, and she, too, grew up with a legacy of good cooking... and a whole lot of interesting characters in her ancestry. Her grandfather was John Runnells Briscoe, a Baptist preacher and missionary as well as a farmer and blacksmith. Grandmother told about the time her grandfather was working in a blacksmith shop when a Mr. Watson and two other men approached him about preaching at a meeting. Rev. Briscoe, being a rather poor man, had no decent shoes and no money with which to buy any. He agreed to hold the meeting when Mr. Watson made him moccasins out of the blacksmith apron he was wearing.

Another time Rev. Briscoe helped to organize a new church in a settler's log cabin. The structure had a low ceiling, and cured bacon hung from the rafters. It seems that Briscoe got a little carried away while he was preaching, and his arms got to waving so wildly that he struck a side of bacon, which fell to his feet. Unperturbed, he picked up the bacon, laid it on the table and covered it with his handkerchief. Then he propped his Bible on the bacon and went right on preaching!

Rev. Briscoe was married three times and a widower twice, and his children had to practically raise themselves. My grandmother recalled hearing her father, Ephraim Wray Briscoe, tell about the time that he and his brother let the fire in their fireplace go out. The boys had to walk several miles to the nearest farm to "borrow" fire. To get it home, they put the coals in a bucket, covered them with ashes, and carried the bucket home with a stick through the handle, each boy holding an end of the stick. Another time, when the boys were seven and nine, they were left alone on the family farm to tend a herd of horses for five months.

Understandably, Ephraim Wray Briscoe grew up to be a very responsible adult, and was County Clerk in Hunt County in 1902 when he died of pneumonia. The Commissioners Court met the next day to appoint his successor. His widow, Lallie, was mentioned as a possibility. Now, this was back in the days before women were allowed to vote or hold public office. But the County Commissioners agreed that Lallie was capable of handling the job. After receiving the go-ahead from the Attorney General of the State of Texas, Lallie Briscoe became the first woman in Texas to hold an elective office.

Lallie was no women's activist or suffragette! My aunts and uncles have described her as "a lady born to sit." Her mother was born in Mississippi in a well-to-do family with lots of maids, cooks and other servants. Although Civil War Reconstruction changed things, Lallie's mother raised both her daughters as if she expected them to be able to live a similar lifestyle. When her older sister's boyfriend moved to Greenville in 1883, Lallie, her widowed mother and her sister took a train west to visit him. They liked what they found and decided to stay, especially since Lallie's mother had dreams of each of her daughters making a good marriage to a wealthy man. Lallie met and married Ephraim Briscoe and had four children (one of whom was my grandmother, Gertrude). After he died, Lallie had no means to support herself or her children, making the next few years difficult ones for her. Fortunately, she met and married the kind Mr. C.C. Carlisle, a local businessman. A longtime bachelor, Mr. Carlisle was proud of Lallie and her family — now his family. Eventually, they had a daughter (also named Lallie) who became Grandmother's adored little sister.

Even though she was raised to be a lady, Lallie had a practical streak in her makeup. At an early age she began to write down recipes in a red leather-bound book which she added to for the rest of her years. This little volume has been passed on and sworn by for four generations. To Lallie, it was fitting that she set down recipes for breads and desserts as well as those dishes which featured her special touches.

If you take into account the order in which the recipes are

recorded, then Lallie must have learned bread baking first. Many of the recipes she recorded probably go back to her family in Mississippi. Here are some of the best:

Spoon Bread

2 cups milk
½ cup cornmeal
1 teaspoon salt
½ teaspoon baking powder

½ teaspoon sugar
2 tablespoons butter or margarine, melted
3 eggs, separated

Preheat oven to 375°. Butter a 1½-quart casserole. Heat milk in a saucepan over medium heat until tiny bubbles appear around the edge of pan. Stir in the cornmeal and cook until thick, stirring constantly. Add the salt, baking powder, sugar and butter. Beat the egg yolks and add to the cornmeal mixture. Remove from heat. Beat the egg whites until soft peaks form and fold into the batter. Pour into prepared dish and bake uncovered at 375° for 25 – 30 minutes or until a knife blade comes out clean when inserted in the center. Spoon onto plate and serve with gobs of butter. *SERVES: 6 – 8*

Sally Lunn Bread

3 tablespoons butter or margarine
3 cups milk
1 package dry yeast
½ cup warm water (105° – 110°)

2 eggs
1 tablespoon sugar
4 cups flour
1 teaspoon salt

If you want to serve hot bread for dinner, plan to begin preparation about 2 hours before serving time. Grease well a tube or bundt pan. Combine butter and milk in a small saucepan and heat just until butter is melted; cool. Dissolve yeast in warm water. In a large mixing bowl, beat eggs until light. Add milk mixture and remaining ingredients. Pour in dissolved yeast and beat well to make a smooth batter. Pour into prepared pan, cover and set in a warm place. Let rise for 1 hour, or until batter is nearly to the top of the pan. Place pan in a 450° oven and bake for 10 minutes. Reduce heat to 400° and continue baking for another 40 – 45 minutes. Remove from pan and slice hot at the table. *SERVES: 8*

Anadama Bread

2½ cups water
½ cup yellow cornmeal
3 teaspoons salt
3 tablespoons shortening
½ cup molasses
2 packages yeast
½ cup warm water
(105° – 110°)

6 – 7 cups flour
¼ cup butter or
  margarine, melted
1 tablespoon yellow corn
  meal
½ teaspoon salt

In a large saucepan, bring 2½ cups water to a boil. Stir in cornmeal and salt. Cook over medium heat, stirring constantly, until mixture thickens — 2 – 3 minutes. Remove from heat. Add shortening and molasses; cool to lukewarm. Dissolve yeast in warm water; let stand 5 minutes. Stir dissolved yeast into cooled cornmeal mixture. Add 5 cups of the flour, beating with a spoon or electric mixer. Turn dough out onto a floured surface and work in the remaining flour with hands. Knead dough until smooth, then place in a greased bowl, turning dough once so the top surface is oiled. Cover and let rise in a warm draft-free place until doubled, about 1 hour. Punch dough down, cover and let rest 10 minutes. Shape into 2 loaves and put into two greased 9×5×3-inch loaf pans. Brush with melted butter. Combine the remaining cornmeal and salt; sprinkle over loaves. Cover and let rise until doubled, about 35 – 40 minutes. Bake at 375° for 30 – 40 minutes until browned and loaves sound hollow when tapped. Remove from pan and cool on cooling rack or serve hot. Anadama Bread makes great toast for breakfast!
MAKES: 2 loaves

Hot Water Cornbread

1 cup yellow cornmeal
1 teaspoon salt
1 teaspoon sugar

¾ cup boiling water
1 tablespoon shortening
Vegetable oil for frying

In medium bowl, combine cornmeal, salt and sugar. Add boiling water and shortening; stir until shortening melts. Pour oil to a depth of ½ inch in a large skillet and heat to 375°. Shape cornmeal mixture into flattened balls using a heaping tablespoon as a measuring guide. Fry each in hot oil, turning once, until crisp and golden brown — about 5 minutes. Drain on paper towels. Serve at once with lots of butter. *MAKES: 1 dozen*

Lallie often entered recipes for the dishes she considered her specialties. Others were gathered from women she knew at church, or neighbors and friends she would call on every Sunday afternoon. Lallie maintained the custom of social calls as long as she was able.

Tomato Aspic

1 envelope gelatin
1¾ cup tomato juice, divided
¼ teaspoon onion salt
½ teaspoon sugar
½ teaspoon Worcestershire sauce
2 tablespoons lemon juice
⅛ teaspoon Tabasco
⅛ teaspoon onion juice
½ cup mayonnaise
3 drops Tabasco
½ teaspoon onion salt
Capers for garnish

Sprinkle gelatin over ¼ cup tomato juice to soften. Heat the remaining 1½ cups tomato juice to boiling and combine with softened gelatin. Stir until dissolved. Add onion salt, sugar, Worcestershire sauce, lemon juice, Tabasco and onion juice. Pour into an 8-inch square pan and chill until firm. Combine mayonnaise, remaining Tabasco and onion salt until blended. When ready to serve, cut aspic into 8 portions, topping each serving with a dollop of seasoned mayonnaise. Garnish with a whole caper.
SERVES: 8

Grandmother's Jellied Chicken

- 1 3-4 pound chicken
- 1 onion, peeled
- 1 carrot, scraped
- 1 stalk celery
- 1 sprig parsley
- 1 teaspoon salt
- 6-8 whole peppercorns
- 1 clove garlic, peeled
- 2 envelopes gelatin
- ¼ cup cold water
- 1 tablespoon Worcestershire
- 1 teaspoon salt
- ½ teaspoon pepper
- Mayonnaise

Place chicken in a large pot with enough water to cover. Add onion, carrot, celery, parsley, salt, peppercorns and garlic. Bring to a boil, reduce heat and simmer 1 hour, or until chicken is tender. Remove chicken and let it cool. Strain broth and return to pot. Bring to a boil and allow to boil until broth is reduced to 1 quart. Remove chicken from bones and cut into small pieces across the grain, discarding skin. Soften gelatin in cold water. Add to hot broth, stirring until dissolved. Add Worcestershire, salt and pepper. Taste, adding more salt if desired. Pour broth over chicken and mix lightly. Pour into an 8-cup mold or 2-quart flat baking dish and chill until set. Cut into squares and serve, garnished with mayonnaise. (Do not pass this up because of its simplicity. That is the secret of its goodness.) *SERVES: 6-8*

Corn Pudding

- 1 17-ounce can cream-style corn
- 1 teaspoon sugar
- ½ teaspoon salt
- 2 cups milk
- 2 tablespoons flour
- 2 tablespoons butter, melted
- Dash nutmeg
- 4 eggs, beaten lightly

Preheat oven to 350°. Butter a 2-quart baking dish. In a large mixing bowl, combine all ingredients, adding eggs last, stirring until well-blended. Pour into the prepared dish. Bake at 350° for 50-55 minutes or until a knife inserted in the center comes out clean. Serve hot. *SERVES: 6-8*

Recipes were often entered into the book with no title — just a comment about the dish.

"Good Cabbage Dish"

1 medium head of cabbage, coarsely chopped
¼ cup flour
1 teaspoon salt
¼ teaspoon pepper
1 cup grated Cheddar cheese
2 cups milk
1 cup soft bread crumbs
2 tablespoons melted butter or margarine

Cook cabbage in enough water to cover until tender — about 10 minutes. (Or steam in a vegetable steamer, if you prefer.) Drain; set aside. Preheat oven to 350°. Butter a 2-quart flat baking dish. Combine flour, salt and pepper in a small mixing bowl. Place half the cabbage in the baking dish, sprinkle with half the flour mixture and ½ cup of the cheese. Repeat layers. Pour milk over cabbage. Combine bread crumbs and melted butter, mixing until crumbs are lightly coated. Sprinkle over cabbage. Bake at 350° for 30 minutes, or until crumbs are browned and mixture is bubbly. This tastes especially good with barbecue or baked ham. *SERVES: 8*

Lallie wrote down sensible recipes. They were the type that many women who grew up at their mothers' sides in the kitchen just seemed to know how to prepare. She must have hoped that some day her book would be used to teach her daughters or granddaughters the practical side of cooking. The simple way she noted how to make three types of white sauce has proved valuable many times for those old-fashioned recipes that simply call for a "thin" white sauce or "medium" white sauce. And, of course, a good white sauce is the basis for many dishes, like creamed chicken or vegetable casseroles.

"How To Make White Sauce"

THIN SAUCE:
1 tablespoon butter or margarine
1 tablespoon flour
¼ teaspoon salt
1 cup milk or cream

MEDIUM SAUCE:
2 tablespoons butter or margarine
2 tablespoons flour
¼ teaspoon salt
1 cup milk or cream

THICK SAUCE:
3 tablespoons butter or margarine
3 tablespoons flour
¼ teaspoon salt
1 cup milk or cream

Melt butter in a heavy-bottomed saucepan over medium heat. Stir in flour and salt. Cook 2 minutes, stirring constantly. Add cold milk or cream. Reduce heat and simmer until mixture thickens, stirring constantly — about 8-10 minutes. Season as desired with pepper, dry mustard, nutmeg or other seasonings. Or add 1 cup grated cheese or 1 cup sautéed sliced mushrooms for flavor variations.
MAKES: 1 cup

Desserts were another category that Lallie perfected. Apple Crumb Betty, Southern Chess Pie and Vinegar Pie were some of Lallie's best. Don't let the title on that last one fool you. Vinegar Pie has a delicate creamy taste and smooth texture. In fact, I enjoy serving it to company and watching the reaction when I inform my guests they're eating vinegar pie.

Southern Chess Pie

1 cup (2 sticks) butter or margarine, softened
2 cups sugar
4 eggs, separated
1 tablespoon cornmeal
2 tablespoons heavy cream
Few grains of salt
1 9-inch unbaked pie crust (deep-dish type if using a commercial crust)

Preheat oven to 400°. Cream butter and sugar together until light. Add beaten egg yolks. In a small bowl, combine cornmeal and cream, blending to a smooth paste. Add to butter mixture. Beat egg whites with salt until stiff, then fold into batter. Pour into unbaked pie crust and bake 5 minutes at 400°. Reduce heat to 350° and bake 55 – 60 minutes longer. Cool. *SERVES: 8*

Apple Crumb Betty

4 cups (4 – 6) apples, peeled, cored and sliced
Juice of 1 lemon
1 cup graham cracker crumbs
1 cup brown sugar
½ cup (1 stick) butter or margarine, softened
1 teaspoon cinnamon

Preheat oven to 325°. Place sliced apples in an ungreased 8-inch square pan. Sprinkle with lemon juice. Combine the remaining ingredients and spread over the apples. Bake in a 325° oven for 45 – 50 minutes. Serve hot or at room temperature. *SERVES: 6 – 8*

NOTE: This is even better topped with cinnamon ice cream. (see page 269)

Vinegar Pie

1½ cups half and half
2 eggs
¼ cup sugar
1½ teaspoons white vinegar
¼ teaspoon salt
1 9-inch unbaked pie crust (deep-dish type if using a commercial crust)
Nutmeg
Sweetened whipped cream (optional garnish)

Preheat oven to 400°. Heat half and half until bubbles form around edges; set aside to cool to lukewarm. Beat eggs, gradually adding sugar in a steady stream. Continue to beat until sugar is dissolved and mixture is smooth. Add vinegar and salt, then stir in warm half and half. Pour mixture into pie crust and sprinkle the top generously with nutmeg. Bake at 400° for 5 minutes, then reduce heat to 350° and bake for 25 – 30 minutes, or until filling is just barely set. Cool, then chill pie. Serve cold with lightly sweetened whipped cream as a garnish, if desired. *SERVES: 8*

While going through Lallie's old recipes for this book, I came across a recipe for making homemade vinegar. I've added this recipe primarily as a curiosity (the pie recipe itself calls for white vinegar), and for its old-fashioned charm: "put into an earthen jar, one gallon warm water, 2 cups sugar and a cake of yeast. Add red apple peelings to make a pretty color or rinsings from the kettle where preserves have been made. Vinegar is ready in two weeks during warm weather."

When I asked my aunt and uncles what they remembered most about the cooking of Mama Carlisle (their name for Lallie), the unanimous answer was "teacakes!" She would make them several times a week, and everyone remembered eating tea cakes as after-school snacks. They also told me that during the years of sugar rationing, she would often use her one-cup ration of sugar to make teacakes. I think this is one of the best simple cookies I have ever tasted, and it is now a favorite of my sons, too. However, they find the idea of round teacakes a bit too plain, so we have discovered that teacakes taste even better when baked in the shape of hearts, bells, dinosaurs, or even the state of Texas!

Mama Carlisle's Teacakes

3 cups flour
1½ teaspoons cream of tartar
1 teaspoon baking soda
¼ teaspoon salt
½ cup (1 stick) butter or margarine, softened

1 cup sugar
2 eggs
1 teaspoon vanilla
2 tablespoons milk or cream

TOPPING:
⅓ cup sugar   Grated rind of 1 orange

Preheat oven to 350°. Sift dry ingredients together and set aside. In a large mixing bowl, cream butter and sugar until light. Add eggs, one at a time, beating until smooth after each. Add vanilla and beat again. Add dry ingredients alternately with milk or cream, mixing until a smooth soft dough is formed. Turn out onto a floured surface and roll dough to ¼-inch thickness. Cut into circles with 3-inch biscuit cutter and place on lightly greased cookie sheets. Combine remaining sugar and grated orange rind and sprinkle a little over each cookie. Bake at 350° for 10 – 12 minutes. *MAKES: 3 dozen*

Another dish that my mother and her siblings fondly recall is Mama's Split Biscuits and Syrup. During the Depression, nothing was thrown away, especially food. If there were biscuits left over from breakfast they were served another way at dinner or supper, as a snack, or even the following morning for breakfast. This was a favorite everyday sweet.

Mama's Split Biscuits And Syrup

Preheat oven to 325°. Split leftover biscuits in half and butter each half generously. Place in well-greased pan with the buttered side up. Pour cane syrup over and around biscuits until it is about ¼-inch deep in pan. Bake at 325° for 45 minutes to 1 hour. The syrup will cook down until it is almost candied. Remove biscuits from pan at once and place on a buttered platter. Serve hot.

The crusts trimmed from sandwiches were also turned into a treat for the grandkids.

Cinnamon Sticks

Bread trimmings from sandwiches (or bread slices cut into long strips)
Vegetable oil for frying
½ cup sugar
2 tablespoons cinnamon

Fry bread trimmings in hot oil (375°) until light brown; drain on paper towels. Place in a paper bag with the sugar and cinnamon; shake well. Add more sugar and cinnamon if necessary. Serve at once. These make great snacks or a good breakfast treat.

Pearl Jordan was a cousin who traveled from Greenville to the New Mexico territory in the early 1900's. She and Mama Carlisle stayed close and continued to share recipes through the mail instead of during the Sunday afternoon visits they enjoyed before Pearl headed west. Pearl was an excellent cook, as her recipe for fudge cake shows.

Legacy Fudge Cake

½ cup (1 stick) unsalted (sweet) butter, softened
¾ cup sugar
2 eggs
1 tablespoon vanilla
2 ounces unsweetened chocolate, melted
1 cup flour
½ teaspoon salt
1 cup chopped pecans

Preheat oven to 325°. Grease an 8-inch square cake pan (or a 12-cup muffin tin for cupcakes). Cream butter and sugar until fluffy. Add eggs one at a time, beating well after each addition. Blend in vanilla. Add melted chocolate and blend. Stir in flour and salt, beating until smooth. Stir in pecans. Pour into prepared pan and bake 30 minutes at 325° (20 – 25 minutes for cupcakes). Remove from oven and cool. When cool, frost with the following icing:

ICING:
½ cup (1 stick) unsalted (sweet) butter, softened
3 tablespoons cold strong coffee
1½ teaspoons vanilla
5 tablespoons cocoa
2½ cups powdered sugar

Cream butter, then add coffee and vanilla. Add cocoa and powdered sugar, beating until smooth. Spread on cooled cake (or cupcakes). *SERVES: 8 – 12*

HINT: Spread any remaining frosting between vanilla wafers or other plain cookies for a delicious sandwich cookie! (It may also help to keep the cake safe from the family until company comes.)

Mary Horton and Lallie "Mama" Carlisle carried on a tradition of good cooking handed down from their mothers. But even more important, each began the practice of setting down recipes for future generations to keep. And the love of recipes and cookbooks was a gift Lallie passed on to her daughter, Mary Gertrude, who passed it on to her daughter, Mary Jane, who shared it with me.

"He had a goat cart that he would bring to town to run errands, which often took him through the neighborhood where Gertrude lived."

Chapter Two

Gertrude and Hal
A woman is to be loved and not understood

Thank goodness the Hortons and Lallie Carlisle were patient folks, because it took a long time for Hal Horton and Gertrude Briscoe to decide to get married. Hal, who was my grandfather, was born on Puddin Hill in 1886. An influenza epidemic several years later took both of his parents, so his mother's parents, Larkin and Belle Hunter, moved their family to Puddin Hill to take care of Hal, his sister and brother. Life was not easy, for the land that James Horton had settled had been divided up in the succeeding generations and had to support more families. Nevertheless, Hal worked hard, setting his sights on an education and, in 1910, earned a law degree from the University of Texas. He returned to Greenville to hang out his shingle.

Hal's heart, meanwhile, was firmly in the grip of Mary Gertrude Briscoe. She, too, was a Greenville native, born in 1889. They met when she was about 12. He had a goat cart that he would bring to town to run errands, which often took him to his aunt's house in the same block where Gertrude's family lived. Hal always said that he was never sure who the real goat was after he got mixed up with Gertrude.

Gertrude was a stubborn, independent sort who was determined that she would be able to support herself before she would ever consider getting married. That strong determination came from watching her mother struggle after her father's death in 1902. Lallie Dyer Briscoe had been raised to be a lady and a good wife for some good man. When her husband died, she did everything from taking in boarders to selling ladies' hosiery to make ends meet. Gertrude vowed she would "be able to make a living," and she kept her promise, attending college and graduating in 1907 with a teacher's certificate.

Hal proposed, and Gertrude said, "Maybe," then went off to teach. If you asked Hal (I called him "Pop"), they were engaged for seven years. If you asked Gertrude (whom I called "Grandmother"), they were "good friends" for six and engaged for one. She was busy teaching, and had decided that Hal wasn't established enough to support her, anyhow.

The romantic stalemate ended in 1912, when Hal accepted a job offer from one of his classmates at law school. Sam Rayburn, who had grown up 30 miles away in Bonham, had just been elected to the U.S. House of Representatives in Washington, and asked Hal to go along as his secretary. The opportunity was too good to pass up, so Hal packed for Washington, leaving Gertrude and her independence behind. Within a year she had capitulated, and they were married in January of 1913. Sam Rayburn served as best man. Grandmother recalled that there were white roses blooming in the yard that January day, so she picked a bouquet to carry in her wedding. Pop was a great romantic, and every year, thereafter, on their anniversary, a bouquet of white roses appeared.

Hal and Gertrude left that day for Washington. Their adventures as a young couple enjoying the excitement of the capitol city were wonderful. Grandmother used to tell of attending the meetings of the National Geographic Society and hearing speeches given by explorers returning from the far corners of the globe. She also relished the chance to go to functions at the embassies and to attend luncheons for the wives of those working in the government. Grandmother found that the food served in Washington sparked her inherent interest in trying new tastes and recipes. Cooking became a challenge and a creative outlet for her, and she collected recipes from many sources. The following recipe became a lifelong favorite of hers. Although old-fashioned in style, there's nothing old-fashioned about the delicious taste — it has become a favorite supper in my house.

Herbed Cornbread Ring With Creamed Chicken

CORNBREAD RING
- 2 tablespoons butter or margarine
- ½ cup chopped celery
- ½ cup chopped onion
- 1 cup yellow cornmeal
- 1 cup flour
- 2 teaspoons baking powder
- 1 teaspoon salt
- ½ teaspoon thyme
- ½ teaspoon poultry seasoning
- 1 cup milk
- 2 eggs, beaten
- ¼ cup butter or margarine, melted
- 2 tablespoons diced pimiento, drained

To make cornbread ring, preheat oven to 400°. Grease a 2-quart ovenproof ring mold or tube pan. Melt butter in a skillet over medium-high heat and sauté celery and onion until softened, about 3 minutes. Set aside to cool. Combine cornmeal, flour, baking powder, salt and seasonings in a mixing bowl and stir to blend. In another bowl, combine milk, eggs and melted butter or margarine. Pour into dry ingredients and stir until just blended. Add the sautéed vegetables and pimiento. Pour into prepared pan. Bake at 400° for 25-30 minutes until browned. Remove from oven and let stand for 5 minutes, then unmold onto large platter. Fill center of ring with creamed chicken.

CREAMED CHICKEN
- 3 tablespoons butter or margarine
- 3 tablespoons flour
- 2 cups milk
- 1 chicken bouillon cube
- 3 hard cooked eggs, sliced
- 3 cups cooked, diced chicken (or turkey)
- Freshly ground pepper to taste
- 1 4-ounce can mushrooms, drained (optional)
- Chopped parsley for garnish

Melt butter in a large saucepan over medium heat. Stir in flour and cook, stirring constantly, for 2 minutes, taking care that mixture does not become browned. Add milk and chicken bouillon cube and cook, stirring constantly, until sauce is thickened and bouillon cube is dissolved. Stir in eggs and chicken. Season to taste with pepper. (Add mushrooms, if desired.) Spoon filling into the center of bread ring and garnish with chopped parsley. *SERVES: 6*

Pop left Sam Rayburn's service a year or so later to take a job as an attorney for the Interstate Commerce Commission. He always loved to tell about a case he had to handle — the decision of just when a calf became a cow and was able to be sold separately from its mother. (Pop never did explain what his decision was or how he arrived at it, saying it made a much better story when the listener had to ponder the question.)

With the outbreak of the Great War in 1916 they returned to Greenville for Pop to enlist in the Army. He was commissioned a Captain in the company from the Greenville area and went off for training. Gertrude mustered all her independent spirit during this difficult time, since Hal Jr. was born soon after they returned from Washington. Pop left for France in 1918, and while he was gone, Sarah was born. He returned at the end of the war to meet the baby girl whose life he had only shared in letters. Instead of returning to law practice, Pop started a grain and feed business.

Even when Pop came home, Grandmother stubbornly refused to let go of her own dreams of earning a living. They compromised with the understanding that she could continue to work and bring in some money so long as it was done at home. Pop probably doubted the wisdom of his decision many times as Grandmother turned the house into everything from a design studio making elegant children's clothes for Neiman Marcus, to a custom wedding cake shop, to a centerpiece for elaborate iris gardens and, finally, to an antique shop.

Jack was born in 1924 and Mary (Mother) in 1925. That same year, Sarah caught the measles and the illness destroyed the bones in one hip, leaving her unable to walk for the next four years. The efforts to help Sarah recover made Grandmother realize that many children with similar illnesses might not be able to get the necessary treatment due to their parents' financial considerations, or a lack of knowledge of just how to get help. Grandmother became very involved in founding the Texas Society for Crippled Children and became known around East Texas as the "Easter Seal Lady."

Sarah recalls that Grandmother made her dozens of raisin sandwiches to help keep the iron levels in her blood high enough to satisfy her doctors. When she told me about them, I was skeptical, but she insisted that they were so good she never got tired of them (thank goodness). She was right, they are good.

Raisin Sandwiches

1 cup raisins
½ cup pecans
1 teaspoon lemon juice

2 tablespoons cream
16 slices bread

Combine the raisins, pecans, lemon juice and cream in the container of a food processor and process until blended and spreadable. Or put raisins and pecans through food grinder, place in small bowl and combine with cream and lemon juice. Spread on eight slices of bread, topping with remaining bread slices. Trim crusts, then cut each sandwich into quarters. Serve with milk or tea for a mid-afternoon snack. *MAKES: 8 sandwiches*

In spite of the anxieties over Sarah's illness, Mother says she remembers a house full of good times and laughter. Their house stood on several acres of land at the eastern edge of town, where there was plenty of room for horses, cows, chickens and Grandmother's flowers. Mother remembers that Grandmother was intrigued by the delicate taste flowers added to her cooking, so she kept the yard filled with roses and scented geraniums. And Mother said that if you checked out the kitchen, you could always find Crystallized Roses, Rose Petal Butter or one of Grandmother's cakes delicately infused with the taste of Rose Geranium leaves. Mother says she asked Grandmother what kind of cake recipe she used. Grandmother replied, "Oh, just plain ol' cake." It's been called that for years.

Crystallized Rose Petals

Rose petals
Egg whites

Water
Sugar

Gather rose petals from just-opened roses early in the morning. (This assures you of the freshest, most fragrant roses.) Carefully wash petals and pat dry with paper towels. Combine an egg white and one teaspoon of water in a small bowl and beat until thoroughly blended. Brush each petal with egg white mixture. Sprinkle petals thoroughly with granulated sugar and lay on wax paper to dry.

NOTE: Use as a garnish or decoration on cakes, tarts or other desserts, or to add color to a party tray. For an especially pretty decoration, place 5 petals together to form a rose, then fill in the center with yellow icing or yellow-tinted sugar crystals.

Alfajores

2 cups cornstarch
½ cup flour
1 teaspoon baking powder
⅔ cup butter or
    margarine, softened
1 cup sugar
1 egg

2 egg yolks
1 teaspoon vanilla
2 teaspoons grated lemon
    rind or 4 drops lemon
    extract
1 tablespoon brandy

Sift the cornstarch, flour and baking powder together; set aside. In a large mixing bowl, cream butter and sugar until light. Add the egg and egg yolks, beating until well blended. Add vanilla, lemon rind and brandy and beat again. Add dry ingredients, mixing to form a smooth dough. Chill dough 4 – 5 hours until it is quite firm. Preheat oven to 325°. Pat or roll the dough on a floured board until it is ¼-inch thick. Cut into rounds with a 1½-inch cookie cutter. Place 2 inches apart on greased cookie sheets. Bake at 325° for 12 – 15 minutes. Cookies will spread and brown around the edges. Remove from pans and cool. Sandwich two cookies together with either rose petal butter or dulce de leche. *MAKES: about 4 dozen cookies (2 dozen sandwich cookies)*

DULCE DE LECHE
1 15-ounce can sweetened
    condensed milk

Empty the can of milk into the top of a double boiler. Cover tightly and set over simmering water. Cook 2½ hours, until milk has caramelized. Milk will turn a caramel color at the edges, then slowly turn golden throughout. Check water in the bottom of the double boiler occasionally to see that it has not boiled dry. Spread cooled cookies with the mixture while it is still warm. Let cool. Refrigerate any remaining milk. *MAKES: about 1½ cups*

Rose Petal Butter

¾ cup rose petals, firmly packed or 2 teaspoons rose flavoring (available at candy or cake decorating stores)

2 tablespoons half and half
1 cup (2 sticks) unsalted (sweet) butter, softened

Select fragrant red or deep pink roses. Gather these early in the morning before the sun strikes them. Carefully check to see that there are not any bugs and wash very gently, blotting with paper towels to dry. Clip the hard white tip from each petal (this is bitter). Place the petals in a blender or food processor with the half and half and blend until finely chopped. Add softened butter and mix until blended. Cover and refrigerate overnight to allow flavors to blend. Remove rose petal butter from refrigerator about an hour before serving so it can soften. Spread butter onto slices of white bread with the crusts trimmed for tea sandwiches. It is also good on warmed slices of pound cake. Or use as a filling between two Alfajores cookies (see preceeding recipe.) Refrigerate any remaining butter.
MAKES: 1½ cups

Just Plain Ol' Cake

3 cups flour
½ teaspoon baking soda
½ teaspoon baking powder
¾ teaspoon salt
1 cup shortening (butter or margarine may be used)
2 cups sugar

4 eggs, at room temperature
1 teaspoon vanilla
1 teaspoon grated lemon rind, or 2 – 3 drops lemon extract
1 cup buttermilk

Preheat oven to 350°. Grease a 10-inch tube or bundt pan; set aside. Sift together flour, soda, baking powder and salt; set aside. Cream shortening and sugar until light. Add eggs, vanilla and lemon rind and beat until well-blended. Add dry ingredients alternately with buttermilk and beat until smooth. Pour batter into prepared pan and bake at 350° for 60 – 65 minutes. Cool in pan 10 minutes, then remove from pan and cool completely. SERVES: 12 – 16

HINT: *Grandmother used to put fresh rose geranium leaves in the bottom of her greased tube pan before pouring in the batter. The light rose flavor of this herb gave a unique taste to her pound cakes. Rose geranium is an herb plant, usually available from nurseries or at herb farms.*

Grandmother's Mint Syrup

½ cup sugar
½ cup water
3 tablespoons chopped fresh mint leaves
2 tablespoons fresh lemon juice
½ cup fresh orange juice
1 tablespoon brandy

Bring sugar and water to a boil and allow to boil 5 minutes. Pour boiling syrup over mint leaves and allow to stand until liquid has cooled. Strain syrup, and add lemon juice and orange juice. Strain again to remove any bits of mint or citrus that remain. Stir in brandy. Chill. *MAKES: 1 cup*

HINT: This syrup is delicious served over any combination of fresh melon balls as a salad or first course. It is also delicious poured over lemon or pineapple sherbet for dessert. Grandmother also added a tablespoon of syrup to a glass of iced tea or lemonade for a refreshing taste.

The noontime meal (always called dinner) was the main meal of the day. The table was never set for just the family, because there were few dinners that somebody didn't bring company home with them. Grandmother always made sure there was ample food, and her reputation as a good cook meant that invitations were never turned down. When Mother was young, Grandmother always had a cook to help her. Many times the specialties of the cook became family favorites. Such was the case of Black Chicken, a recipe from Bernice Roland, who cooked for Grandmother for many years. It is so easy to make . . . and so good! The best part is the gravy, especially when served over rice or with baked potatoes.

Black Chicken

¼ cup butter or margarine
1 large fryer, cut up
1 medium onion, finely chopped
1 clove garlic, minced
2 tablespoons Worcestershire
2 tablespoons black molasses
½ teaspoon salt
¼ teaspoon pepper
1 4-ounce can mushrooms with liquid
2 tablespoons cornstarch
¼ cup cold water
Cooked rice or potatoes

Preheat oven to 275°. In a large skillet, melt the butter over medium heat. Brown chicken on all sides and remove. Sauté onions and garlic in butter until translucent. Place chicken in a baking dish and top with onions and garlic. Combine Worcestershire, molasses, salt and pepper and drizzle the mixture over the chicken. Add mushrooms and their liquid. Cover and bake at 275° for 1 hour. Remove chicken pieces and keep warm. Pour pan drippings into a saucepan. Combine cornstarch and cold water, stirring until smooth. Pour into saucepan and simmer over medium heat until thickened. Serve with rice or potatoes. This makes a good party dish because it will hold a long time.
SERVES: 4-6

NOTE: If you are planning to serve baked potatoes with the Black Chicken, prepare them and put them in the oven to bake along with the chicken. Both will be done at the same time.

Every dinner included hot rolls. One of Grandmother's real talents in the kitchen was bread-making. Her Parkerhouse rolls, fresh from the oven and always wrapped in a linen napkin, were snapped up almost before she could set them on the table.

Grandmother's Parkerhouse Rolls

2 packages yeast
¼ cup warm water
   (105° – 110°)
3 eggs
1 cup sugar
1 cup (2 sticks) butter or margarine, melted
1 cup mashed potatoes (leftover or instant mashed potatoes can be used)

1½ cups warm water
1½ teaspoons salt
7 – 8 cups flour
½ cup (1 stick) butter or margarine

Sprinkle yeast over ¼ cup warm water; let stand 5 minutes. In a large mixing bowl, beat eggs until light in color. Add dissolved yeast, sugar, melted butter, potatoes, water and salt. Beat until smooth. Add flour a cup at a time, until a smooth dough is formed. Turn dough out onto a floured board and knead briefly. Roll dough to ⅜-inch thickness and cut with a 3-inch round cutter. Reroll and cut trimmings. With the back side of a table knife, make a deep crease across the roll, a little off center. Melt the remaining ½ cup butter and brush the surface of each roll. Fold larger side over the smaller and place 1 inch apart on a greased baking sheet. Brush tops of rolls with melted butter, cover and let rise in a warm, draft free place until doubled in size, about 45 minutes. Bake at 350° for 15 – 20 minutes, or until browned. *MAKES: 4 dozen*

HINT: Grandmother used to freeze a batch of these rolls by placing them on a waxed paper-lined cookie sheet and, when frozen, storing them in plastic bags. Before mealtime, Grandmother would place as many frozen rolls as needed on a greased pie plate or a baking sheet. She would boil a pot of water, take it off the heat, set the pie plate of rolls on top of the pot, cover it and let the rolls thaw and rise. Larger pans of rolls were set on top of a heating pad set on high, and covered. The rolls would be ready to bake in about an hour.

As far as Pop was concerned, Grandmother's rolls were made for soaking up gravy. He said that there were three ways to eat gravy or pan drippings. First, you could split the rolls and pour the gravy over them (best with a cream gravy or other thick gravy), or you could soak the rolls in the juices left on the serving plate, letting the bread act as a sponge to absorb the liquid. But the best way, in his opinion, was to "sop" the rolls. He used to say that sopping was similar to soaking, except that you "motioned the bread around" over the plate to be sure you got the best of the juices. There's no doubt that he was an expert on the subject. And when it came to the best "soppin' material," it was pan-broiled steak. Grandmother would sear the steak on both sides in a hot iron skillet, then make a wonderful gravy from the pan drippings. It's interesting that there has been so much recent attention given to this technique for cooking a steak, as evidenced by the popularity of cajun-style, blackened steaks. Just be sure to have lots of rolls on hand when you try this recipe.

Broiled Steak

Use T-bone, porterhouse or sirloin steaks, cut an inch or more thick, allowing at least 6-8 ounces per person. Heat a large iron skillet (be sure it is larger than steaks) until very hot. Sprinkle the bottom of the skillet generously with salt and drop in steaks. Sear first side for about one minute, or until well-browned, then turn and sear the other side. Continue to cook steaks, turning occasionally, until they reach the desired doneness. Reduce heat, if necessary, so that outsides of steaks don't burn. Just before steaks are done, top each with 1 tablespoon of butter and cook until the butter has melted. Pour a 4-ounce can of mushrooms and their liquid over the steaks (add a second can if you have more than 4 steaks in the skillet — or happen to really like mushrooms). Remove steaks from skillet to heated platter. Pour gravy from skillet into a gravy boat and serve over steak and hot rolls or biscuits.

There were other dinnertime favorites, too:

Baked Chops With Cherries

4 thick loin pork chops
Salt
Pepper
⅓ cup light rum
1 cup raw rice
1 16-ounce can sweet pitted cherries, undrained
¾ cup red wine
1 tablespoon sugar
1 teaspoon grated lemon peel
¼ teaspoon cinnamon

Preheat oven to 350°. Sprinkle pork chops with salt and pepper. Brown chops on both sides in a heavy bottomed skillet. Pour rum over chops and cook until rum is reduced by half. Place uncooked rice in an 8-inch square baking dish. Drain juice from cherries, reserving ½ cup. Combine drained cherries and reserved juice with remaining ingredients. Pour ½ of sauce mixture over rice and arrange chops on top. Pour remaining sauce over chops. Cover and bake 1 hour at 350°. *SERVES: 4*

Chicken A La Chasseur

2 – 2½ pound chicken, cut up (or chicken pieces)
Lemon juice
Salt and pepper
1 tablespoon butter or margarine
1 tablespoon olive oil
¼ pound fresh mushrooms, sliced or 1 4-ounce can mushrooms, drained
1 shallot, chopped
2 tablespoons brandy
1 cup dry white wine
2 fresh tomatoes, peeled, seeded and chopped
½ cup chicken broth
2 tablespoons minced parsley
Pinch dried tarragon

Rub chicken pieces with lemon juice, then lightly sprinkle with salt and pepper. Combine butter and olive oil in a heavy skillet, heating over medium heat until butter is melted. Add chicken pieces and brown on all sides. Add sliced mushrooms and cook for 5 minutes, or until mushrooms are wilted. Add shallot, brandy, white wine, tomatoes, chicken broth and 1 tablespoon of the minced parsley. Cover and simmer on low heat for about 20 – 25 minutes, or until chicken is tender. Remove chicken to serving platter and keep warm. Let sauce simmer 10 minutes or until reduced by half. Pour sauce over chicken. Combine the remaining parsley and tarragon and sprinkle over all. This can be made ahead and reheated. *SERVES: 4*

Broccoli Pudding

2 cups cooked, finely chopped broccoli or 1 10-ounce package chopped broccoli, cooked and drained
½ cup mayonnaise
1 tablespoon butter or margarine, melted
1 tablespoon flour
3 eggs
1 cup half and half
½ teaspoon salt
¼ teaspoon white pepper

Preheat oven to 375°. Butter a 6-cup heat-proof mold or casserole. In a large mixing bowl, combine the cooked broccoli, mayonnaise and melted butter, stirring gently. Sprinkle the flour over the mixture and fold it in. In a separate mixing bowl, beat eggs until light, then add half and half, salt and pepper. Stir egg mixture into broccoli. Pour into prepared dish. Place dish in a larger pan with a deep rim. Carefully pour boiling water into the larger pan to a depth of 1 – 2 inches. Bake at 375° for 30 – 35 minutes, or until a knife inserted in the center comes out clean. If baked in a mold, loosen edges and turn out onto a serving platter. Cut in slices to serve. *SERVES: 8*

NOTE: Refrigerate any leftovers and serve as a cold side dish, garnished with mayonnaise.

Broiled Peaches

1 29-ounce can peach halves, drained

SELECT 1 OF THE FOLLOWING FILLINGS:

¼ cup grated sharp Cheddar cheese
½ cup sour cream
2 tablespoons chopped green chilies

OR

½ cup brown sugar
½ cup chopped pecans

Preheat broiler. Place drained peach halves, cavity side up, in an ungreased baking dish. Combine selected filling ingredients and mix until well-blended. Spoon into peach halves. Place under broiler and cook until bubbly, watching carefully so that topping doesn't burn. *SERVES: 8*

Two Timin' Potatoes

6 medium potatoes, peeled and coarsely shredded or chopped (or use 1 32-ounce package Potatoes O'Brien in place of potatoes, peppers and onions)
1 green pepper, finely chopped
½ small red bell pepper, finely chopped (optional, — gives color and flavor)
3 green onions, chopped
1 teaspoon salt
1 teaspoon pepper
1½ cups half and half
½ cup (1 stick) butter or margarine

Preheat oven 225°. Grease a 2-quart flat baking dish. Combine the shredded potatoes with the peppers, onions, salt and pepper (or use the bag of Potatoes O'Brien). Pour into prepared baking dish. Heat the half and half and butter in a small saucepan over low heat until the butter has melted. Remove from heat and pour over the potato mixture. Bake, uncovered, at 225° for 4 – 5 hours. Check after 4 hours, adding milk if the mixture seems dry. The potatoes will hold in the oven for another hour. Serve as a side dish where you would normally serve potatoes.
SERVES: 6

NOTE: Refrigerate any leftover potatoes and serve the next morning for breakfast. Heat potatoes in a skillet with about ¼ cup butter or margarine. Great with eggs and bacon as a new twist to hashbrowns.

Grandmother saved fancy desserts for special occasions, but she often prepared simple sweets to end a meal for the family. Her Apricot Milk Pie was easy to fix, and she made it extra special by adding orange juice and grated orange peel to her pie crust.

Apricot Milk Pie

Unbaked orange pie crust
1 cup sugar
4 tablespoons flour
1 21-ounce can apricots
2 tablespoons apricot juice
1 cup sweetened condensed milk

Mix sugar and flour. Sprinkle half over crust. Drain apricots, reserving juice and chop coarsely. Spread over flour mixture. Combine remaining sugar and flour mixture with 2 tablespoons reserved apricot juice and pour over apricots. Drizzle sweetened condensed milk over pie. Bake at 350° 40 – 45 minutes until bubbly. Cool. *SERVES: 8*

ORANGE PIE CRUST
¾ cup sifted flour
1½ teaspoons sugar
¼ teaspoon salt
1½ teaspoons grated orange peel
¼ cup butter or shortening
2 – 3 tablespoons orange juice

Sift flour, sugar, salt. Add orange peel. Cut in butter or shortening until mixture resembles coarse cornmeal. Gradually add just enough orange juice to bind ingredients together. Chill dough at least 30 minutes. Roll pastry out on floured surface until it is a circle slightly larger than the pie pan. Lightly oil pie pan, then gently ease crust into pan and crimp the edges.

Lemon Jelly was another dessert that Grandmother served all the time, but because of its versatility, the family never tired of it. Sometimes it was served as a pudding, other times as a filling for a lemon tart, and still again, sandwiched between cookies or spooned over slices of cake. But the way everyone liked it best was when she combined lemon jelly and whipped cream, then used the mixture to frost an angel food cake.

Lemon Jelly

1 cup sugar
5 egg yolks, beaten
Grated rind of 2 lemons
½ cup (1 stick) butter or margarine
Juice of 3 lemons

Combine all ingredients in the top of a double boiler set over simmering water. Cook, stirring constantly, until mixture is thick and smooth. Remove from heat, let cool, then chill. *MAKES: 1½ cups*

This is a versatile filling, and may be used in the following ways:

1. Use as a filling for tarts, topping each tart with a dollop of whipped cream.

2. Spread between layers of white cake or angel food cake (especially good for wedding cakes).

3. Thin with heavy cream to a pourable consistency and serve as a lemon sauce over fresh raspberries, blueberries, or other fresh fruit.

4. Whip 1 cup of heavy cream and fold into lemon jelly. Frost top and sides of an angel food cake.

Occasionally, even Grandmother decided that cooking a big dinner every day was lots of work. On those days, Pop came home to a meal of leftovers. Never one to complain, Pop was well-known for his sense of humor. But one day he wanted to gently make a point. Beginning to bless the meal, he opened with his customary, "Bow your little heads." A pause... "Dear Lord, bless all these old friends. Amen." Needless to say, even with Pop's hint, there were many more meals with "old friends" as long as Grandmother ruled in the kitchen!

Mother's brother, Jack, had the responsibility for the cow and the chickens. He sold the extra eggs for spending money, and even earned enough to pay for a trip to the 1939 World's Fair in New York. Of course, Grandmother was proud of his efforts, as noted on a copy of her recipe for Lemon Pie. Although she specified "Jack Horton" brand eggs, the recipe still results in a nice, lemony pie when store-bought eggs are used.

Lemon Pie

1 lemon
3 eggs, "Jack Horton" brand
1 cup sugar
3 tablespoons butter or margarine, melted
1 9-inch unbaked pie crust

Grate a thin layer of peel from lemon (yellow only). Juice lemon, removing seeds, and set both juice and grated peel aside. Beat eggs until light, then gradually add sugar, beating until thick. Add melted butter, lemon juice and peel. Pour into unbaked pie crust. Bake at 400° for 5 minutes, then reduce heat to 350° and bake for 25–30 minutes. Remove from oven and cool. SERVES: 8

Grandmother's Favorite Pie Crust

3 cups sifted flour
1 teaspoon salt
1¼ cups shortening
1 egg, slightly beaten
6 tablespoons water
1 teaspoon vinegar

Combine flour and salt in a mixing bowl or the work bowl of a food processor. Cut in shortening until mixture resembles coarse meal. Stir in beaten egg, then add water and vinegar. Stir or process until mixture will hold together. Divide dough into 3 balls. Chill 30 minutes. Roll each ball out on a floured surface until it is a circle slightly larger than the pie pan. Lightly oil pie pan, then gently ease crust into pan and crimp edges. If a baked crust is required, prick surface evenly with a fork and bake in a preheated 450° oven for 8–10 minutes, or until browned. MAKES: 3 crusts

NOTE: Wrap any dough you don't need and freeze it for later use. It's even more convenient if you roll out the dough and line extra pie tins, then wrap and freeze them. When you need a pie crust, simply pull out a prepared crust and proceed.

Jack Horton-brand eggs were also excellent for pickling, and Grandmother always kept a jar of pickled eggs in the refrigerator. They were usually served with supper, added to lunch pails or taken on picnics. Even my memories of Grandmother's kitchen include that ever-present jar of pickled eggs set on the table with supper. They are easy to make, and a nice change from deviled eggs.

Pickled Eggs

12 hard cooked eggs
2 cups juice from dill pickles
  or pickled beets

Peel eggs, then put into a large jar or non-metal container with a tight fitting lid. Try to select a container that will allow the eggs to fit as close together as possible. Pour pickle juice over eggs. Cover and refrigerate at least 5 days. Serve as an accompaniment to meats, chicken or sandwiches. Beet pickle juice makes beautiful eggs. *MAKES: 1 dozen*

Perhaps one of the more unusual (and often told) family stories is Mother's explanation of how she learned to love caviar at a very young age. It seems that Pop learned that one of the local stores he sold some feed to was about to declare bankruptcy, and he was going to lose the money owed to him. Pop called Grandmother and told her to go to the store and charge several hundred dollars worth of groceries (in those days the stores would bill you at the end of the month for whatever you had picked up). She was to make up a story about needing to stock up for a party or something, so that the store owner would not get suspicious and stop her. After Grandmother had bought everything she thought she would need, she added a case of caviar to her purchases in order to reach the dollar amount Pop had specified. Mother said the family ate caviar very nonchalantly through that whole summer. Grandmother often made caviar "pie", as the kids called it, for a special company treat. Her creation makes a delicious addition to a buffet or holiday party table. It's an attractive way to show off caviar . . . and makes a little go a long way, in case you don't have a pantry full to offer your guests!

Caviar Pie

9 slices fresh white bread, crusts trimmed
1 tablespoon butter or margarine, melted
8 hard cooked eggs, peeled and chopped coarsely
2 tablespoons mayonnaise
2 tablespoons sour cream
¼ cup very finely chopped onion
½ teaspoon salt
¼ teaspoon pepper
¼ cup sour cream
1 2-ounce jar caviar — black, red or golden

Preheat oven to 325°. Lay three slices trimmed bread side by side, with edges overlapping about ¼-inch. Roll bread flat with a rolling pin. Repeat twice more with remaining bread slices to form three long rectangles. Overlap rectangles along long edges about ¼-inch to form a large square. Roll with rolling pin to press together, then press firmly along all seams with fingertips to insure they are joined together. Invert a 9-inch pie plate onto the square and cut around edge with a sharp knife to form a large circle. Place circle on an ungreased cookie sheet, brush with melted butter and top with a second cookie sheet (this will keep the edges from curling). Bake at 325° for 15 minutes until lightly browned. Let cool completely before removing top cookie sheet. While crust is cooling, prepare egg salad by combining eggs, mayonnaise, 2 tablespoons of sour cream, onion, salt and pepper, blending gently until well mixed. Spread over crust in an even layer, then spread remaining sour cream over egg salad. Gently spoon or spread caviar over the top of the pie. Chill. At serving time, cut into wedges. *SERVES: 10 – 12*

Mother also remembers the fun that she and her friends had at taffy pulling parties. Grandmother would cook up a big batch of the candy and pour it out to cool. When the clear liquid had cooled and was firm enough to handle, Mother and her friends would butter their hands and stretch the taffy again and again until it was creamy white and satiny smooth. After cutting and wrapping each piece, the guests took home a taste of the afternoon's work to share with their families.

Sugar Taffy

3 cups sugar
⅔ cup water
⅓ cup vinegar
2 teaspoons butter
1 teaspoon vanilla or a few drops of peppermint flavoring

2 - 3 drops food coloring (optional)

Generously butter a large pan or platter; set aside. Combine sugar, water and vinegar in a large saucepan and bring to a boil. Cook, without stirring, until mixture reaches 268° - 270° on a candy thermometer (the soft crack stage). Remove from heat and add butter, stirring until melted. Pour onto prepared pan and let mixture cool. When it is cool enough to handle, add flavoring and food coloring. Coat hands generously with butter and pull taffy, stretching and folding it over until mixture changes from a clear to a satiny, opaque appearance. Cut in individual pieces and wrap each piece in a small square of waxed paper or plastic wrap. *MAKES: 4 - 5 dozen pieces*

Like her mother before her, Grandmother considered herself a bread baker whose skill was unequaled in Greenville. Judging from the response of her friends, her assessment was not unjustified. In addition to her regular baking of Parkerhouse Rolls, she would often make special breads for other meals.

Golden Dumpling Bread

1 cup milk
2 packages yeast
¼ cup warm water (105° – 110°)
3 eggs, beaten
½ cup sugar
1 teaspoon salt
1 teaspoon grated lemon rind, or ¼ teaspoon lemon extract

4½ – 5 cups flour
1 cup (2 sticks) butter or margarine, melted
1 cup chopped nuts
1 cup sugar
1 cup apricot preserves

Heat milk in saucepan over medium heat until tiny bubbles appear around the edge of the pan. Set aside to cool to lukewarm. Sprinkle yeast over warm water; let stand 5 minutes. In a large mixing bowl, or the work bowl of a food processor, beat eggs until light in color. Add dissolved yeast, ½ cup sugar, salt, lemon rind and cooled milk. Beat until smooth. Gradually add flour. After flour is incorporated, work ½ cup of the melted butter into dough. Turn out onto a floured surface and knead until smooth and pliable. Shape dough into a ball and place in an oiled bowl, turning over once so top surface of dough is oiled. Cover and let rise in a warm, draft-free place until doubled in bulk, about 45 minutes. Punch dough down, knead briefly, cover and let rise again until doubled — about 45 minutes. Pour remaining melted butter into a pie plate. Pinch off pieces of dough and roll into 1½-inch balls. Dip into melted butter. Place ⅓ of the buttered dumplings in the bottom of well greased tube or bundt pan. Combine nuts and sugar and sprinkle half of the mixture over the dumplings. Spoon half of the apricot preserves over the sugar layer. Repeat layers. Cover with the remaining third of the dumplings. Cover and let rise until doubled, about 30 minutes. Bake at 350° for 50 – 55 minutes. Cool in pan 10 minutes before turning out onto plate. Serve hot. Remaining bread can be wrapped in foil and reheated. *SERVES: 8*

Anadama Batter Bread

¾ cup boiling water
½ cup yellow corn meal
3 tablespoons shortening
⅓ cup molasses
2 teaspoons salt
1 package yeast
¼ cup warm water
   (105° – 110°)

1 egg
2½ cups flour
1 tablespoon butter or
   margarine, melted
1 tablespoon cornmeal
¼ teaspoon salt

In a large mixing bowl, combine first 5 ingredients, stirring until shortening has melted. Set aside to cool to lukewarm. Sprinkle dry yeast over warm water; let stand 5 minutes. Add dissolved yeast, egg and 1 cup of the flour to cornmeal mixture and beat until smooth. Add remaining flour, mixing until a smooth, thick batter is formed. Spread batter into a greased 8½ × 4½ × 2¾-inch pan. Brush with melted butter. Combine remaining cornmeal and salt and sprinkle evenly over top of loaf. Let rise in a warm, draft-free place until doubled, about 1½ hours. Bake at 350° for 35 – 40 minutes, or until loaf is browned and sounds hollow when tapped. Remove from pan and cool on rack or serve hot. *MAKES: 1 loaf*

Bread baking was a skill she felt important to pass along, so Grandmother encouraged us grandkids to join her in the kitchen. She found this bread recipe in a newspaper back in the 1930's, and often made it when we were there to help. I loved to drop the bag of dough into a bucket of water and wait for it to float to the top. Perhaps it was a subtle way of teaching me just how yeast worked in bread dough. All I knew was that when the cooking lesson ended, I was so proud to show off these delicious rolls.

Excellent Tea Rolls

ROLLS:
3 cups sifted flour
½ teaspoon salt
½ cup (1 stick) butter or margarine
2 packages yeast
1 teaspoon sugar
¼ cup warm water (105° – 110°)
¼ cup evaporated milk
3 eggs, beaten
1 teaspoon vanilla
1 cup chopped nuts
½ cup sugar
Cheese cloth or a loosely woven cup towel

GLAZE:
½ cup powdered sugar
2 – 3 tablespoons evaporated milk

In a large bowl, combine 1½ cups of the flour and salt. Cut in butter until mixture resembles coarse cornmeal (like you would make a pie crust). Dissolve yeast and sugar in warm water. Let stand 5 minutes. Combine with evaporated milk. Add to the flour-butter mixture and beat well. Cover and let stand for 20 minutes. Add eggs, vanilla and remaining 1½ cups flour. Stir until smooth. Tie the dough loosely in cheese cloth or towel and drop into a pail of cool water (70° – 80°). In about 1 hour, the dough will rise to the top of the water. Remove from the pail and turn onto a plate. Preheat oven to 425°. Combine nuts and sugar in a small bowl; set aside. Cut off pieces of the dough about the size of an egg and roll in nut-sugar mixture. Twist the dough into figure eights. Place on greased cookie sheets about 2 inches apart, and let stand for 5 minutes. Bake at 425° for 10 – 15 minutes, until browned. While rolls are baking, combine powdered sugar and evaporated milk, blending until smooth. Drizzle over hot rolls. Serve at once.
MAKES: 2 dozen

Mother's favorite bread was the Sweet Rye Bread that Grandmother would make. Its dense texture and mildly sweet flavor made it perfect for toasting or making ham sandwiches. Mother loved this bread so much that one Christmas, Grandmother gave her a certificate for fifty-two loaves (one loaf a week) to be baked and given in regular installments over the next year.

Sweet Rye Bread

2 cups whole milk
½ cup sugar
1½ teaspoons salt
½ cup dark molasses
½ cup shortening
1½ teaspoons caraway seed
1 teaspoon anise seed
2 packages yeast
¼ cup lukewarm water (105° – 110°)
1 cup rye flour, sifted
6 – 6½ cups white flour

Heat milk in saucepan over medium heat until tiny bubbles appear around the edge of the pan. Remove from heat and add sugar, salt, molasses, shortening, caraway and anise seeds. Stir until shortening has melted and set aside to cool. Dissolve yeast in lukewarm water. When milk mixture has cooled, add the dissolved yeast and rye flour. Set mixture aside to rise about 1 hour. Work in the white flour a little at a time, kneading dough until smooth and elastic — at least 5 minutes of good kneading. Place dough in an oiled bowl, turning once so that oiled surface is on top. Cover and let rise in a warm draft-free place until doubled, about 1 hour. Punch dough down and knead briefly in bowl. Divide into 2 loaves and place in greased 9×5×3-inch loaf pans. Let rise in a warm draft-free place until doubled. Bake loaves in a preheated 375° oven for 15 minutes then reduce heat to 350° and continue baking 20-30 minutes longer until loaves sound hollow when tapped. Remove from pans and cool. *MAKES: 2 loaves*

Grandmother's skill for bread baking was not shared by her good friend Mrs. H.L. McLow. But Mrs. McLow's specialty was cookies. Many of her cookie recipes, two of which are included here, turned up in Grandmother's recipe box. Grandmother and Mrs. McLow often swapped freshly baked bread and cookies, since each thought the other could do a better job. Pop was especially partial to the oatmeal cookies which Mrs. McLow always baked in muffin tins. Pop named them "Sinkers", because they reminded him of the weights he used on his fishing line. He thought they were similar in both shape and weight!

McLow's Sinkers

¾ cup butter or margarine, softened
¼ cup sugar
¼ cup honey
½ teaspoon vanilla
1 egg
1 cup flour
½ teaspoon cinnamon
½ teaspoon nutmeg
½ teaspoon baking soda
½ teaspoon salt
3 tablespoons buttermilk
½ cup pecans or walnuts
½ cup raisins
½ cup snipped dried apricots
1 cup uncooked quick rolled oats

Preheat oven to 350°. Grease 3 small-sized 12-cavity muffin tins. In a large mixing bowl, cream butter, sugar and honey together until light and fluffy. Stir in vanilla and egg, beating until smooth. In another bowl, sift together flour, cinnamon, nutmeg, baking soda and salt. Gradually add dry ingredients to butter mixture, alternating with buttermilk, until well blended. Stir in nuts, raisins, apricots and oatmeal. Spoon about 1 tablespoon of batter into each muffin tin cavity, making sure that batter does not fill each cup more than ¾ full. Bake at 350° for 12 – 15 minutes. Let sit in pans for 5 minutes, then remove sinkers from pans and allow to cool before serving. These can also be baked as drop cookies — drop about 2 tablespoons of batter onto well greased cookie sheets. Bake as instructed above. *MAKES: 3 dozen*

NOTE: A delicious variation on the flavor of this cookie can be obtained by substituting ½ cup miniature chocolate chips for the apricots.

McLow's Chocolate Fingers

½ cup flour
2 tablespoons cocoa
½ teaspoon baking powder
2 eggs, separated
2 tablespoons butter or margarine, softened
½ teaspoon vanilla
Pinch of salt
¾ cup sugar
¼ cup finely chopped pecans
¼ cup powdered sugar

Preheat oven to 350°. Grease an 8-inch square cake pan. Sift together flour, cocoa and baking powder; set aside. Beat egg yolks and butter until thick. Stir in vanilla and set aside. In a separate bowl, beat egg whites and salt with an electric mixer until frothy. Continue beating and gradually add sugar in a steady stream, beating until sugar is dissolved and mixture is thick. Fold into egg yolk mixture. Sift dry ingredients over eggs and fold in. Pour into prepared pan and sprinkle with pecans. Bake at 350° for 20-25 minutes. Cool. Cut into 1″×2″ strips and roll each strip in powdered sugar. *MAKES: 24*

Another cookie recipe in Grandmother's recipe collection makes a crisp oatmeal cookie with a lacy texture. The recipe came from Wilhelmina Warren who, along with her husband, Fletcher, was a close friend. The Warrens served with the State Department for many years, and Mr. Warren held posts as ambassador to Turkey, Greece, Paraguay and Uruguay during his career. Mrs. Warren was responsible for coordinating all dinners, receptions and other functions at the embassies where her husband was posted. Her talent for gracious entertaining has had a great influence on my family. She has shared many of her ideas with Grandmother, Mother and me.

Alexandrites

1 egg
1 cup sugar
½ cup (1 stick) butter or margarine, melted
2 tablespoons flour
¼ teaspoon salt
¼ teaspoon baking powder
1 teaspoon vanilla
1 cup uncooked quick rolled oats

Preheat oven to 350°. Line greased baking sheets with a piece of waxed paper. Lightly grease the waxed paper. Beat egg; add sugar and melted butter. Add dry ingredients and mix well. Add vanilla and oats. Drop each tablespoon of batter 3 – 4 inches apart on prepared pans. (These cookies really spread.) Bake for 12 minutes in 350° oven. As soon as you remove them from the oven, pull the waxed paper off onto a cool surface. This prevents the cookies from sticking. *MAKES: 3 dozen*

Mrs. Warren gave another very special recipe to Grandmother. Greek Lemon Soup was one acquired during the days that she and Mr. Warren were posted in the Mediterranean. It's so easy to make and always an elegant beginning to a meal.

Greek Lemon Soup

4 cups chicken broth
½ cup raw rice
2 teaspoons salt
2 egg yolks
2 tablespoons lemon juice
1 lemon, sliced thinly (for garnish)

Bring chicken broth to a boil in a large saucepan over medium heat. Add rice and salt, reduce heat and simmer, covered, for 20 minutes. Remove from heat. Beat egg yolks in a small bowl with an electric mixer. Slowly add lemon juice, and beat until light. Continue beating and gradually add 2 cups of the hot chicken mixture. Pour egg yolk mixture into remaining chicken broth and heat over very low heat until soup has thickened slightly. Do not allow soup to boil. Serve at once, garnishing each serving with a thin slice of lemon. SERVES: 6 - 8

Grandmother's half-sister, Lallie Carlisle Davis, shared the family interest in cooking and collecting recipes. She carried on the tradition of making a cookbook like her mother, Mama Carlisle. In 1931, she gave Grandmother a small book of favorite recipes as a Christmas gift. Lallie was also a painter, and added character to the book with a variety of clever illustrations. Many of the recipes were old family favorites conveniently set down in one place. Others Lallie had discovered on her own.

Molded Chicken Salad

2 envelopes gelatin
¼ cup cold chicken broth
1½ cups hot chicken broth
1 tablespoon lemon juice
½ cup salad dressing (not mayonnaise)
½ teaspoon salt
¼ teaspoon white pepper
½ cup heavy cream, whipped
2 cups diced, cooked chicken
1 cup frozen peas, thawed
½ cup chopped celery
½ cup chopped almonds
2 tablespoons chopped black olives
2 tablespoons capers
Additional salad dressing and whole black olives for garnish

In a large mixing bowl, soften gelatin in cold broth. Add hot broth and stir until gelatin is dissolved. Let cool. Add lemon juice, salad dressing, salt and pepper, stirring until smooth. Fold in whipped cream. Gently stir in remaining ingredients. Pour into a 2-quart flat baking dish. Chill until set. Cut into squares and garnish each serving with a dollop of salad dressing and a whole black olive. SERVES: 8

Corn Creole

4 tablespoons butter or margarine
2 tablespoons chopped onion
2 tablespoons chopped green pepper
4 tablespoons flour
2 egg yolks, slightly beaten
1 14½-ounce can tomatoes, undrained and chopped
1 teaspoon salt
1 cup frozen whole kernel corn
2 teaspoons chopped parsley

Melt butter in a large heavy skillet over medium heat. Sauté onions and peppers until onions are transparent. Add flour and stir with wire whisk until smooth, about 1 minute. Stir in egg yolks. Add chopped tomatoes, salt, corn and parsley. Simmer uncovered about 12 minutes, stirring often. SERVES: 6

Old-Fashioned Fruit Salad Dressing

This recipe originally called for plain vinegar, but I have found the taste much improved by adding raspberry vinegar or white wine vinegar.

2 egg yolks
½ cup sugar
½ cup raspberry vinegar or white wine vinegar
½ teaspoon salt
¼ teaspoon cayenne
2 teaspoons butter or margarine
1 cup heavy cream

Mix egg yolks, sugar, raspberry vinegar, salt and cayenne in a double boiler set over hot water and cook until mixture thickens. Add butter, stirring until melted. Remove from heat and let cool, then chill. At serving time, whip cream until soft peaks form. Fold into chilled, cooked mixture. Combine with an assortment of fresh and/or canned fruit. (I like to use sliced bananas, drained mandarin oranges, seedless grapes and fresh melon chunks.)
MAKES: 2 cups

Lallie's Lemon Almond Cookies

1½ cups slivered almonds
1 cup (2 sticks) butter or margarine, softened
1 cup sugar
2 eggs
1 teaspoon baking powder
2 cups flour
Grated rind of 1 lemon
Whole almonds for garnish

Grind almonds in a blender or food processor until the texture of cornmeal. Set aside. Cream butter and sugar together in a mixing bowl until light and fluffy. Add eggs and beat until smooth. Stir baking powder and flour together and add to butter mixture. Stir in ground almonds and lemon rind. Divide dough in two, and shape each section into a long roll. Wrap each roll in waxed paper and chill until firm — several hours or overnight. At baking time, preheat oven to 300°. Slice chilled dough ¼-inch thick, and place cookies 2 inches apart on ungreased cookie sheets. (Press an almond into the center of each cookie for garnish, if desired.) Bake at 300° for 15–20 minutes until lightly browned, watching carefully to see that cookies do not burn on the bottom. MAKES: 4–5 dozen

NOTE: I make a stronger almond-flavored cookie by omitting the lemon rind and adding 2 teaspoons almond extract to the cookie dough. This cookie dough freezes beautifully, and is great to keep on hand.

Hot Chocolate

3 ounces unsweetened chocolate
½ cup cold water
¾ cup sugar
⅛ teaspoon salt
1 teaspoon vanilla
1 cup heavy cream
Hot milk

Combine chocolate and water in a saucepan over low heat. Stir until chocolate is melted. Add sugar and salt, stirring until mixture is smooth. Bring to a boil, stirring constantly, and cook 5 minutes. Remove from heat and add vanilla. Cool completely. At serving time, whip heavy cream and fold into chocolate mixture. Ladle about 3-4 tablespoons of sauce into each cup and fill with hot milk. *MAKES: 6 – 8 servings*

NOTE: This recipe makes a perfect chocolate dessert sauce all by itself. Just leave out the hot milk and spoon over ice cream.

Two of the more unique entries in Lallie's book were listed on a page titled "Invalid Cookery". Mother confirmed that these were commonly prepared by both Grandmother and Lallie to help nurse someone back to health after an illness. In fact, both are still used today. Egg in Nest is a breakfast favorite (and we don't have to be under the weather to enjoy it). Beef Tea is prepared when an easily digestible source of nourishment is needed for someone who has been ill. I guess you could say that Beef Tea is the same type of all-purpose medicine for my family that chicken soup is for many other families.

Egg in Nest

INGREDIENTS FOR EACH SERVING:
1 egg, separated
⅛ teaspoon salt
Dash of pepper
1 slice toast, well buttered
Chopped parsley for garnish

Preheat oven to 300°. Beat egg white and salt together until stiff. Fold in pepper. Pile egg white on toast, making a depression in the center. Slide in the unbroken yolk. Bake on an ungreased cookie sheet in a 300° oven 15 – 20 minutes or until white is lightly browned and yolk is set. Sprinkle with chopped parsley. *SERVES: 1*

Beef Tea

1¾ – 2 pounds round steak, not tenderized (bottom round is best)

Salt and pepper

Trim all fat off round steak; cut into ½-inch cubes. Put cubes into a quart jar with a tight-fitting lid, packing the jar as full as possible. Cover tightly with lid. Place jar in a deep saucepan and add as much water as possible, so that the meat is cooked in a water bath. Bring to a boil, reduce heat and simmer gently for 3 hours, adding hot water to the saucepan as necessary. Remove jar from water and let cool until jar and meat can be handled. Drain off all liquid and reserve. Scrape as much grey film off the meat as possible, adding it to the broth. Chill broth and skim fat off the top. To serve, blend broth in a blender until smooth, then reheat. Season to taste with salt and pepper. *MAKES: about 1 cup*

NOTE: Save the cooked cubes of beef and use in a salad, or add to a stroganoff-type sauce and serve over noodles.

Lallie and Grandmother continued to share recipes whenever they found good ones. About 15 years after she made the little cookbook, Lallie and her husband, George Davis, an Army officer, spent several years in Japan as part of the occupation forces after World War II. When they returned, Lallie brought this recipe, which she called Skimpy Shrimp.

Skimpy Shrimp

6 slices buttered bread, cut into cubes
1 pound cooked shrimp or 4 4¼-ounce cans shrimp, drained
4 cups (16 ounces) grated Swiss cheese

3 eggs
1 cup milk
1 teaspoon prepared mustard
½ teaspoon salt

Preheat oven to 350°. Grease a 2-quart flat baking dish. Place bread cubes in bottom of casserole, top with shrimp and sprinkle with cheese. Beat eggs, milk, mustard and salt together. Pour over top. Let stand 45 minutes. Bake at 350° for 40 – 45 minutes. Cover loosely with foil if top browns too quickly. Serve at once. Sam's Salad (see index) goes nicely with this casserole. *SERVES: 6*

World War II had seen Pop re-enter the service, serving most of the war years as executive officer of Camp Gruber in Muskogee, Oklahoma. One of Camp Gruber's functions was to house prisoners of war captured in Europe. Pop's infamous sense of humor showed up once again in one of the ways he claimed to have kept order in the camp. He always told us that he would show the prisoners "Cowboy and Indian" movies for entertainment. When the films were over, he reminded them that they were in Oklahoma Indian territory. Of course, most prisoners were unaware that the days of Indian uprisings were over . . . and Pop never volunteered the information. He claimed to have a remarkably good record where discipline was concerned. (Pop was later declared the winner in the annual Hunt County Liars' Contest many times, so I've never been sure whether he told this story straight, or was just spinning a good one.)

Grandmother and Pop lived in a wonderful old home that they had spent countless hours working on when Mother was a young girl. All the woodwork in the house was black walnut, cut from Puddin Hill trees. Grandmother supervised the work as the wood was kiln-dried by a coffin maker, then made into doors, door frames, bookcases and pillars. The back room, once an old porch, was the best place in the house. The family dining table was on one side of the room, Pop's chair and reading lamp on the other, and the rest was taken up by bookcases and the table holding Grandmother's latest project. I spent many happy hours beside Grandmother "helping" her with whatever she was working on, and often getting a lesson or lecture about whatever was on her mind.

The back room was always welcoming and comfortable — a very special place to everyone. Every grandchild (or kid of any age) knew where the candy was kept. A three-tiered cut glass candy jar always held the special treats which Grandmother made. The top layer, easily opened by little hands, held the Minted Pecans — my favorite. The second layer offered up Roasted Pecans. And the third layer contained the favorite of my father and most of the other grownups, Candied Orange Peel. Grandmother was a master at this confection, and now that I've grown up, I can appreciate it. There is no bitterness from the peel — just a wonderful sweet orange flavor.

Grandmother's Minted Pecans

1 cup sugar
½ cup water
⅛ teaspoon salt
¼ cup light corn syrup

6 large marshmallows
2 tablespoons green Creme de Menthe
2½ cups pecan halves

Combine sugar, water, salt and corn syrup in a saucepan. Bring to a boil over medium heat until a candy thermometer registers 238° (the soft ball stage). Remove from heat and add marshmallows and Creme de Menthe. Stir until marshmallows melt, then add nuts and stir until they separate. Turn out onto pan and separate with a fork. Let cool completely and store in an airtight container. *MAKES: 3 cups*

NOTE: For variety, substitute amaretto, rum, brandy or any other liquor or liqueur for the creme de menthe.

Roasted Pecans

¼ cup butter or margarine
1 pound pecan halves
1 – 2 teaspoons salt

Melt the butter in a heavy iron skillet over low heat. Add the pecans and stir constantly until nuts are well-coated with butter and evenly browned. Remove from heat, stir in the salt and spread on waxed paper to cool. *MAKES: 2 – 3 cups*

Grandmother's Candied Orange Peel

5 – 6 oranges
Water to cover
1 tablespoon lemon juice
3 cups water
3 cups sugar
1 teaspoon vanilla
Additional sugar (about 1 cup) for rolling

Lightly grate the outside of each orange to release the oil in the peel (save grated peel for other uses by storing in a plastic bag in the freezer). Quarter each orange, remove peel from each quarter and cut peel into ½-inch wide strips. Place orange peel in a large saucepan and cover with water. Bring to a boil and cook for 10 minutes. Drain peel and repeat the process. (This removes any bitter taste from the peel). Drain again. Make a sugar syrup by combining the lemon juice, 3 cups of water and 3 cups of sugar in a large saucepan; bring to a boil. Cook syrup to 228° on a candy thermometer. Remove from heat, add drained orange peel and bring to a boil again. Reduce heat and simmer peel in syrup until most of the syrup is absorbed and peel has become translucent — one to two hours. Stir occasionally to make sure that peel does not scorch. Drain peel and roll each piece in granulated sugar. Let dry several hours on waxed paper. Store in an airtight container.
MAKES: 6 – 8 dozen candies

When Pop turned seventy-eight, he decided that it was time to retire, so he sold his grain and feed business and settled back to enjoy life. His "enjoyment" lasted about six weeks, then he found things were too dull. He felt the only way to handle his boredom was to tackle a demanding project. Returning to law practice offered him that challenge, but Pop realized that he was terribly out of date when it came to all the legal changes that had occurred since 1910. The best way to correct the situation was to go back to law school; so that's just what he did! Pop enrolled in law classes at the University of Texas. Grandmother willingly closed up the house in Greenville for the semester, and they moved into the married students' apartments on campus. While Pop attended classes, Grandmother delighted the wives of the other law students by dispensing recipes, entertaining tips and the kind of advice that only comes from years of experience.

They returned to Greenville after that venture, and Pop opened a law practice that kept him happy until he retired again at age 87. Even then, he moved his office to a bedroom in the house, where he "went to work" each day. He read and wrote his memoirs, and chatted with those who came by for a visit. I can remember being at the house at noon, when Pop would call down the stairs, "Gertrude, can I come home for dinner yet?" If she said yes, then he would join us at the table.

Grandmother was not about to be outdone by this display of over-seventy energy. When she turned eighty, she realized that she'd better face the fact that one day, hard as it was to imagine, she might get old. When that happened, she wanted to be prepared with a project that would keep her busy and make sure folks kept coming by the house. So she embarked upon yet another of her in-home careers — an antique shop. It started out with a few pieces of porcelain and cut-glass and grew into a business that saw her regarded as an expert on cut-glass. Because of her knowledge, her collection and, most of all, her reputation as a charming hostess, folks did come to see her. What they found captivated them. Grandmother and Pop loved nothing more than to sit and visit with the customers, especially if they could be talked into staying for a cup of tea. Tea was served from an antique china teapot (with the price tag visible), and accompanied by an antique silver tray filled with her special tea breads and muffins. Grandmother explained the price tags by saying she believed beautiful things were to be used and enjoyed, not stuck on a shelf somewhere. She didn't have to explain her cooking.

Apricot Nut Bread

2 cups flour
4 teaspoons baking powder
1 teaspoon salt
2/3 cups sugar
1 cup chopped pecans or walnuts
3/4 cup finely chopped dried apricots
2 eggs, well beaten
1 cup milk
1/4 cup vegetable oil

Preheat oven to 375°. Grease a 9×5×3-inch loaf pan. Sift flour, baking powder, salt and sugar into a large bowl. Add nuts and apricots, tossing lightly; set aside. In a small bowl, combine remaining ingredients. Add to dry ingredients, stirring only until flour is moistened. Turn into prepared pan. Push batter up into corners of pan, leaving the center slightly hollowed so loaf will be even after baking. Allow batter to stand in pan for 20 minutes, then bake at 375° for 1 hour. MAKES: 1 loaf

Cranberry Orange Bread

2 cups flour
1½ teaspoons baking powder
1 cup sugar
½ teaspoon baking soda
½ teaspoon salt
1 orange
2 tablespoons vegetable oil
Water
1 egg, beaten
1 cup chopped fresh cranberries
1 cup chopped nuts

Preheat oven to 325°. Grease a 9×5×3-inch loaf pan. Sift together flour, baking powder, sugar, soda and salt; set aside. Grate thin layer of peel from orange (try not to get any of the white part). Juice orange into a measuring cup (remove seeds if any). Add oil and enough water to make ¾ cup. Add beaten egg to liquid. Combine with dry ingredients, stirring until just blended. Stir in nuts, peel and chopped cranberries. Pour into prepared pan and bake at 325° for 1 hour. Store 24 hours before serving. When ready to serve, slice thin and spread with butter or cream cheese. This bread is also good toasted. *MAKES: 1 loaf*

Date-Nut Muffins with Orange Glaze

MUFFINS:
3 eggs, slightly beaten
¾ cup sugar
2 tablespoons flour
1 cup chopped pecans
1 cup chopped dates

GLAZE:
¾ cup powdered sugar
¼ teaspoon grated orange rind
4 – 5 teaspoons orange juice

To make muffins, preheat oven to 350°. Grease 3 small-sized 12-cavity muffin tins or use paper liners. In small bowl, beat eggs and sugar until light. Add flour, blending until smooth. Stir in pecans and dates. Spoon mixture into prepared muffin tins and bake at 350° for 20 minutes. Cool 5 minutes before removing from pans. Glaze while still hot. To make glaze, combine all ingredients in a small bowl, stirring until smooth. Spread a small amount of glaze on each muffin. *MAKES: 3 dozen*

Both Grandmother and Pop lived to be 89. Pop died two years before Grandmother, and she was grateful to have the antique shop to keep her busy. She continued to be very active until she was killed in an automobile accident in Dallas. It occurred two blocks from the biggest antique show of the year, to which she had been en route. We all said that anyone who could die two blocks from heaven surely made it the rest of the way. We believe she did. On her coffin was a simple bouquet of a dozen white roses.

Grandmother and Pop left us and everyone they touched a remarkable legacy. They brought together two very special heritages and combined them into a solid union. They taught us that the real wealth in life is an understanding and appreciation of one's family, that the tally of friends counts far more than any pile of dollars, that giving back to the community is an obligation (but one which brings much satisfaction and pleasure), and that marriage is built on laughter, acceptance, love and plenty of good cooking.

When my husband Mike and I married, Grandmother and Pop asked us to dinner several nights before the wedding. They each had a gift for us — something that expressed their individual philosophies of marriage. Pop gave Mike a framed picture that had hung on the wall of his office for many years. It said, "A woman is to be loved and not understood." Grandmother gave me a copy of a cookbook produced in 1923 by her church. She opened it to this passage and told me to take it to heart:

HOW TO COOK HUSBANDS

A good many husbands are entirely spoiled by mismanagement in cooking, and so are not tender and good. Some women go about it as if their husbands were bladders, and blow them up. Others keep them constantly in hot water. Others let them freeze by their carelessness and indifference. Some keep them in a stew by irritating ways and words. Others roast them. Some keep them in a pickle all their lives. It can not be supposed that any husband will be tender and good managed in this way, but they are really delicious when properly treated. In selecting your husband you should not be guided by the silvery appearance, as in buying mackerel, nor by the golden tint, as if you wanted salmon. Be sure and select him yourself, as tastes differ. Do not go to the market for him, as the best is always brought to the door. It is far better to have none unless you will patiently learn how to cook him. A preserving kettle of the finest porcelain is the best, but if you have nothing but an earthenware pipkin it will do, with care. See that the linen in which you wrap him is nicely washed and mended, with the requisite number of buttons and strings nicely sewed on. Tie him in the kettle by a strong silken cord called comfort; duty is apt to be weak. Husbands are apt to fly out of the kettle and be burned and crusty on the edges, since, like crabs and lobsters, you have to cook them while alive. Make a clear, steady fire out of love, neatness and cheerfulness. Set your husband as near this as seems to agree with him. If he sputters and fizzes, do not be anxious. Some husbands do this until they are quite done. Add a little sugar in the form of what confectioners call kisses, but no vinegar or pepper on any account. A little spice improves him, but it must be used with judgement. Do not stick any sharp instrument into him to see if he is becoming tender. Stir him gently; watch the while lest he lie too flat and close to the kettle, and so become useless. You can not fail to know when he is done. If thus treated, you will find him very digestible, agreeing nicely with you and the children, and he will keep you as long as you want, unless you become careless and set him in too cold a place.

"When Hal got his wings, Grandmother, Jack and Mother drove Lelloine to California for the wedding."

Chapter Three

The Rest of the Horton Crowd

Mother's family has many good cooks who have been influenced by Grandmother and her skills in the kitchen. The result is that, whether it be a visit from an out-of-town relative, a birthday, or just because a good "catch-up" is needed, any assembly of family members usually becomes an occasion for a meal.

Grandmother and Pop loved nothing better than having all their children and grandchildren together. Close friends, relatives of in-laws, distant cousins or those that might be kin through friendship were considered part of the family. Anyone who had no family member nearby was taken in and made to feel welcome. I can't remember an Easter, Thanksgiving or Christmas that my relatives didn't make sure that everyone they knew had a place to be on the holiday. If not, they were included at our table.

During my childhood, Grandmother and Pop's house was the center of the family. It was just a few blocks from our home, so Mother and I would usually stop by every day for a quick visit. Pop always greeted me with his special greeting, "Hello, Pud. I've been a-missin' you." It didn't matter whether it was the second visit that day or the first in a week — Pop had always been a-missin' me.

Many times the family got together for an impromptu supper, with everyone bringing something. If no one felt like cooking then Dad was elected to pick up pizzas. When I was in college, I usually called home twice a week to talk to Mom and Dad. If they weren't home, I always called Grandmother's house. Nine times out of ten, if it was at supper-time, I would find that Grandmother and Pop had put the extra leaves in the table to accommodate everyone. Occasionally, whoever answered the telephone would be sitting right next to Mom or Dad, but the phone went around the table so that everyone could say hello. (Thank goodness Dad helped with the phone bill.)

The gatherings aren't as frequent now that Grandmother and Pop are gone, but I think that my family has done a remarkable job of staying close. Any time that someone known to all the family comes to town, there's still what we call a "gathering of the clan." And birthdays are occasions to be celebrated with lots of loved ones around. Of course, no celebration is complete without food. Good eating is the secondary purpose for getting together. (There are those who argue that the Horton bunch uses the get-together merely as an excuse for a meal.)

Mother and her sister, Sarah Horton Plunket, share a love of cooking and entertaining. Sarah overcame her years of illness to study portrait photography as a young woman. Upon completion of her studies, she opened her own studio. When she married Paul Plunket and began to raise a family, Sarah followed Grandmother's lead and moved the cameras into her home to continue her career. The living room served as a studio, and a closet served as a darkroom. Even in this limited space, Sarah turned out beautiful work.

When her daughter and son were in high school, Sarah once again established a studio, this time with Paul at her side (or in the darkroom). Their work has won many honors, and Sarah has earned the rank of Master Photographer as a result of both her hard work and talent with a camera.

In spite of having a busy career, Sarah loves to entertain and to cook. A number of the recipes that I continually reach for in my recipe collection are labeled "From the kitchen of Sarah Plunket". Her recipes range from delicious, easy to prepare suppers like Kosher Cabbage, to unique recipes like her Pickled Smoked Turkey. A word about Kosher Cabbage before you read the recipe; the first ingredient listed is bacon. That's not exactly kosher, and everyone in my family knows it. But this recipe has been called Kosher Cabbage for over forty years, and if I were to change the name now, there would be a family uprising.

Kosher Cabbage

8 strips bacon
1 large onion, chopped
1 cup chopped celery
1 green pepper, chopped
1 medium head cabbage, coarsely chopped
1 28-ounce can tomatoes
1½ cups water
1 teaspoon turmeric
½ cup vinegar
⅓ cup sugar
1 teaspoon salt

Fry bacon in a large saucepan or Dutch oven; remove and crumble. Add onion, celery and pepper and sauté in bacon drippings until soft. Add remaining ingredients and bring to a boil. Reduce heat and simmer slowly, uncovered, for 1 hour, stirring occasionally. Add crumbled bacon.
SERVES: 8

NOTE: Kosher Cabbage makes a delicious side dish, but it is even better served over a wedge of freshly baked cornbread. Accompany with dill pickle spears and a light dessert for a nice supper.

Sarah makes a smoked turkey that is unlike any I've ever tasted. She created the recipe with a pickling marinade normally used to prepare corned beef. The secret is to soak the turkey in this marinade for at least 10 days, and it's better if soaked even longer — up to three weeks. Then it's slowly cooked on a smoker-grill to insure moistness and flavor. Although it is good served hot, we prefer to serve the turkey cold — it makes wonderful sandwiches, especially on the Puddin Hill Store's Italian Cobblestone Bread (see page 142.) Sarah usually serves Sweet-Sour Beans, a cold marinated bean salad with the turkey.

Pickled Smoked Turkey

8 – 10 pound turkey
2 teaspoons saltpeter (potassium nitrate-found at the pharmacy)
¼ cup warm water
2 tablespoons sugar
2 teaspoons paprika
1 tablespoon mixed pickling spices
4 – 5 bay leaves
2 quarts water
2 cloves garlic
½ cup salt
1 medium onion, sliced

Place turkey in turkey-size browning bag or heavy plastic bag (use a double thickness for protection). Dissolve saltpeter in warm water and blend in the remaining ingredients. Pour marinade over turkey, seal and refrigerate, marinating 10 – 21 days, turning once every day. Be sure to keep in refrigerator. The longer it marinates, the more distinctive the flavor. When ready to cook, drain and dry turkey with a cloth. Cook in smoker or over grill according to manufacturer's instructions. Slice and serve hot, or chill turkey meat and use on a cold cut platter or for sandwiches. *SERVES: 10 – 12*

NOTE: The same recipe can be used with a beef brisket When ready to cook, drain (reserving marinade) and dry with a cloth. Using a Dutch oven or heavy pot, brown brisket in 4 tablespoons butter. Add 2 cups of marinade and simmer for 2 hours or until tender. Remove and wrap in foil. Refrigerate until cold. Slice thin and serve with rye bread, cheese and pickles.

Sweet-Sour Beans

2 16-ounce cans whole green beans, drained
1 medium onion, thinly sliced
1 clove garlic, minced
1 cup sugar
1 cup vinegar
½ cup salad oil

Combine green beans, onion and garlic in a large bowl. In a small saucepan, bring sugar and vinegar to boil, cooking until sugar is dissolved. Remove from heat, stir in oil, and pour over beans. Cover and refrigerate several hours. This will keep for several weeks in the refrigerator. *SERVES: 8*

NOTE: Drained, canned kidney beans may also be used with, or in place of, the green beans.

Paul's brother, Jack Plunket, has lived for many years in Mexico City, and Sarah and Paul visit them frequently. These trips are usually a boon for the recipe boxes of the family. Delores, Jack's wife, knows Sarah's love of cooking and often plans meals that feature the dishes of central Mexico. Sarah has a real gift for recreating dishes she has tasted on her travels. She returns from these vacations filled with culinary inspiration.

Mexico City's cuisine is remarkably different from Tex-Mex, due to the influence of Emperor Maximillian who attempted to establish a French kingdom in Mexico in the 1860's. The French influence shows up in the subtle tastes of Mexico City's dishes. Although the classic Mexican spices like cumin and chili powder are used, it is with much more restraint.

Shrimp Picadillo

¼ cup butter or margarine
¼ cup chopped onion
1 green pepper, chopped
⅔ cup chopped celery
1 clove garlic, minced
½ teaspoon cumin
2 teaspoons Worcestershire
1 teaspoon dry mustard
1 teaspoon chili powder
2 pounds cooked, peeled shrimp (frozen cooked shrimp may be used)

Melt butter in large saucepan over medium heat. Add onion, green pepper, celery and garlic and sauté until tender. Add remaining ingredients, reduce heat and simmer until liquid has almost evaporated. Serve with tostados or corn chips. *SERVES: 6 – 8*

NOTE: If you are using frozen cooked shrimp, cooking may bring out extra liquid. If so, spoon off all but about 1 cup liquid and simmer as instructed.

Chili Nuts

¼ cup butter or margarine
2 tablespoons Worcestershire sauce
1 tablespoon chili powder
½ teaspoon cinnamon
1 teaspoon salt
4 cups unroasted nuts (pecan halves, peanuts, almonds)

Preheat oven to 300°. Melt butter in a large skillet over medium heat. Add Worcestershire, chili powder, cinnamon and salt; stir to blend. Add nuts and stir until they are coated with mixture. Pour nuts onto a large rimmed cookie sheet and spread in a single layer. Bake at 300° for 25 – 30 minutes, stirring every 10 minutes until toasted. Cool and serve as cocktail nibbles. *MAKES: 4 cups*

On one of their trips to Mexico, Sarah and Paul visited a resort known for its good food. Sarah returned from Villa Montaña in Morelia, Michoacan, and served a side dish of baked radishes in a cheese sauce that she had tasted there. It was delicious — the hit of the evening. The radishes, which lose some of their hot taste when boiled, are complimented by the cheese sauce. As is befitting, the name gives a tip of the sombrero to both the Mexican and French cultures:

Radishes Con Queso Au Gratin

4 cups cleaned radishes (about 6 bunches or 4 cello bags)
2 tablespoons butter or margarine
2 tablespoons flour
1 cup milk
½ teaspoon salt
¼ teaspoon white pepper
⅛ teaspoon cayenne
1 teaspoon prepared mustard
2 tablespoons dry vermouth
1 cup (4 ounces) grated Cheddar cheese
2 tablespoons butter or margarine
2 slices bread, cubed

Wash radishes. Remove stems and root ends. Place in a large saucepan with enough water to cover. Bring to a boil and cook 10 minutes; drain. In a medium saucepan, melt butter over medium heat. Add flour and cook 1 minute, stirring constantly. Add milk, reduce heat and simmer until thickened — about 5 minutes. Remove from heat and add seasonings, mustard and vermouth, stirring until smooth. Add cheese and stir until melted. Stir in radishes. Pour into a buttered 6-cup casserole. Preheat oven to 350°. In a small skillet, melt butter, add bread cubes and toss until coated. Spread cubes over the radish mixture. Bake at 350° for 20 minutes, or until bread cubes are browned and mixture is bubbly. *SERVES: 8*

Finally, after all this discussion about the subtleties of the cuisine of central Mexico, I include one recipe from Delores Plunket's kitchen that is hardly subtle, her potato salad generously laced with fresh jalapeño peppers. If you are not up to this much spicy heat in your food, replace the jalapeños with mild chopped green chilies to taste. But if you are one of those strong-willed folks who eat jalapeños like others eat popcorn, then you will find this recipe to your liking.

Delores Plunket's Papitas

SALAD:
2 pounds new potatoes
2 tablespoons oil
1 onion, sliced thin
5 cloves garlic, minced
2 bell peppers, sliced in thin strips

1 – 5 jalapeños, seeded and sliced (quantity depends on your heat tolerance)

DRESSING:
1 tablespoon dry mustard
1 teaspoon pepper
2 teaspoons salt

¼ cup oil
2 tablespoons vinegar

Boil unpeeled potatoes in water to cover until tender. Drain and cool until easy to handle, then slice each potato into large chunks. Heat oil in a heavy skillet over medium heat and sauté onion, garlic, and both peppers until tender. Combine with warm potatoes. In a small bowl, blend dressing ingredients with a wire whisk until smooth. Pour over warm vegetables, tossing gently. Refrigerate several hours to let flavors blend. Allow papitas to stand at room temperature one hour before serving. SERVES: 6 – 8

Sarah's daughter, Trudy Hutton, found Russian cooking to be an influence in her kitchen. Trudy and her husband, Tom, spent nine months in the Soviet Union on a cultural and scientific exchange program in 1974 and 1975. Tom, a neurologist, was offered the chance to represent the United States in a research fellowship with a leading Russian doctor. So he, Trudy and baby son, Andy, eagerly took the opportunity of a lifetime to study and live in Moscow. As is typical of the cooks in my family, Trudy returned with this recipe among her memories. Now a busy attorney, she still enjoys preparing this stew-like dish, as we all do, because it is quick to fix, yet special enough to serve to company. Trudy recommends serving her mother's coleslaw recipe with the ragout.

Balkan Sausage Ragout

2 tablespoons olive oil
2 large onions peeled and sliced
2 large green peppers, seeded and sliced
1 4-ounce jar diced pimiento, drained
1½ teaspoons paprika
½ teaspoon marjoram
½ teaspoon oregano
½ teaspoon caraway
1 bay leaf
½ teaspoon pepper
1½ teaspoons salt
1 pound fully cooked smoked sausage, sliced ½-inch thick
2 potatoes, peeled and cubed
2 cups tomatoes (if fresh or whole, whirl in blender or processor)
2 medium zucchini, cubed
2 tablespoons chopped parsley
Sour Cream

Heat olive oil in a large saucepan or stockpot on medium heat. Add onion and green pepper and sauté for 10 minutes, stirring occasionally. Add pimiento and spices; bring to a boil. Add sausage, potatoes, and tomatoes. Cover, reduce heat and simmer for 30 minutes. Add zucchini and simmer 10 minutes. Remove bay leaf before serving. Ladle into bowls and sprinkle with parsley. Granish each serving with a dollop of sour cream. Add black bread and coleslaw for a complete meal. *SERVES: 6*

Cabbage Slaw with Lemon Dressing

1 lemon
3 tablespoons sugar
½ cup mayonnaise (not salad dressing)
½ cup sour cream
1 medium head green cabbage
2 tablespoons poppy seed

Grate the peel from the lemon, taking care to get only the yellow layer. Squeeze juice from lemon. Combine grated peel, juice and sugar and let stand for at least an hour. Blend mayonnaise and sour cream, then add lemon-sugar mixture, stirring until smooth. Shred or chop cabbage coarsely and combine with dressing and poppy seed. Toss until cabbage is well coated with dressing. The lemon dressing is also good served over a combination of chopped apples, shredded cabbage, raisins and walnuts or pecans. *SERVES: 8*

Both of Mother's brothers did very well when it came to falling in love, because they latched onto talented women who were also good cooks. Hal's wife, Lelloine, and Jack's wife, Joyce, join the others who have married into the family in making up the band known as the "out-laws." This term came about when Mother and Dad were about to be married. When they announced their engagement, Lelloine and Paul, Sarah's husband, suddenly announced (with tongue in cheek) that they liked the family just the way it was.

They were not certain that they wanted to let anyone else marry into such an elite group. Therefore, Dad had to work hard to win their favor. It became a great game with teasing and bribes being offered at every turn, until inevitably, the wedding day came. Lelloine and Paul finally decided at the wedding reception that they had better agree to let Dad into the family because, after all, Pop had spent a small fortune to get Mother married! The tradition of the "out-laws" has continued with every wedding since. The band has grown larger and includes several generations now, which only means that the newest member-to-be must gain the favor of more people. However, once the wedding vows have been said, the "out-laws" realize that they must vote. The verdict is always grudgingly favorable. As a consolation, the newly-added "in-law" becomes the leader of the "out-laws" and gets to lead the next initiation.

Those who have become "out-laws" have added greatly to the family with their personalities and their talents. Both Hal and Jack married capable, independent women (wonder where they got the role model?) who have managed both families and businesses with equal skill.

As the first "out-law" in the family, Lelloine couldn't have been more welcomed by Grandmother and Pop, who were worried that Hal wouldn't "get up Fool's Hill." They were so glad that Hal had managed to find such a lovely young woman. Grandmother welcomed her as a daughter even before she and Hal married. Several years after they were married, Lelloine told Hal, "I don't know what you'll do if we ever have marital problems, because if that happens, I'm going home to YOUR mother!"

Hal and Lelloine married the summer before Pearl Harbor was attacked. Hal was stationed in Sacramento, California, where he was in the Air Force. When he got his wings, Grandmother, Jack and Mother drove Lelloine to California for the wedding. Grandmother always said she wanted to make sure that girl didn't get away!

Lelloine's days in Sacramento were typical of those of a young, newly-married officer's wife. She learned about life on a military base, and made friends with other wives in similar positions. And, being intimidated by Grandmother's formidable reputation as a good cook, Lelloine was proud to be able to send a recipe from California to her new mother-in-law that was not already in those bulging recipe boxes.

Tomato Juice Cake

2 cups flour
1 teaspoon baking soda
1 teaspoon cinnamon
½ teaspoon cloves
½ teaspoon nutmeg
½ cup (1 stick) butter or margarine, softened

1 cup sugar
3 eggs
1 cup tomato juice
1 cup currants or raisins
1 cup pecans or walnuts

Preheat oven to 350°. Grease a 13×9-inch cake pan. Sift together flour, soda, cinnamon, cloves and nutmeg; set aside. Cream butter and sugar until light and fluffy. Add eggs one at a time, beating thoroughly after each addition. Alternately add flour mixture and tomato juice, beginning and ending with flour mixture. Stir in currants or raisins and nuts. Pour into prepared pan. Bake for 25 – 30 minutes or until tester inserted in center of cake comes out clean. Cool in pan, then top with icing. *SERVES: 12-16*

ICING:
3 ounces cream cheese
2 tablespoons orange juice
1 teaspoon grated orange rind

¼ cup butter or margarine, softened
1 16-ounce package (heaping 3 cups) powdered sugar

Combine all ingredients in a mixing bowl and beat with an electric mixer until smooth. Add more powdered sugar if frosting is too runny.

Hal's attempts at helping Lelloine cook his favorite dishes were not always productive. Once he told Lelloine that he really wanted ham with red-eye gravy. That was easy, because every East Texas girl knew how to pan-fry a ham steak, then dilute the pan drippings with cold coffee. But Hal said that it wasn't right. Lelloine tried again. She still couldn't please Hal. He insisted that red-eye gravy had milk in it. Lelloine couldn't find anyone who had ever heard of red-eye gravy with milk in it. About the time she was at her wits end, they were transferred back to Texas. Lelloine promptly went to Grandmother and asked for a cooking lesson on red-eye gravy. Grandmother proceeded to make it just as Lelloine did — with coffee, not milk. Exasperated, Lelloine ordered Hal into the kitchen, where it was finally discovered that what he really wanted was cream gravy. He didn't even know his own mother's cooking! You can imagine Lelloine's indignation. (For a good ham and red-eye gravy recipe, see page 110.)

Lelloine ignored Hal's culinary advice from then on and continued to share her best new "finds" in recipes with Grandmother and her friends.

Curried Chicken Salad

1½ cups cooked rice
2 tablespoons mayonnaise
2 teaspoons vinegar
¼ cup minced onion
½ teaspoon curry powder
2 cups cooked, diced chicken

¼ cup chopped green pepper
1 cup chopped celery
¼ teaspoon salt
Dash pepper
¾ cup mayonnaise

Combine rice, the 2 tablespoons of mayonnaise, vinegar, onion and curry powder. Chill several hours. Add remaining ingredients and serve immediately, or refrigerate until serving time. This salad is especially good served with Olive Nut Bread. SERVES: 6 – 8

Olive Nut Bread

2½ cups flour
⅓ cup sugar
4 teaspoons baking powder
½ teaspoon salt
1 cup milk

1 egg, beaten
1 cup sliced, stuffed green olives
1 cup broken walnuts
2 tablespoons chopped pimiento

Preheat oven to 350°. Grease a 9×5×3-inch loaf pan. Sift together flour, sugar, baking powder and salt. In a separate bowl, beat the milk and egg together until well-blended. Add to dry ingredients, stirring until just blended. Mix in olives, walnuts and pimiento. Pour into prepared pan and bake at 350° for 55 – 60 minutes. Cool in pan 5 minutes, then remove and cool completely. Slice thinly and spread with cream cheese to make delightful luncheon or tea sandwiches. MAKES: 1 loaf

Pop wasn't the only one to retire once, or even twice. Hal followed in his footsteps. After a career in the Air Force Reserve, Hal bought an oil distributor's franchise in Bonham, Texas. Later, he purchased a moving company and warehouse. Lelloine, while helping Hal with the businesses, found herself accepting the title of Railway Express agent for Bonham. This meant that she was entitled to a license to carry a gun at all times, if she so desired. Somehow, the thought of a gun-totin' Lelloine (who is about as ladylike as they come) was enough to bring chuckles to everyone who knew her.

Hal sold his businesses and thought he would retire, too. But opportunity knocked in a most unusual way. Their son, Hal R., (known to the family by the nickname "Red"), and his family moved to Alaska at the time the Alaska pipeline was being built. Red found his father a job with the pipeline crews, and Hal decided that this was too good a chance to pass up, so he headed north. Lelloine divided her time between Anchorage and Bonham. Hal asked Lelloine to try and make the sourdough rolls that he had learned to love while working on the pipeline. It is now one of her most-requested recipes.

Sourdough Rolls

2 packages dry yeast
1 cup warm water
 (105° – 110°)
6 cups self-rising flour
½ cup shortening
2 cups buttermilk
½ cup sugar

Dissolve yeast in warm water. In a large mixing bowl or the work bowl of a food processor, combine flour and shortening, working until mixture resembles course meal. Add remaining ingredients and dissolved yeast, working until a smooth dough is formed. Put dough in large container with a lid or a greased plastic bag with enough room for expansion. Refrigerate for at least 24 hours, but longer if a more pronounced flavor is desired (as much as one week). To bake, remove as much dough as needed. Roll dough into balls the size of an egg and place in greased muffin tins. Allow to rest about 30 minutes while oven is preheated to 375°. Bake at 375° for 20 – 25 minutes, until golden brown. Serve at once. *MAKES: 2 dozen rolls*

This recipe came from Red's wife, Beth, and daughter, Terry. It's an easy recipe they enjoy fixing for the family on Saturday mornings.

Terry Horton's Dutch Babies

⅓ cup butter or margarine
4 eggs
1 cup milk
1 cup flour
1 tablespoon sugar
½ teaspoon nutmeg

Preheat oven to 425°. Place butter in a 10-inch skillet and set inside preheated oven to melt butter. If you don't have an iron skillet, be sure to select a skillet with an ovenproof handle. Mix batter quickly while the butter melts. Place eggs and milk in the container of a blender or food processor and blend on high speed for about 30 seconds. Add flour, blending again to make a smooth batter. Remove skillet from oven and swirl butter to coat bottom completely. Pour batter into hot skillet, using a hot pad to hold skillet. Sprinkle with sugar and nutmeg. Return to oven and bake 15-20 minutes or until puffed and well-browned. Serve at once. Great with powdered sugar or fresh fruit or both! *SERVES: 3-6*

HINT: You may also omit the sugar and nutmeg and bake as directed. Fill with a savory filling like Chicken a la King or taco meat, lettuce and tomato for a great main dish.

When Hal heard that I was working on this cookbook, he was determined not to be outdone by his wife, and wanted to let the world know that Gertrude Horton's sons could cook, too. So he shared these two recipes for his "specialties".

Fried Whole Okra

20 small fresh okra pods
1 cup buttermilk
¾ cup all-purpose flour
½ teaspoon baking powder
⅛ teaspoon pepper
¼ cup cornmeal
½ teaspoon salt
Cooking oil for deep frying

Wash okra and trim stems. Drain well. Place in a shallow container. Pour buttermilk over okra and set aside. Combine next 5 ingredients, mixing well. Heat 1 inch of oil in a heavy skillet (or use a deep fat fryer) to 360-370°. Remove each pod from buttermilk and carefully roll in cornmeal-flour mixture. Drop okra a few at a time into hot oil and fry 3-5 minutes, turning once. Drain on paper towels. *SERVES: 4*

Funnel Cakes

2 eggs, beaten
1 teaspoon baking soda
2 cups flour
½ teaspoon salt

2 – 2½ cups milk
1 tablespoon vanilla
Powdered sugar

Combine all ingredients except powdered sugar in a large mixing bowl and beat with an electric mixer until smooth. If mixture is too stiff, it will not flow through the funnel. Gradually add extra milk as necessary to make a thinner batter. Pour oil into a large skillet to a depth of 1 inch. Heat to 360° – 370°. Place a funnel cake ring in the hot oil. Pour ¼ – ½ cup of the batter into the funnel. Hold the end of the funnel about 2 – 2½ inches above the oil and, with a circular motion, drop batter into the ring, controlling the flow by placing your finger over the tip of the funnel. Keep the funnel moving so the cake will be light and lacy. Cook until golden brown, turning once. Remove from oil and drain on paper towels. Sprinkle hot cake generously with powdered sugar. Eat plain or with jelly, honey or syrup. Repeat cooking procedure with remaining batter. *MAKES: 10 – 12 cakes*

NOTE: If you do not have funnel cake rings, use clean tuna fish cans with the top and bottom removed.

Mother's other sister-in-law, Joyce, enjoys cooking for groups of six or eight friends. Joyce was a home demonstration agent with the Texas Department of Agriculture before she married Jack. Much of her professional time was spent in education and demonstration on the subjects of nutrition and cooking. Joyce enthusiastically shared some of her favorites with me, many of which are just right for informal entertaining or good family meals. These dishes are easily made ahead and will hold in the oven until you are ready to serve them.

Cheese Puffs

½ cup (1 stick) butter or margarine
1 cup (4 ounces) grated sharp Cheddar cheese
2 egg whites
1 loaf French bread cut into 1-inch cubes

Preheat oven to 400°. Melt cheese and butter in the top of a double boiler over simmering water. Beat egg whites until stiff and fold into melted cheese. Remove from heat and dip bread cubes into mixture. Place on ungreased cookie sheet and bake 8 – 10 minutes at 400° until puffs begin to brown. Serve warm. *SERVES: 8*

NOTE: These can also be frozen before baking by placing dipped bread cubes on a waxed paper-lined tray to freeze. When frozen, store in a large plastic bag. At serving time, place frozen puffs on a cookie sheet and bake 10 – 12 minutes.

Cornbread Crepes With Mexican Beef

CREPES:
1 cup flour
½ cup cornmeal
1½ cups milk
3 eggs
⅛ teaspoon salt

SAUCE:
2 pounds ground chuck
½ cup chopped onion
½ cup chopped celery
1 17-ounce can cream-style corn
2 8-ounce cans tomato sauce
1 1½-ounce envelope Taco seasoning mix
1 cup (4 ounces) grated Cheddar cheese
1 2¼-ounce can sliced ripe olives

To make crepes, combine all ingredients and mix well. Pour ¼ cup batter into hot, lightly oiled crepe pan and cook until top is dull and underside is lightly browned. Turn and cook about 15 seconds on second side. Preheat oven to 350°. Brown meat, onion and celery in large skillet. Pour off drippings; stir in corn. Combine tomato sauce and taco mix. Add 1¼ cups tomato sauce to meat and corn. Spread remaining sauce in a 13×9-inch baking dish. Spoon 2 tablespoons meat mixture onto each cornmeal crepe and roll. Place seam side down on top of tomato sauce. Spoon remaining meat mixture over crepes. Sprinkle with the grated cheese and bake 20 minutes at 350°. Garnish with ripe olives. *MAKES: 10 – 12*

Yellow Squash Casserole

2 cups Stella's cornbread mix (see Page 77) or 1 6-ounce envelope cornbread mix
2 eggs, lightly beaten
1 cup milk
¼ cup butter or margarine, melted
3 cups cooked, mashed yellow squash
½ cup chopped green onion
½ cup chopped green pepper
1 10-ounce can cream of mushroom soup
1 cup sour cream
3 tablespoons butter or margarine, melted

Prepare and bake cornbread according to Stella's recipe, using first 4 ingredients (or use an envelope of cornbread mix, prepared and baked according to package directions). Let cool, then crumble. Preheat oven to 350°. Spread about ⅔ of the crumbled cornbread into bottom of a buttered 3-quart flat baking dish. Combine remaining ingredients except butter and pour over cornbread. Sprinkle the remaining cornbread on top. Drizzle with melted butter and bake 20 – 30 minutes at 350°. *SERVES: 10*

Joyce collects recipes for cookies, and her favorites are different from those found in most cookie jars. The recipe for Orange Slice Cookies is one that she learned from her mother. It calls for the gumdrop-like orange slice candy, which forms a nice contrast to the crunch of oatmeal-coconut cookie dough.

Orange Slice Cookies

½ cup shortening
½ cup (1 stick) butter or margarine, softened
1 cup brown sugar
1 cup sugar
1 teaspoon vanilla
2 eggs
2 cups flour
1 teaspoon baking soda
1 cup coconut
2 cups corn flakes
1 cup uncooked quick rolled oats
1 cup chopped pecans
1 cup chopped orange slice candies (dust with flour to keep from sticking together)

Preheat oven to 350°. Cream shortening, butter and sugars. Beat in vanilla and eggs one at a time. Sift and stir in dry ingredients. Stir in coconut, corn flakes, oats, nuts and orange slices. Drop by small teaspoons on lightly greased cookie sheets. Bake for 10 minutes at 350°. Remove from baking sheet while still hot, and cool on racks or waxed paper. *MAKES: 6 dozen*

Gussied-Up Grahams

12 whole graham crackers
1 cup (2 sticks) butter or margarine
1 cup brown sugar
1 cup chopped nuts

Preheat oven to 325°. Line a jelly roll pan with graham crackers. Boil sugar and butter 3 minutes and stir in pecans. Quickly pour over graham crackers. Bake 10 minutes at 325°. Remove graham crackers from pan and transfer to waxed paper to cool. Cut each cracker in half with the edge of a spatula while still warm. *MAKES: 2 dozen*

Orange Pecan Cookies

3 cups sifted flour
2 teaspoons baking powder
½ teaspoon baking soda
½ teaspoon salt
¾ cup butter or margarine, softened
½ cup sugar
1 cup brown sugar, packed
2 eggs
1 tablespoon grated orange rind
½ cup sour cream
1 cup chopped pecans

Preheat oven to 375°. Sift together flour, baking powder, soda and salt and set aside. Cream butter, then gradually add sugars, beating until smooth. Add eggs and orange rind and beat well. Stir in sour cream, then blend in dry ingredients. Add pecans. Drop by rounded teaspoons onto greased baking sheets. Bake at 375° for 10 – 15 minutes. Frost while warm and garnish with pecan halves.

ICING:
2 cups sifted powdered sugar
2 teaspoons grated orange rind
⅛ teaspoon salt
3 – 4 tablespoons orange juice
Pecan halves

Combine powdered sugar, grated orange rind and salt in a small mixing bowl. Add orange juice a little at a time until the icing has a spreadable consistency. *MAKES: 5-6 dozen*

In my childhood memories of Joyce's kitchen, the strongest image is of the birthday cake she always made for her daughter, Judy, and son, Jack, Jr. It was so beautiful and tasted so good. Swirls of whipped cream lavishly covered a tender angel food cake. But the creamy covering held a hidden treasure of chocolate chunks and almonds. It would disappear in a flash! I used to think that it must have taken Joyce hours to make that cake. Imagine my surprise to learn (when I was old enough to ask for the recipe) that she had all us kids fooled — it took minutes. Whether it is for a birthday, company, or just when a quick dessert is needed, Joyce's cake is still a big hit.

Joyce's Birthday Cake

1 10-inch angel food cake (may be store-bought)
2 cups heavy cream
⅓ cup powdered sugar
1 8-ounce chocolate bar with almonds, coarsely chopped

Place cake on serving plate; set aside. Whip heavy cream until frothy, then slowly add powdered sugar, beating until mixture will hold soft peaks. Fold in chopped chocolate. Frost top and sides of cake generously with whipped cream mixture, piling any remaining cream on the top. Refrigerate until serving. SERVES: 12

Finally, every family has one relative whose actions and antics raise eyebrows. My family is no exception. Stella, my grandmother's cousin was like an aunt to all of us. After losing her only son many years ago, she took in all of "Cousin Gertrude's" family. Stella had married a well-to-do businessman, and she enjoyed the finer things in life. I remember that Stella's life seemed very glamorous to me as a child. When I was about eight, she invited me to be her guest for a day at the original Neiman-Marcus store in downtown Dallas. What an experience that was! We wandered from floor to floor of the store while Stella introduced me to someone in each department (it seemed that she knew every salesperson in the whole store). We had lunch in the Zodiac Room, where Stella entertained me with tales of her friend, Helen Corbitt, the director of restaurants for Neimans. I was ever-so-properly guided on my manners during lunch, and Stella appeared to be quite proud of me when we had finished. I still remember how grown up and lady-like I felt that day.

Stella's sense of elegance extended into her life in many ways, although it was often a bit much for Greenville and the Horton crowd. She enjoyed thinking she was the arbiter of good taste in our small town. To make sure that everyone knew that she was so anointed, Stella wrote a weekly column on entertaining, cooking and social news for the local newspaper. And, when she decided to sell her house and move into an apartment, she chose the top floor of the downtown hotel, the Cadillac, as her new residence. After remodeling two "suites" to give her more space, she invited everyone to visit her in the "penthouse." Greenville had never had a penthouse before.

Another of Stella's eccentricities that both amused and frustrated Grandmother and the rest of the family was how fickle she could be. She loved to have a "favorite" family member to lavish her attentions upon. This endorsement could take the form of little gifts, invitations to the "penthouse" for supper, or even being named in her will (news of which she willingly shared with the favorite... and the rest of the family). Of course, she expected the same sort of attention in return, and when the chosen person could not or would not reciprocate, her affections were quickly directed to another family member. Mother's family finally labeled this behavior Stella's "Relative of the Month Club."

In spite of her maddening eccentricities, Stella could be charming. An invitation to a meal at her place was always an occasion. Stella's friendship with Helen Corbitt was only part of a lively interest she had in cooking and in food. She and Grandmother enjoyed sharing with each other any newly discovered recipes. Stella's taste leaned to a more elegant style of cooking than did Grandmother's, with meals usually being served in several courses, and always on silver serving pieces.

Indian Chicken Balls

4 ounces cream cheese, softened
2 tablespoons mayonnaise
1 tablespoon chutney
1 tablespoon curry powder
½ teaspoon salt
1 cup cooked, diced chicken
1 cup sliced, blanched almonds
½ cup flaked coconut

Beat cream cheese in a small mixing bowl until smooth. Add mayonnaise, chutney, curry powder and salt; blend. Stir in chicken and almonds until well blended. Chill mixture until it is firm enough to handle — about 1 hour. Shape into balls about 1 inch in diameter. Roll in coconut. Chill several hours before serving. These may be made ahead and stored, tightly covered, in the refrigerator until serving time. *MAKES: 3 dozen*

Rum Sausages

½ cup brown sugar
½ cup soy sauce
1 5-ounce package tiny cocktail sausages
½ cup rum

Combine brown sugar and soy sauce, stirring until smooth. In a large skillet, saute sausages on one side over medium heat. Turn sausages and cover with soy sauce mixture. Simmer 10 minutes in sauce. Add rum, simmer 1 minute, then remove from heat and ignite to flambé. When flames die down, transfer to serving dish. Keep warm and serve with toothpicks or cocktail forks. *SERVES: 6 – 8*

Chilled Cream of Shrimp Soup

1 medium onion, chopped
¼ cup chopped celery
1 small carrot, chopped
½ small bay leaf
4 cups (1 quart) water
3 chicken bouillon cubes
½ pound cooked shrimp, peeled and deveined
½ teaspoon salt
¼ teaspoon white pepper
1 cup half and half
2 tablespoons sherry
Chives, finely chopped, for garnish

In large pot, cook onion, celery and carrot with bay leaf in 1 quart water until very tender. Add bouillon cubes, shrimp, salt and white pepper and cook about 2 minutes. Remove bay leaf. Purée in blender or processor until smooth; chill. Just before serving, stir in half and half and sherry. Garnish each serving with chives. *SERVES: 4*

Cumberland Sauce For Baked Ham

⅓ cup red currant jelly
¼ cup port or Madeira wine
¼ cup orange juice
2 tablespoons lemon juice
2 teaspoons dry mustard
1 teaspoon ground ginger
2 teaspoons paprika
3 tablespoons grated orange rind

Melt jelly in a small saucepan over low heat. Remove from heat and add remaining ingredients, stirring until smooth. Cool. Serve sauce at room temperature or chilled over slices of cold ham. Or use the sauce as a glaze for baked ham, brushing over the ham several times during the last 30 minutes of baking. *MAKES: 1 cup*

Crabmeat, Ham And Rice Salad

SALAD:
- 2 cups cooked, chilled rice
- ½ cup crabmeat or sea legs, flaked
- ½ cup finely chopped ham
- ½ cup finely chopped celery
- 2 hard cooked eggs, peeled and coarsely chopped

DRESSING:
- 1 tablespoon chopped chives
- ¼ cup chopped parsley
- 2 teaspoons olive oil
- 2 teaspoons white wine vinegar
- ½ cup mayonnaise
- ½ teaspoon salt
- ¼ teaspoon pepper

Combine the salad ingredients in a mixing bowl; set aside. In a small bowl, combine the ingredients listed for dressing, blending thoroughly. Pour over salad and toss to coat. Chill. Serve with fresh fruit and bread sticks.
SERVES: 6-8

Breast Of Chicken With Oysters

- 6 chicken breasts, skinned and boned
- ½ cup (1 stick) butter or margarine
- 12 large mushrooms, sliced
- 4 green onions, chopped
- 1 clove garlic, minced
- 3 tablespoons flour
- 1 14½-ounce can chicken broth
- ¼ cup white wine
- ½ teaspoon salt
- ¼ teaspoon pepper
- 1 pint oysters, drained

Preheat oven to 350°. Pound chicken breasts to ¼ to ½-inch thickness. Melt butter in a heavy skillet over medium heat and brown chicken. Remove chicken and add mushrooms, onions and garlic. Cook until mushrooms have softened. Add flour and stir until smooth, being careful not to let it brown. Add chicken broth, wine, salt and pepper, stirring until thick. Place browned chicken in a baking dish, cover with sauce and bake for 30 minutes at 350°, or until tender. Five minutes before serving, add oysters and cook until the oysters begin to curl. Dish may be prepared ahead up to the point of adding oysters. Reheat and add oysters 5 minutes before serving.
SERVES: 6

Imperial Chicken

1½ cups dried bread crumbs
⅓ cup grated Parmesan or Romano cheese
¼ cup chopped parsley
1 clove garlic, minced
2 teaspoons salt
¼ teaspoon pepper
1 fryer, cut up, or 4 chicken breast halves
½ cup (1 stick) butter or margarine, melted

Preheat oven to 350°. Mix bread crumbs, cheese, and seasonings together. Dip chicken pieces in melted butter, then into crumb mixture, making sure that each piece is well coated. Arrange pieces in a shallow baking dish so that they do not overlap. Pour any remaining butter over the chicken. Bake at 350° for 45 minutes. *SERVES: 3 – 4*

Stella's cornbread mix recipe is a good basic that she kept made up and stored in her pantry at all times. She used it any time that a skillet of cornbread was needed and when a recipe called for a package of cornbread mix. Stella's recipe has become a quick and convenient staple in my kitchen. I keep a chart listing quantities needed for preparing any amount taped to my container of cornbread mix.

Stella's Cornbread Mix

CORNBREAD MIX:
2 cups yellow cornmeal
2 cups flour
4 teaspoons sugar
4 teaspoons salt
4 teaspoons baking powder

CORNBREAD:
2 cups cornbread mix
1 cup milk
2 eggs, lightly beaten
¼ cup butter or margarine, melted

For mix, sift all ingredients together several times. Place in an air-tight container. To make cornbread, preheat oven to 450°. Grease a 10-inch skillet, an 8-inch square pan or a 12-cup muffin tin. Measure cornbread mix into a mixing bowl. In a separate bowl, combine milk, beaten eggs and melted butter, blending well. Pour over mix and stir until just blended. Pour batter into prepared pan and bake at 450° for 15 minutes for muffins or 20 – 25 minutes for skillet or 8-inch pan. *MAKES: 1 pan or 1 dozen muffins*

HINT: For a crisp crust, grease the skillet with shortening and place in the oven to heat while making batter. Pour batter into hot skillet and bake.

In her last years, Stella and Mother became quite close. Mother understood that Stella, with no family, needed love and care. Stella continued her demanding ways until the end. And Mother was surprised to discover she was the "Relative of the Month" when Stella died. While most of her money was left to charity, Stella did leave Mother a few sentimental odds and ends (like her collection of sixty custom-made Neiman Marcus hats and 43 leather handbags). There was one real treasure trove bequeathed to Mother — Stella's collection of books and papers. In it were nine file card boxes of recipes. The contents of those boxes became part of the collection of recipes that formed the foundation for this book.

It's rather sad... Greenville doesn't have a penthouse anymore.

"The tally was: 500 pounds of fruit cake made and sold, two exhausted students and the realization that this might be a golden opportunity."

Chapter Four

Sam And Mary
All the nuts aren't in the fruit cakes

Although I have heard and told the story of the early days of my parents' marriage and business many times, I still find it fascinating. It took tenacity and creativity for them to turn a family recipe for fruit cake into what is now a large mail-order company. But they both learned those qualities in their upbringing.

Sample Buck Lauderdale (yes, that's really Dad's name) hails from Somerville, located in east central Texas, between Waco and Houston. If you ask Dad to tell you where Somerville is, the answer will always be, "Oh, it's just right down there between Gay Hill, Snook and Dime Box."

Somerville was a company town, with a creosote plant owned by the Santa Fe railroad being the only industry. Railroad ties and telephone poles were treated with a thick coating of the smelly, sticky black liquid creosote, which made them waterproof and termite resistant, thus preventing decay and destruction of rail or utility lines. Dad always remembered the terrible odor that came from the plant, saying that it didn't matter which direction the wind was from — you could always smell Somerville's perfume. Naturally, Dad's father worked at the creosote plant, as did almost every other man in town.

Dad was one of six children, and he remembers his childhood as a lean one, especially during the Depression years. There was not always lots of extra money. But, thanks to a garden, two cows and some chickens, there was at least plenty of food on the table. Dad has always said that his mother was one of the most creative cooks he ever knew. She could fix beans seven different ways — one for each day of the week!

Dad also recalls an incident in school during a science and health class that made him realize how little money his family had. The teacher, in attempting to stress the importance of good nutrition, had asked each student to tell the class what he or she had eaten for breakfast. As Dad heard his peers tell about having toasted light bread or "Post Toasties" and milk for breakfast, he felt smaller and smaller — his breakfast had been biscuits and gravy! He says he lied to the class, telling them he had eaten toast and eggs. Of course, he now realizes that he probably had the tastiest breakfast of all. Today, he never misses the chance to order biscuits and gravy at a restaurant.

In spite of the hardships, Dad's parents did everything they could for their children. Pop and Granny Lauderdale were honest, hardworking folks who had a strong sense of moral values. They passed these on to their children. I can recall a conversation that Grandmother Horton and I once had about Dad's parents. "You be sure you hold them in high regard," she said, "because they raised a good man in your daddy. Your Granny Lauderdale is a fine woman. Just because you don't see them as often as you see us doesn't mean you can't appreciate those folks." Alas, I was only ten years old when they died. The few memories I have, I cherish.

In high school, Dad realized that athletics would be his ticket to college. Somerville's baseball team had won the state championship. As a result, Dad, who played outfield, was offered a work-study scholarship to the University of Texas in 1940. An athletic scholarship in those days meant that the University helped you find a job to meet expenses. There were no free rides. Dad went to work in Tommy Knight's restaurant in Austin. He attended classes during the first part of the day, practiced baseball in the afternoon and worked until late at night. Then he went back to his room and studied.

Dad says it took him ten years and four summers to get a college degree, but that was because he interrupted his education to volunteer for the Army during World War II. After serving in the Pacific Theater, he returned to Austin to finish school. Although the scholarship was gone, the job at Tommy Knight's was still available. The G.I. Bill helped out, too, paying $70 a month toward his expenses.

In Somerville, church had been one of the binding forces in the Lauderdale household. When Dad got to Austin, he immediately became involved in a church, and continued to be active when he returned from the war. It's a good thing he did, for that is where he and Mother met.

Mary Jane Horton's background couldn't have been more different. Her father was a businessman and civic leader in Greenville. Although the Depression meant a general tightening of the belt, times were not nearly as lean for Mother's family as they were for Dad's.

Mother was very much the tomboy in her early years. Her best friend was her brother, Jack. Eighteen months older than Mother, Jack was usually the leader in their childhood antics. He was always putting odds and ends of junk together which, when fueled with imagination, could become the grandest playthings. Mother fondly recalls the time he took half the space away from the chickens in the henhouse to create a "palace". He and Mother played there until Grandmother finally put her foot down, making them return the roosting places to the hens.

Mother and Jack developed a strong partnership in another endeavor. During the war years, gasoline rationing severely cut down on their ability to use the car to get around town. Mother had a brown and white paint horse named "Tony" that was saddle broke. Jack bought a buggy from a widow in the country, promising Mother she could ride with him if he could hitch the buggy to her horse. Mother agreed, but said the horse was skeptical. He had never had anything follow him around quite like the buggy did. However, Tony soon learned to pull the buggy, making Jack and Mother two of only a handful of high school students in Greenville who had "wheels" during the war. Although not the most popular mode of transportation with his girl friends, Jack found the promise of a buggy ride proved to be effective with another generation. He soon had every one of Grandmother's and Mama Carlisle's friends offering to bake cookies and pies in exchange for a chance to relive the days of their girlhood.

When she graduated from high school, Mother went to the University of Texas to study foods research. She says that she had dreams of being the next "Betty Crocker". She headed for Austin, where she studied under Dr. Gene Spencer, who taught food chemistry. One Christmas, Grandmother baked some fruitcakes using Great-grandmother Mary Horton's recipe. Mother gave one to Dr. Spencer as a Christmas gift. After tasting the pecan-laden confection, Dr. Spencer told Mother that if she ever needed to make some extra money, just make and sell that fruitcake!

Mother and Dad met at University Christian Church in Austin, and were soon engaged. When they married in August of 1948, Mother was just starting work on her Master's Degree. Dad was studying chemical engineering, hoping to get a job somewhere in Texas' strong petroleum industry. Just before the wedding, Grandmother went down to Austin to make sure that the newlyweds would have a proper place to live. While dining at Green Pastures, a well-known Austin restaurant, Grandmother and Mother began visiting with the owner, Mary Faulk Koock. The Koocks had converted the old Faulk homeplace into the restaurant, with the kitchen and dining rooms taking up the entire downstairs. Mrs. Koock, her husband Chester, and six children lived upstairs. She desperately needed someone to help her with the restaurant, especially since the children were all young, and another child was on the way. Mrs. Koock offered Mother a job, and at Grandmother's suggestion, set to converting one of the out-buildings on the property into living space for Mother and Dad.

The days at Green Pastures were some of the most entertaining of Mother's and Dad's marriage! While Mother and Mrs. Koock worked in the kitchen, Dad helped baby-sit the Koock children after classes and studies. He frequently loaded five or six kids into the Koock's old Plymouth and headed off to the store, with all passengers singing "Somewhere Over the Rainbow" at the top of their lungs. And the cast of characters that passed through or dined at the Koock family table provided more amusement than the best playwright could have dreamed up. Mother was used to having an ever-changing crowd sit down to meals at home in Greenville, but the Koock's guests surpassed even the best that Pop brought home.

When Mother and Dad married, Pop told Dad that he and Mother were on their own with the statement, "Sam, I don't take returns on damaged merchandise." Soon the income from the G.I. Bill didn't seem to be enough to get them through each month. That's when Mother remembered Dr. Spencer's advice. She and Dad talked Grandmother and Pop into lending them the money to buy the cases of pineapple, cherries and dates they would need to get started. Using the restaurant kitchens in the off-hours, they baked a few cakes, wrapped them attractively using cellophane, yellow ribbon and copper mesh (the sort also used for making "Chore Girl"-type pot scrubbers), and sold them to folks around Austin under the name "Mary of Green Pastures".

The fruit cake project kept Mother and Dad quite busy that holiday season. They even called on Mother's sorority sisters to help package the cakes. When Christmas finally came, the tally was: 500 pounds of fruit cake made and sold, two exhausted students, some money in the bank, and the realization that this might be a golden opportunity for them to establish their own company.

Dad finished school and he and Mother decided to move to Greenville and give the business a try. Dad went to work for Pop at the feed company to provide a steady income until they were on their feet. Grandmother, who loved minding everyone else's business, helped them turn the laundry room of her home into a kitchen. They renamed the company "Mary of Puddin Hill" in honor of Great-grandmother Mary Horton. The first few years were filled with both struggles and successes. Mother wrote letters in longhand to everyone she, Grandmother, or their friends knew. The letters told about the wonderful pecan fruit cake they were baking, and how easy it was to order it through the mail. The letters worked — during that holiday season they sold 1,100 pounds of cake. The next year saw them bake and sell 10,000 pounds! Mother says it nearly killed her and Dad as they tried to get everything made and shipped out. But they knew success was theirs at last.

A couple of years later, the highway department made a decision that would give Mother and Dad's fledgling business a big boost. The bill establishing the Interstate Highway system had just been passed, so plans were mapped out for Interstate 30, the highway connecting Dallas and Little Rock, Arkansas, to pass through Greenville. As luck would have it, the new highway cut off a corner of the farm right next to Pop's part of Puddin Hill. That property was owned by a cousin, and was part of the land originally belonging to James and Mary Horton. Mother and Dad bought it and built a new bakery where Puddin Hill sloped down to meet the highway.

By the time I came along in 1954, business had picked up enough so Mother and Dad could make a living from it. Dad left Pop's business about a year before I was born, devoting all his time to Mary of Puddin Hill. Each summer was spent on the road, selling cakes to companies for customer and employee gifts. Mother came up with a clever way to attach a sample slice of fruit cake to Dad's business card which helped to get him beyond the receptionist in many cases.

Mother and Dad moved into a neighborhood primarily made up of young families. Many evenings one or two families would get together for supper. Informality was the key, especially since the children were included. This dish of Mother's was often on the menu. Adults and kids alike enjoyed it.

Mexican Chicken With Fruit Sauce

- 3 – 3½ pounds chicken pieces
- Salt and pepper
- 3 tablespoons butter or margarine
- ½ cup blanched slivered almonds
- ½ cup white raisins
- 1 cup crushed pineapple, drained
- ¼ teaspoon ground cinnamon
- ⅛ teaspoon ground cloves
- 1½ cups orange juice
- ¼ cup Triple Sec or Cointreau
- 1 tablespoon flour
- 2 tablespoons cold water
- 1 avocado, peeled and sliced (for garnish)
- 4 cups cooked white rice

Sprinkle chicken pieces with salt and pepper. In a large skillet, melt the butter over medium heat and brown the chicken pieces on both sides. Add almonds, raisins, pineapple, cinnamon, cloves, orange juice and Triple Sec. Cover and simmer on low heat for 40 – 45 minutes, until juices run clear when chicken is pierced with a fork. Remove chicken pieces to platter and keep warm. Thicken remaining juices in pan by dissolving flour in cold water to make a smooth paste, stirring paste into pan drippings in the skillet and simmering until thickened. To serve, place chicken in a serving dish and pour about ½ cup of the sauce over the chicken. Garnish with avocado slices. Pass remaining sauce. Serve chicken with rice, dousing both with more delicious sauce! SERVES: 6

HINT: *Use instant flour to thicken all sauces and gravies. It dissolves quickly and easily to make a smoother sauce.*

When several families got together, it was "Potluck" time. Everyone brought something to contribute to the meal. Mother's Banana Nut Cake was so popular with the neighbors, that before long, protests were raised if she didn't bring it.

I make it a practice to keep all the ingredients on hand to make this cake. Then, whenever there are a few leftover bananas around, my family gets a treat (the caramelized coconut-pecan topping is their favorite part).

Banana Nut Cake

½ cup (1 stick) butter or margarine, softened
1½ cups sugar
1 tablespoon vanilla
2 eggs
1 cup mashed bananas

1 teaspoon baking powder
1 teaspoon baking soda
2 cups flour
2 tablespoons buttermilk
1 cup pecan pieces

Preheat oven to 325°. Grease and flour a 10-inch tube or bundt pan. Cream butter and sugar together until light and fluffy. Stir in vanilla. Add eggs and bananas and beat until smooth. Sift baking powder, soda and flour together and add to batter alternately with buttermilk. Stir in pecans. Pour into pan and bake for 40 – 50 minutes, until cake tester inserted in the center comes out clean. Remove cake and turn oven temperature up to 400°. Prepare topping and spread over cake as directed.

TOPPING:

1 cup brown sugar
1 cup coconut
¼ cup pecan pieces

6 tablespoons butter or margarine, softened
4 tablespoons milk

Mix ingredients until well blended and spread on hot cake. Return cake to oven and bake until topping is browned — about 10 minutes. Watch carefully to see that it doesn't burn. Remove from oven and allow cake to cool completely before removing from pan. Turn out onto serving plate. This is a very moist cake, so don't think you've underbaked it. It also freezes beautifully. *SERVES: 12 – 16*

The neighborhood gatherings soon grew into monthly parties with each couple bringing a snack. By that time, Mother was building her own reputation as a good cook. Everyone knew about her fruit cake recipe (which, of course, was a closely guarded secret), but soon discovered her talent for cooking was not limited to sweets.

Mary's Cheese Ball

- ¾ cup (3 ounces) blue cheese, crumbled
- 2 3-ounce packages cream cheese, softened
- 1 5-ounce jar processed Old English cheese spread
- 1 tablespoon grated onion
- 1 teaspoon Worcestershire sauce
- ⅔ cup ground pecans
- ⅓ cup chopped parsley

Have cheeses at room temperature. Combine all three cheeses with onion and Worcestershire sauce; blend thoroughly. Add ⅓ cup of the pecans and 2 tablespoons of the parsley and stir well. Shape into a ball and place in a bowl lined with plastic wrap and cover. Chill several hours or overnight. About an hour before serving time, remove ball from plastic wrap and roll in a mixture of the remaining pecans and parsley. Serve with crackers. *MAKES: 1 6-inch cheese ball*

HINT: Crumble any leftover cheese ball into a mixture of ½ cup sour cream and ½ cup mayonnaise (more may be needed if you have lots left over), to make a wonderful dressing for a Romaine lettuce salad.

Creamy Shrimp Dip

- 1 8-ounce package cream cheese, softened
- 3 tablespoons chili sauce
- 4 teaspoons onion juice
- ½ teaspoon lemon juice
- 4 teaspoons Worcestershire sauce
- ¼ cup milk
- ½ pound cooked tiny shrimp, or 2 4¼-ounce cans cocktail shrimp, drained

Combine first six ingredients in a food processor or blender and mix until smooth. Add shrimp and mix for a few seconds more until blended through and shrimp is chopped fine. Chill and serve with crackers or pita chips (see instructions under Gone-in-a-minute Breadsticks, page 211). *SERVES: 10 – 12*

The neighbors were even willing to pay to enjoy Mother's cooking, as Dad once discovered. Grandmother and Pop had some out-of-town company coming for supper, and Mother offered to prepare the meal. Because they were very close friends, she had planned a special menu, a three-inch thick sirloin steak to be marinated, then grilled, and a salad with her delicious Parmesan dressing. Mother said she paid about $9.00 for the steak — a lot of money thirty years ago. Something came up suddenly, and Mother had to take the guests to Dallas to catch a flight home. She called Dad from the airport, telling him to invite some of the neighbors for supper. He did, and when she returned home three couples were waiting to enjoy the steak. Mother said it was a delicious meal. But after supper, Dad suddenly declared, "Okay, pay up!" Mother was shocked to learn that Dad's invitation had been for the "best steak and salad you'll ever get, for the bargain price of only $3.00 a couple."

Beef Or Chicken Teriyaki Marinade

4 steaks or 4 chicken breasts, skinned and boned (your choice)
⅔ cup vegetable oil
⅔ cup soy sauce
⅔ cup bourbon
1 clove garlic, mashed
¼ teaspoon ginger

Combine oil, soy sauce, bourbon, garlic and ginger. Pour into an 8-inch square baking dish or a large heavy lock-top type plastic bag. Place steaks or chicken in marinade. Allow to marinate 1 – 4 hours, turning occasionally. Remove from marinade and grill over hot coals until desired doneness is reached. *SERVES: 4*

HINT: Mother keeps the leftover marinade in her refrigerator and reuses it. She puts the steaks in a bag, pours the marinade over and allows them to marinate until supper time. A tossed salad and rolls make this a quick and easy supper!

Parmesan Salad Dressing

4 eggs
1 2-ounce can anchovies or 2 tablespoons anchovy paste
1 clove garlic, chopped
¾ cup olive oil
6 tablespoons lemon juice
3 tablespoons red or white wine vinegar
1 teaspoon dry mustard
½ teaspoon Worcestershire sauce
1 teaspoon pepper
½ teaspoon salt
½ teaspoon sugar
1 cup grated Parmesan cheese
¼ cup chopped parsley

Drop eggs in boiling water for 3 minutes; cool. Scoop egg out of shell and put into blender or food processor. Combine with remaining ingredients, blending well. Chill and serve over salad greens or cooked shrimp. *MAKES: 2 cups*

NOTE: Even if you don't like anchovies, you'll enjoy this dressing. It has a nice garlic-Parmesan flavor similar to a Caesar salad dressing.

Other specialties from Mother's kitchen include these dishes. The eggplant and shrimp casserole recipe was sent to her by a Puddin Hill customer and rice farmer in Louisiana. Her quick-to-fix curried chicken is especially good when served with the California Salad.

Eggplant On Parade

1 large eggplant, or two small ones
3 beef bouillon cubes
2 cups hot water
¼ cup bacon drippings or oil
1 medium onion, chopped
1 small green pepper, chopped
½ cup chopped celery
1 cup raw rice
2 tablespoons Worcestershire sauce
2 drops Tabasco sauce
1 cup cooked shrimp, peeled and deveined (or 2 4¼-ounce cans shrimp, drained)

Preheat oven to 375°. Grease a 2-quart casserole. Peel eggplant and cut in 1-inch cubes. Cook in enough water to cover until tender, about 8 minutes; drain. Dissolve beef bouillon cubes in hot water; set aside. Heat bacon drippings in a skillet over medium heat and sauté onion, pepper and celery until soft. Remove from heat, add cooked eggplant, rice, Worcestershire sauce, Tabasco, shrimp and dissolved bouillon. Pour into prepared casserole, cover tightly and bake at 375° for 1 hour and 15 minutes.
SERVES: 6

NOTE: For variety, try substituting ½ pound browned ground beef or ½ pound cooked, chopped chicken livers for the shrimp.

Hurry Curry

3 tablespoons butter or margarine
1 onion, finely chopped
2 10½-ounce cans cream of chicken soup
1 soup can water
2 cups cooked, diced chicken
1 tablespoon curry powder, or to taste
6 – 8 cups cooked rice

CONDIMENTS: Plan on about one cup each of an assortment of the following curry toppings.

Chopped apples
Hard cooked eggs (chopped)
Chutney
Coconut
Peanuts
Crumbled canned onion rings
Shoestring potatoes
Raisins
Sweet pickle relish

Melt butter in a small skillet over medium heat and cook onion until translucent. Combine with remaining ingredients except rice in a large saucepan over low heat and simmer 10 – 15 minutes, stirring occasionally, until heated through. Serve over cooked rice with selection of condiments, allowing guests to top their curry with any or all they choose. SERVES: 6 – 8

California Salad with Honey-Lime Dressing

DRESSING:
1 cup mayonnaise
½ cup honey
¼ cup fresh lime juice
1 cup heavy cream

SALAD:
2 grapefruit, peeled and sectioned
3 avocados, peeled and cut into chunks
2 cups seedless green grapes

For dressing, combine mayonnaise, honey and lime juice, stirring with a wire whisk until blended. Whip cream until soft peaks form, then fold into mayonnaise mixture. Combine with fruit and toss gently. SERVES: 8

NOTE: This dressing may be used with any combination of fresh fruits. It is especially good with citrus and melon.

Dad displays considerable skill in the kitchen, too. He particularly enjoys cooking outdoors. Although he could always cook a mean steak, Dad really takes pleasure in trying new recipes. One of his specialties is lamb, marinated and grilled. It so impressed one of Mother's friends that she asked Dad to prepare the lamb for a dinner in her Dallas home honoring Princess Irene of Greece. He and Mother have created an entire menu around this dish. The lamb is accompanied by Dad's special salad and a side dish of curried fruit. Bananas in a rum sauce served over ice cream complete the meal.

Grilled Lamb

5 – 7 pound shoulder or leg of lamb (Have butcher bone it for you.)
¾ cup red wine vinegar
¼ cup white vinegar
¼ teaspoon seasoned salt
¼ cup vegetable oil

1 clove garlic, minced
¼ teaspoon black pepper
¼ teaspoon sage
¼ teaspoon thyme
1 teaspoon parsley
½ teaspoon paprika

Open boned lamb out into a flat piece. Trim off as much fat as possible and cut off any tendons or coarse bits. Work the lamb into a long, flat slab about 2 inches thick by cutting into the thickest sections to open them out. Flatten with a meat mallet. (Lamb should look like a brisket of beef when finished.) Place lamb in a large plastic bag. Combine remaining ingredients and pour over lamb. Close bag and marinate for at least 4 hours, turning occasionally. After marinating, remove lamb and grill over a fire (laid out flat like steak) allowing approximately 45 minutes to each side. *SERVES: 8*

Sam's Salad

1 cup Poppy Seed Dressing (see following recipe)
1 cup sour cream
8 cups iceberg lettuce, washed and torn into bite-sized pieces

1 small onion, chopped fine
1 cup sliced, pimiento-stuffed olives or salad olives

Combine Poppy Seed Dressing and sour cream, beating with a wire whisk until smooth; chill. At serving time, toss lettuce, onion and olives with dressing. (Commercial Poppy Seed Dressing may be used if desired.) *SERVES: 8*

Poppy Seed Dressing

¾ cup sugar
1 teaspoon dry mustard
1 teaspoon salt
⅓ cup vinegar
4 teaspoons onion juice
1 cup salad oil
5 teaspoons poppy seeds

Combine sugar, mustard, salt, vinegar, and onion juice, beating with a wire whip or an electric mixer until sugar has dissolved. Add oil in a thin stream, beating constantly until thickened and smooth. Stir in poppy seeds. Chill and serve over fresh fruit. *MAKES: 1½ cups*

HINT: For a different taste, replace the poppy seeds with celery seeds.

Curried Fruit

1 15½-ounce can pineapple chunks
1 21-ounce can apricot halves
1 16-ounce can sliced peaches
1 16-ounce can sliced pears
1 10-ounce bottle maraschino cherries, drained
3 tablespoons butter or margarine
1½ cups brown sugar
3 teaspoons curry powder

Drain fruit in a colander for 2 hours. Preheat oven to 325°. Melt butter in a small saucepan. Slowly blend in sugar and curry powder. Put drained fruit in a 13×9-inch baking dish. (Try to serve fruit in the dish it is cooked in.) Spoon sugar mixture over fruit and bake 45 minutes at 325°. Serve hot. *SERVES: 8*

Acclaimed Flamed Bananas

3 tablespoons butter or margarine
¾ cup brown sugar
¼ cup dark rum
3 large bananas
¼ cup light rum
Vanilla ice cream

Heat butter and sugar in a large saucepan over medium heat, stirring until sugar is dissolved. Add dark rum. Slice bananas crosswise into pan. Cook, stirring frequently, 7–8 minutes. Heat light rum in a small saucepan. Ignite rum and pour over bananas, stirring until the flames die down. Serve hot over ice cream. *SERVES: 6–8*

Dad considers his real culinary forté to be breakfast foods. When he and Mother married, they discovered a seemingly insurmountable difference. Dad loved to get up very early every morning. Or, as Mother says, he thinks it's a mortal sin to sleep past five o'clock. Dad also preferred to have someone to share the sunrise with. Mother was not very cheerful about being dragged out of bed, and even less cheerful about cooking at that time of day. So a compromise was struck. (Mother says it has been one of the keys to the success of their marriage.) Dad would get up and cook breakfast, but no matter what hour of the morning it was, Mother had to get up and eat with him. She could go back to bed after breakfast, if she wished, but she had to join him at the table. It was also understood that the first time that Mother refused, barring illness, she had to take over breakfast duties. Mother has endured breakfasts served at all hours of the morning. The rules applied to me, too. I learned to sit at the table and eat while almost asleep. As soon as breakfast was over, I stumbled back to bed. Dad is really quite good in the kitchen, occasionally turning out some eye-opening breakfast dishes.

Baked Eggs

INGREDIENTS FOR EACH SERVING:
1 egg
1 tablespoon sour cream
   or yogurt
1 teaspoon butter or
   margarine
Salt and pepper to taste

Preheat oven to 350°. Break egg into a buttered ramekin. Top with sour cream or yogurt, and butter. Sprinkle with salt and pepper and bake at 350° 15 – 20 minutes or until center is set. (This recipe will not microwave.) *SERVES: 1*

Skinny Blender Muffins

2 eggs
1 medium banana
1 teaspoon baking soda
4 heaping teaspoons Sugar Twin (or 3 packages artificial sweetener)
⅔ cup powdered dry milk
⅓ cup Grape-Nuts
⅓ cup bran cereal
1 teaspoon vanilla

Preheat oven to 350°. Spray a 12-cup muffin tin with non-stick spray. Combine all ingredients in a blender or food processor and blend until smooth. Pour into prepared muffin tin, allowing batter to fill each cup halfway. Bake at 350° for 12 – 15 minutes. Serve at once. *SERVES: 2*

The next recipe is really two meals in one. Mother prepares the beef dish for supper. Dad uses the leftover sauce to top scrambled eggs the next morning. Breakfast is definitely the best part! I've adjusted the recipe so the quantities listed are sure to make enough sauce for breakfast.

Beef Steaks In Wine Sauce — And Breakfast The Next Day

4 beef cube steaks (about 6 ounces each)
¼ cup butter or margarine
1 onion, chopped
2 10½-ounce cans mushroom gravy
1½ cups red wine
1 8-ounce package medium width egg noodles, cooked and drained

Brown steaks on both sides in a large skillet. (You may add a tablespoon of the butter if necessary). Remove steaks from skillet and set aside. Add butter to skillet and sauté onion until translucent. Add gravy and red wine, stirring to blend thoroughly. Return steaks to skillet, cover and simmer over low heat for 15 – 20 minutes until steaks reach desired doneness. Remove steaks to a platter and simmer sauce uncovered for another 5 minutes. To serve, place steaks on bed of cooked noodles and pour half the sauce over them. Remember, you want to save half the sauce for breakfast! *SERVES: 4*

BREAKFAST THE NEXT DAY

Remaining sauce
8 eggs
½ cup milk
2 tablespoons butter or margarine
1 cup (4 ounces) grated Cheddar cheese
Salt and pepper to taste
4 English muffins, split and toasted

Heat remaining sauce in a small saucepan. While sauce is heating, beat eggs with milk. Melt butter or margarine in a large skillet over medium heat and scramble eggs. When eggs are beginning to set, add cheese and continue to cook until eggs are set and cheese is melted. Season to taste with salt and pepper. On each plate, place two halves of a toasted English muffin. Top each muffin with eggs, dividing evenly. Spoon sauce over eggs and serve. *SERVES: 4*

With both she and Dad working full-time in the business, Mother realized that it was too much to try to keep up with the house, me, AND the company — and do it all successfully. She and Dad decided that it was necessary for them to find someone who could be a housekeeper, cook and baby-sitter (in short, someone who could almost walk on water). They found Mamie. She started working for my family when I was about eighteen months old, and I have grown up thinking of her as a second mother. Over the more than thirty years that Mamie has been a part of the household, she and Mother have developed an understanding of each other that is a blend of suspicion and deep affection. There have been dozens of incidents that have generated lots of laughter.

One of the best "Mamie stories" occurred when Mother sent her to find a Christmas gift for Dad. He wanted a one-inch wide black alligator belt, and Mother had not been able to find it. Very soon, Mamie returned with exactly what was wanted. Mother asked Mamie where she had bought it, and Mamie named the store. When asked how she had paid for it, Mamie responded, "I charged it."

"But, Mamie," Mother said, "we don't have a charge account at that store."

"We do now," Mamie replied. Greenville was a small enough town that everyone knew Mamie worked for the Lauderdales.

On another occasion, Mamie found me sobbing uncontrollably in the back yard. My pet duck had become ill and could not move. She tried to settle me down, but I only became more upset. In desperation, she telephoned the veterinarian, who lived in the neighborhood. But the right words just wouldn't come out. She managed to say, "Oh, Dr. Wilkins! I need your help... are you... are you a quack doctor?" He assured her that he was — in every sense of the word — and managed to get the duck started on the road to recovery.

Mamie says that she really isn't all that good a cook. She insists she just cooks "plain ol' soul food." I only know that I was raised on some of the best eatin' one could have.

Mamie's Pot Roast

3 – 4 pound boneless chuck roast
1 teaspoon salt
½ teaspoon pepper (more, if you like)
1 tablespoon Worcestershire sauce
2 tablespoons vegetable oil
1 clove garlic, peeled
4 carrots, scraped and cut in 3-inch lengths
8 small potatoes, peeled
8 small onions (about 1-inch diameter)
3 stalks celery, cut in 3-inch lengths
2 cups beef broth
4 tablespoons cornstarch
½ cup cold water

Preheat oven to 325°. Rub roast on all sides with salt, pepper and Worcestershire sauce (be generous with the pepper, as Mamie says that is the secret to her pot roast). In a large oven-proof pot with a tight-fitting lid, heat the oil over medium heat. Add the garlic clove and sauté until browned; remove. Add the roast, browning on one side. Turn roast to brown on the other side and add the vegetables. Pour in the beef broth, cover and bake at 325° for three hours, or until meat is tender. Remove meat and vegetables to a serving platter and pour pan drippings into a saucepan. Skim off the fat that rises to the top and heat. Dissolve cornstarch in cold water and add to gravy. Cook, stirring constantly, until thickened and smooth. Serve gravy over roast and vegetables. Serve with lots of hot bread or biscuits to soak up the extra gravy.
SERVES: 6 – 8

Fried Chicken

2 – 3 pounds chicken pieces
1 cup buttermilk
1 cup flour
1 teaspoon salt
1 teaspoon pepper
1 teaspoon paprika
Oil for deep frying

Place chicken pieces in a single layer in a baking dish. Pour buttermilk over the chicken, turning each piece so that it is evenly coated. Let stand at least 15 minutes. Combine flour, salt, pepper and paprika and pour into a large plastic bag. Heat oil in a large heavy skillet to 360°-370°. Drain each piece of chicken, put into the plastic bag and shake to coat with flour mixture. Put chicken pieces in oil and cook, turning occasionally, until golden brown and juices run clear when pierced with a fork. Drain on paper towels and keep warm, if necessary, while remaining chicken is cooked. SERVES: 4

When the world became more conscious of fat and excessive calories, Mamie managed to come up with a chicken dish that had the taste of her fried chicken, but with far fewer calories.

Smothered Chicken

4 chicken breast halves, skin removed
1 cup soft bread crumbs
1 cup buttermilk
½ teaspoon salt
½ teaspoon pepper
½ teaspoon paprika
⅛ teaspoon garlic powder

Preheat oven to 350°. Place chicken in a greased 2-quart flat baking dish. Place in oven and brown for 2 – 3 minutes. Turn chicken and brown on the other side. Combine remaining ingredients and pour over browned chicken. Cover and bake at 350° for 45 – 50 minutes. *SERVES: 4*

There is one meal Mamie cooks that has won acclaim from friends far and wide. She first cooked red beans at the request of Dad. He remembered his mother's special way of combining ground beef, chili powder and red beans into a dish that was served over cornbread. Mamie cooked it for him, but served the red beans over cornbread baked from a recipe Mother had just given her. The cornbread was filled with green chilies and corn, then topped with cheese and jalapeño peppers. What a combination! Soon, Mamie was making "beans and bread" for Dad to share with family, friends, customers... anyone he thought worthy was invited to sample this splendid concoction.

Mamie's Red Beans

1 pound dried pinto beans
8 cups water
1 pound ground beef
2 tablespoons chili powder
2 teaspoons salt
½ teaspoon black pepper

Combine beans and water in a large saucepan and allow to soak 6 – 8 hours. Place pan over medium heat, bring to a boil, reduce heat and simmer, covered, about 1½ hours or until beans are tender. While beans are cooking, brown meat in a skillet; drain excess fat. Add meat, chili powder, salt and pepper to beans, cover and simmer an additional ½ hour until thickened. Watch beans during the last ½ hour to make sure that they do not thicken so much as to become dry. Should that appear to be happening, add more water — ½ cup at a time as needed. Serve with Mamie's Jalapeño Cornbread. *SERVES: 8*

A quick note about Mamie's cornbread. It does not have the firm, coarse texture usually associated with cornbread. Instead, it is very moist and tender, and might appear underdone to the uninitiated. Please don't overbake it.

Mamie's Jalapeño Cornbread

1 cup (4 ounces) grated American or Cheddar cheese
2 tablespoons pickled jalapeño peppers, drained and chopped
1½ cups cornmeal
2 tablespoons baking powder
½ teaspoon salt
2 eggs, beaten
1 cup buttermilk
3 tablespoons melted shortening or vegetable oil
1 17-ounce can cream-style corn
1 4-ounce can chopped green chilies (hot or mild)

Preheat oven to 500°. Combine cheese and jalapeños; set aside. In a large bowl, blend cornmeal, baking powder and salt. Combine eggs, buttermilk and shortening or oil in a small bowl and mix thoroughly. Add to dry ingredients, stirring until just blended. Stir in corn and green chilies. Generously grease a 10-inch iron skillet with shortening and place in preheated oven for 5 minutes. Pour batter into hot skillet. Sprinkle reserved cheese and jalapeño mixture over the batter. Bake at 500° for 15 minutes. Remove and let stand 5 minutes before cutting. The cornbread should be very soft in the center and does not have the texture of regular cornbread. *SERVES: 8*

NOTE: You may substitute green chilies for the jalapeños if your system is not up to the heat!

Dad has a punch recipe that he enjoys making for special parties. Just before a party that he and Mother and several neighbors were hosting started, he was mixing a batch of punch concentrate in a gallon-sized glass jar. Beside him, Mamie was at the sink washing dishes. Suddenly, Dad's spoon knocked a hole in the glass jar, spilling the punch concentrate into the sink. As Mamie and Dad stared in disbelief at a sinkfull of Southern Comfort-flavored suds, Mamie calmly said, "You know, I believe this is the first time in my life I've ever had an urge to drink the dishwater."

Southern Comfort Punch

1 1.75-liter bottle of
   Southern Comfort
¾ cup lime juice
1¼ cups lemon juice
½ cup Curaçao
⅓ cup sugar
1 2-liter bottle club soda,
   chilled

Mix Southern Comfort, lime juice, lemon juice, Curaçao and sugar together. Stir to dissolve the sugar. Chill several hours. When ready to serve place punch base in punch bowl and add club soda. Float an ice ring in the punch bowl. *SERVES: 15 – 20*

NOTE: Warning! This punch is very smooth — and very potent! I usually add a little more club soda as the evening progresses. You may add as much as another liter, if necessary.

One special friendship has formed an extended family that Mother and Dad cherish. With Forest and Bobbie Lake they have shared some of the best times of their lives. From raising children, to planning weddings, to traveling together now that the kids are all gone, each stage of life has included the Lakes.

Bobbie and Mother have their mutual interest in cooking as a special bond. In fact, their recipe collections are almost interchangeable after so many years of sharing recipes. But Bobbie deserves credit for the good fare served in her home.

Scallops Sausalito

6 tablespoons butter or
   margarine, melted
2 teaspoons minced
   parsley
2 teaspoons minced chives
1 clove garlic, minced
⅔ cup soft breadcrumbs
1 pound scallops
Lemon wedges

Preheat oven to 350°. Butter 4 individual baking dishes or 1 9-inch glass pie plate. Combine butter, parsley, chives, garlic and breadcrumbs. Spread half the mixture in baking dishes, top with scallops and sprinkle with remaining mixture. Bake at 350° for 25 – 30 minutes. Serve with lemon wedges. *SERVES: 2 – 4*

Alexander A La Forest

Several scoops of a good quality vanilla ice cream
½ jigger rum
½ jigger Cream de Cacao
Crushed ice

Blend ice cream, rum and Creme de Cacao in a food processor or a blender. Gradually add ice to thicken and pour into two champagne glasses. *SERVES: 2*

This dessert has been a favorite of both the Lake and Lauderdale families for many years. Bobbie discovered the recipe, and Mother embellished on it by adding leftover fruit cake to the whipped cream and liqueur mixture. It's no wonder that when this creation is served, a rousing chorus of "Glory, glory hallelujah!" breaks out.

Glory Hallelujah

1½ cups crumbled soft macaroons (or ¾ cup macaroons and ¾ cup crumbled fruit cake)
½ cup sugar
½ cup cognac or Tia Maria
2 cups (1 pint) heavy cream
16 cherries (for garnish)

Combine macaroons, fruit cake, sugar and cognac in a medium mixing bowl. Let stand 30 minutes, stirring occasionally. Whip cream in a separate bowl until soft peaks form and fold into macaroon mixture. Spoon into 16 paper-lined muffin cups. Freeze until firm. Let stand 10 minutes before serving. Garnish with cherries. *SERVES: 16*

I mentioned that Mother used leftover fruit cake in her version of Glory Hallelujahs. Since Mother and Dad decided years ago that they would never sell fruit cake seconds to anyone, they have often found themselves in the unusual position of having some fruit cake left over after the holiday season — sometimes as much as a hundred pounds! There's nothing wrong with the taste of the cakes — usually they have been dropped or damaged in shipment, or are simply extra inventory. This has led to the development of a collection of recipes over the years using leftover fruit cakes.

Although Mother and I have developed these recipes using the Mary of Puddin Hill Fruit Cake, there is no reason that another fruit cake couldn't be used (although the results might not be as tasty). You may also use crumbled fruit cake in place of nuts in many dessert, cookie or cake recipes.

Fruit Cake Bar Cookies With Chocolate Glaze

2 eggs
1 teaspoon vanilla
1 cup sifted powdered sugar
1 tablespoon butter or margarine, melted
¼ cup flour
¼ teaspoon salt
½ teaspoon baking powder
2 cups crumbled fruit cake (or you may use 1 cup fruit cake and 1 cup chopped nuts)

Preheat oven to 325°. Grease an 8-inch square cake pan. Beat eggs until lemon colored with an electric mixer. Add vanilla, powdered sugar and melted butter and beat until blended. Sift flour, salt and baking powder together, then add to egg mixture and beat until smooth. Stir in crumbled fruit cake. Pour into prepared pan. Bake at 325° for 25 – 30 minutes, or until center springs back when gently touched. Remove from oven and set aside to cool. While cooling, prepare glaze.

GLAZE:
2 ounces unsweetened chocolate, melted
1 cup powdered sugar
½ teaspoon vanilla
1 – 2 tablespoons warm water or milk

Blend glaze ingredients in a small bowl until smooth, adding water or milk to achieve a spreadable consistency. Spread over cookies in pan. Allow to cool completely, then cut into bars. *MAKES: 12 – 16*

Fruit Cake Ice Cream

½ gallon good quality vanilla ice cream
2 cups crumbled fruit cake (or more or less to taste)
½ cup bourbon, rum or cognac
Chocolate sauce and toasted fruit cake crumbles (optional)

Soften ice cream until it can be stirred. Blend in fruit cake and bourbon. Refreeze until serving time. Top with chocolate sauce thinned with a bit of bourbon, rum or cognac, if desired, and garnish with toasted fruit cake crumbles. *SERVES: 8 – 12*

Toasted fruit cake crumbles: Spread crumbled fruit cake on a cookie sheet and bake at 350° until lightly toasted — about 8 minutes. Sprinkle over ice cream instead of nuts.

Essence Of Christmas Pie

CRUST:
1½ cups crumbled fruit cake
¼ cup granulated sugar
¼ cup butter or margarine, melted (more if your fruit cake is dry)

Preheat oven to 400°. Combine crumbled fruit cake, sugar and melted butter in a mixing bowl and blend until thoroughly mixed. Pat into an oiled 9-inch pie pan and place in preheated oven. Immediately turn the heat down to 350° and bake for 10 – 15 minutes, watching carefully to see that the crust doesn't get too brown. Cover with foil if it browns too rapidly. Remove from oven and cool.

FILLING:
1 envelope unflavored gelatin
3 tablespoons brandy
1 cup milk
3 eggs, separated
¼ cup sugar
¼ cup bourbon
1½ teaspoons vanilla
Pinch of ground nutmeg
Pinch of salt
3 tablespoons sugar
½ cup heavy cream
Whipped cream and pecan halves for garnish

Sprinkle gelatin over brandy to soften; set aside. Heat milk in the top of a double boiler over simmering water until bubbles form around the edges. In a mixing bowl, beat egg yolks and sugar together until sugar is dissolved. Add ¼ cup of hot milk to the mixture and stir to warm egg yolks. Pour into remaining milk in the double boiler and cook, stirring constantly, until mixture coats the back of a wooden spoon (about 3 – 5 minutes). Remove from heat and stir in the softened gelatin, bourbon, vanilla and nutmeg. Chill mixture, stirring occasionally, until it mounds. Do not let it set. Beat egg whites and salt until just blended, then add remaining sugar and beat until stiff peaks form. Fold ⅓ of the egg whites into the chilled bourbon mixture to lighten it, then gently fold in the remaining egg whites. Beat heavy cream until soft peaks form, then fold into the mixture. Pour into prepared fruit cake crust, and chill several hours until filling is set. Garnish with whipped cream and pecan halves, if desired. *MAKES: 1 pie*

Angel Food Fruit Cake

2 cups heavy cream
¼ cup cocoa
1 cup powdered sugar
1 cup crumbled fruit cake
1 10-inch angel food cake

Combine heavy cream, cocoa and powdered sugar in a large mixing bowl and refrigerate several hours or overnight. Two hours before serving, whip cream mixture until soft peaks form. Fold in fruit cake. Slice angel food cake horizontally into three layers. Spread about 1 cup of the cream between each layer. Use remaining cream to frost top and outside of cake. Chill 2 hours. *SERVES: 8*

Over the years, Mother's interest in cooking has continued to grow. She credits four women with having the greatest influence on her cooking. Her mother, of course, was the first, followed by Mary Faulk Koock, Madaline Hill and Nancy Parker.

During the year Mother and Dad lived in Austin, Mother learned quite a lot about the restaurant business. Mary Koock's dedication to the quality of the food that her kitchen turned out set the course Mother and Dad would follow with their own company. Mrs. Koock taught Mother that people who appreciate quality are willing to spend a little more to get first-rate food. She also believed that starting a business with high standards was easier than trying to raise the standards after a few years. The reason, she said, is because both ownership and employees are trained not to accept substandard ingredients or workmanship. Time and again I have seen the effectiveness of Mrs. Koock's teachings here at Puddin Hill. Because Mother and Dad set high standards in the beginning for the quality of the products from Puddin Hill, those employees now in the kitchen care enough to make sure that nothing goes into any product that is in any way questionable.

Mary and Chester Koock regard Mother and Dad as far more than just former employees. They are like proud parents when visiting Puddin Hill. And Green Pastures Restaurant, by the way, is still one of the finest in Austin.

Mary Faulk Koock's Crab Island Dip

2 cups sour cream
2 teaspoons curry powder
1 teaspoon onion powder
⅛ teaspoon cayenne pepper
½ teaspoon salt
1 cup grated fresh coconut
8 ounces flaked crabmeat or 2 6-ounce cans crabmeat, drained and flaked
2 – 4 tablespoons milk

Combine all ingredients except milk in a mixing bowl and blend well. Add enough milk to make a good dipping consistency. Chill. Serve with corn chips or crackers. SERVES: 10 – 12

NOTE: Fresh coconut is essential to the unique taste of this recipe. Do not substitute sweetened coconut. If fresh coconut is unavailable, use frozen grated coconut or unsweetened shredded coconut.

Madalene Hill's influence has been over Mother's cooking at home. For many years, Mrs. Hill has run a remarkable establishment in Cleveland, Texas, (about an hour's drive from Houston), called Hilltop Herb Farm. Mother had grown up tasting Grandmother's rose petal butter and geranium-infused pound cakes, so Mrs. Hill's extensive knowledge of herbal cookery naturally intrigued her. Mrs. Hill and her daughter, Gwen Barclay, willingly shared their secrets, believing that the more knowledge they shared, the more appreciative and loyal their customers would be. Mother and Dad established a small herb garden in their back yard, and began snipping bits of oregano, mint or basil to add to whatever might be on the stove.

One of the highlights of a meal at Hilltop Herb Farm and later Hilltop Country Inn was the soup. Mrs. Hill created wonderful soups that were smooth and flavorful. Her secret for many of the soups was simple — just make a concoction using leftover vegetables and lettuce, add broth and herbs, heat and puree in a blender. Mother brought the technique back to her kitchen, often cooking a pot of cabbage, broccoli or yellow squash to use as a soup base for the rest of the week. One night, while washing the dishes, Dad coined the name for this soup as he dumped the leftover salad and carrots into Mother's soup pot.

Mary's "Gotta Go" Soup

Leftover vegetables
Leftover lettuce or vegetable salad
Chicken broth
Salt
Pepper
Tabasco sauce
Herbs to your liking

Combine any bits of leftover vegetables (broccoli, cabbage, carrots, green beans, potatoes, etc.), leftover salad (the dressing adds flavor) and enough chicken broth to cover. Bring to a boil over medium heat. Reduce heat and simmer 15 minutes, or until vegetables are tender. Purée soup in blender or food processor, adding more chicken broth or water if necessary to thin soup. Return to saucepan and season to taste with salt, pepper, Tabasco sauce and herbs. If desired, ½ – 1 cup of heavy cream may also be added. Serve hot in mugs as a delicious first course. Garnish with a tablespoon of dry sherry for company.

NOTE: If you do not have enough leftover vegetables to make the soup, add a can of zucchini in tomato sauce or a package of frozen mixed vegetables.

Mrs. Hill's Herb Butter is another feature on both Mother's table and mine. It elevates the obligatory rolls or bread served with supper to delectable heights. Mrs. Hill recommends fresh herbs, of course, but realizes that not everyone has access to them. In that case, she recommends substituting one teaspoon dried herbs for each tablespoon of fresh herbs. Always use fresh parsley in the herb butter to give the mixture flecks of bright green for an appetizing appearance.

Madalene Hill's Herb Butter

1 cup (2 sticks) butter or margarine, softened
1½ teaspoons fresh basil
1½ teaspoons fresh oregano
1½ teaspoons fresh chives
1 tablespoon fresh parsley

Combine softened butter and herbs in a small mixing bowl, stirring until well blended. Chill several hours to let flavors blend. Serve on bread or rolls, use in skillet to cook scrambled eggs, top baked fish or add to steamed vegetables. *MAKES: 1 cup*

Texas Rice is my favorite rice recipe. It is easy to make and tastes so good. Because it holds well, I like to take it when I am asked to bring a dish to a covered dish dinner. And Mrs. Hill's Imperial Mousse is a refreshing dessert.

Texas Rice

¼ cup butter or margarine
1 cup chopped green onion
4 cups cooked white rice
2 cups sour cream
1 cup small curd cottage cheese
1 large bay leaf, finely minced
½ teaspoon salt
Dash pepper
2 4-ounce cans chopped green chilies, drained
2 cups (8 ounces) grated sharp Cheddar cheese
Parsley and paprika for garnish

Preheat oven to 375°. Lightly butter a 13×9-inch baking dish. Melt butter in a small skillet and sauté onion until translucent. Combine onion with remaining ingredients except parsley and paprika in a large mixing bowl, stirring gently until well-blended. Pour into prepared dish and bake uncovered at 375° for 25 minutes, until bubbly and hot. Sprinkle with paprika and parsley before serving.
SERVES: 8

Imperial Mousse

1 envelope gelatin
½ cup cold water
½ cup boiling water
½ cup sugar
2 cups sour cream
½ teaspoon almond extract
1 teaspoon vanilla

Sprinkle gelatin over cold water to soften. Combine softened gelatin, boiling water and sugar in a mixing bowl. Stir until gelatin and sugar are dissolved. Blend in sour cream and flavorings. Pour into a 4 cup mold that has been rinsed with cold water. Chill until set. At serving time, unmold onto a serving plate and serve with one of the following:

   1. 2 cups sliced fresh strawberries combined with ⅓ cup sugar and ¼ cup Grand Marnier.

   2. 2 cups sliced fresh peaches combined with ⅓ cup sugar and ¼ cup amaretto.

   3. 2 cups fresh pineapple tossed with 2 tablespoons gin.

   4. 1 10-ounce packaged frozen raspberries, puréed in a blender or food processor, then strained to remove seeds.
SERVES: 8

When including Nancy Parker in this book, the most difficult decision was not which recipes to include, but which of the hundreds she has shared with us to leave out. Nancy is an extraordinary cook and an even more extraordinary woman. She operated a cooking school in Greenville for many years, attracting women from as far away as Colorado, Kansas, Florida and Minnesota, as well as from all over the Southwest, to take her classes. She also conducted cooking classes and demonstrations for Neiman-Marcus in Dallas. Helen Corbitt had taught cooking classes at the store for years and, when she retired, Nancy was invited to teach.

While she created menus and demonstrated dishes that were worthy of any five-star restaurant in France, Nancy made them accessible to the average cook. She also acknowledged her Southern roots in the dishes she prepared for her classes. Therefore, ham with red-eye gravy or hushpuppies might appear on her menus alongside classical French dishes. Nancy based her recipes on ingredients that were available to every cook, not just those who lived near a gourmet market. And her instruction in basic techniques or "Nancy Parker discoveries" had a dramatic effect on the way that Mother and I and countless others now cook and entertain.

Nancy semi-retired from teaching several years ago, which was a real loss to her many students and friends. She is still active in the culinary world, however, working on her own cookbook and serving as a consultant for houseware and gourmet companies.

Between the two of us, Mother and I did not miss one of Nancy's classes offered in Greenville. We couldn't wait to get home and try out something we had learned (many times it was cooked that very night for supper). Nancy graciously gave me permission to share some of the recipes that are our favorites, plus pass along some of the wonderful tips and tricks that she has taught in her classes.

San Diego Salad

SALAD:
- 5 cups Romaine lettuce, washed and torn into bite-sized pieces
- ¾ pound bacon, cooked crisp and crumbled
- 2 large avocados, sliced
- 2 cups cubed cantaloupe

DRESSING:
- ¼ cup sugar
- ⅓ cup catsup
- ¼ cup white wine vinegar
- 1 teaspoon salt
- 1 teaspoon paprika
- ½ cup oil
- ⅓ cup minced shallots

Combine salad ingredients in a large salad bowl. In a small mixing bowl, combine dressing ingredients and blend with a wire whisk until sugar is dissolved. Pour dressing over salad and toss gently. *SERVES: 8*

NOTE: If cantaloupe is out of season, try this salad with drained mandarin oranges. Fresh spinach can also replace the Romaine lettuce.

New Orleans Pot Roast

- 4 pounds middle round or chuck roast
- 6 large pimiento-stuffed olives
- ½ cup diced salt pork
- 2 large onions, chopped
- ½ cup rum
- 1 stalk celery
- 1 bay leaf
- 2 sprigs parsley
- 4 fresh tomatoes, peeled and chopped (or 1 16-ounce can whole tomatoes, drained and chopped)
- ½ teaspoon basil
- 2 cloves garlic, minced
- ½ teaspoon freshly ground black pepper

Preheat oven to 300°. Make 12 slits, about 1½ inch deep in sides of roast. Cut each olive in half, lengthwise, and insert an olive half into each slit. Tie roast with string at 2-inch intervals to hold shape. Sauté diced salt pork in a large flame-proof casserole with a tight-fitting lid over high heat until browned. Remove pork from drippings and add roast, browning on all sides. Remove roast and drain off all but 1 tablespoon of the drippings. Reduce heat to medium and add onions, cooking until browned. Return pork and roast to pan, add rum and cook 2 minutes, or until alcohol has evaporated. (You may flambé the roast at this point to get a good, crisp outside to the roast. Just be sure the lid is handy to douse the flames, if necessary.) Tie celery, bay leaf and parsley sprigs together to form a bouquet garni to flavor the sauce. Add to pot, along with remaining ingredients. Cover with lid and bake at 300°. for 4 – 5 hours, or until beef can be cut with a spoon. Remove to platter, cut off string and slice. Spoon some of the sauce over the roast, and pass remaining sauce. Should you have any roast leftover, reheat in a bit of the sauce. Leftover roast also makes good sandwiches. *SERVES: 8*

Country Cheese Pie

PASTRY:
3 cups flour
¾ cup cold butter
1 teaspoon salt
2 eggs

FILLING:
1½ cups ricotta cheese
2 cups (8 ounces) grated smoked Edam or Gouda cheese
1½ cups (6 ounces) grated Mozzarella cheese
1½ cups freshly grated Parmesan cheese
4 ounces salami, pepperoni or ham, diced
2 tablespoons chopped fresh parsley
4 eggs, slightly beaten
½ teaspoon salt
¼ teaspoon pepper

GLAZE:
1 egg, slightly beaten
1 tablespoon water

Combine flour and butter in the work bowl of a food processor fitted with a steel blade until mixture resembles coarse cornmeal (or use a pastry blender). Add salt and eggs, process until just combined. Gather dough into a ball, cover and let rest for 30 minutes. While dough is resting, combine filling ingredients, mixing well; set aside. Divide dough into 2 pieces, one larger than the other. Preheat oven to 375°. Grease a pizza pan or cookie sheet. Roll out smaller piece of dough into a 10-inch circle and place on pizza pan. Top with filling, leaving a 1-inch margin around edges for sealing. Roll out remaining dough into a 14-inch circle and place over filling. Fold over and crimp edges to seal. Cut two slits in the top to vent steam. Beat egg and water together and brush over dough. Bake at 375° for 55 – 60 minutes until top is browned and filling is set. Cover with a piece of foil if top browns too quickly. Remove from oven and let cool completely. Serve at room temperature, cut into wedges. *SERVES: 8*

NOTE: This is a wonderful dish to take on a picnic. I often make it in a large pie plate instead of on the pizza pan so that it is easier to carry. Serve with fresh fruit and a hearty red wine.

Zucchini Crisps

1 egg
2 tablespoons lemon juice
½ teaspoon dry mustard
½ teaspoon salt
½ teaspoon basil
½ teaspoon tarragon
1 clove garlic, minced
1¼ cups vegetable oil
4 medium zucchini, unpeeled
1 tablespoon garlic salt
1 cup finely crushed saltine cracker crumbs
1 cup grated Parmesan cheese
Paprika

Prepare herbed mayonnaise by combining egg, lemon juice and seasonings in a blender or food processor. With machine running, add oil in a thin, steady stream. Blend until thickened and smooth, about 30 seconds; set aside. Scrub zucchini, remove tips and cut lengthwise into ¼-inch thick slices. Place in colander and sprinkle with garlic salt. Let stand 5 minutes to remove excess water. Combine cracker crumbs and Parmesan cheese in a plate or on waxed paper. Preheat oven to 400°. Lightly grease 2 cookie sheets. Blot moisture off zucchini slices with paper towels. Dip each slice into herbed mayonnaise, coat with crumb mixture and place ½ inch apart on prepared cookie sheets. Bake 15 – 20 minutes at 400° until slices are browned and crisp. Sprinkle with paprika and serve at once. This is a great side dish for grilled steaks, chicken or fish. (Refrigerate any remaining mayonnaise for another use — it will keep several days.) *SERVES: 8*

Nancy Parker's Simply Delicious Ham

1 fully cooked ham, any size
½ cup brown sugar
¼ cup prepared mustard
1 cup strong black coffee, heated

Preheat oven to 325°. Remove wrappings from ham, place in roasting pan, and bake 20 minutes per pound. Fifteen minutes before the end of cooking time, remove ham from oven. Make ¼ inch deep cuts diagonally across top of ham in both directions. Combine brown sugar and mustard to make a thick paste and spread generously over the top of the ham. Return to oven and bake 15 minutes longer, or until sugar has caramelized. Turn off oven and pour coffee into roasting pan. This deglazes the pan and makes red-eye gravy. Leave ham in the oven another hour. Remove from roasting pan and slice thinly. Pour gravy into a sauceboat to serve. Ham and gravy can be reheated.

One of the best parts of Nancy's classes was when she suddenly decided to prepare another recipe for the class — right then and there. Nancy is the only person I know who could get Safeway to deliver a spaghetti squash and a package of Gruyere cheese to her house within ten minutes just so she could demonstrate a great dish she had dreamed up the previous evening. You see, the grocery stores in our town don't make deliveries.

Nancy Parker's Spaghetti Squash

1 large spaghetti squash
½ cup sour cream
¾ cup grated Gruyere cheese
½ teaspoon salt
¼ teaspoon white pepper
½ cup grated Parmesan cheese
2 tablespoons butter or margarine, melted

Cut squash in half, lengthwise, and scoop out seeds. In a large pot with a tight-fitting lid, pour water to a depth of ¼ inch and bring to a boil. Put squash in cut side down, cover, reduce heat and simmer for 20 minutes, or until squash separates into strands when scraped with a fork. Or cook in a microwave: place squash, cut side down, in a flat baking dish with ¼ inch water; cover with plastic wrap and cook on high for 10 – 12 minutes. Scrape squash from shell with a fork and separate into strands. Preheat oven to 350°. Grease a 2-quart flat baking dish. Combine squash, sour cream, Gruyere, salt and pepper in a large mixing bowl and stir gently until blended. Pour into prepared dish, sprinkle with Parmesan cheese and drizzle with melted butter. Bake at 350° for 20 – 25 minutes until cheese has melted and mixture is bubbly. Serve at once as a vegetable dish. *SERVES: 8*

HINT: Nancy suggests freezing soft cheese like Gruyere or Monterey Jack to make grating with a food processor easier.

Although Nancy demonstrated some wonderful desserts in her classes, in my opinion her forte in sweets was ice creams and sorbets. Each day of her three-day-long sessions, students were treated to a new frozen concoction. My favorites were light and refreshing — designed to cleanse the palate during a meal or as a light dessert.

Grapefruit Sorbet

½ cup water
½ cup honey
2 large grapefruit, peeled and sectioned (or 2 cups canned sections)
1 cup milk
¼ teaspoon salt
1 cup grapefruit juice
Additional grapefruit sections dipped in honey for garnish

Combine water and honey in a small saucepan and boil 2 minutes. Remove from heat and let cool completely. Place sectioned grapefruit in a blender or food processor and puree. Add cooled syrup, milk, salt and juice. Blend. Freeze in an ice cream maker according to manufacturer's directions. Or freeze in a metal pan until firm, then break into chunks and puree in a food processor. (Add 1 egg white to frozen mixture in processor for a fluffier texture, if desired.) *MAKES: 1 quart or 8 servings*

NOTE: Ruby Red or pink grapefruit give this sorbet a more appetizing color.

Pear Mint Sorbet

½ cup water
½ cup honey
1 28-ounce can pears, undrained
¼ cup pear-flavored liqueur
2 tablespoons white Creme de Menthe
1 cup half and half
Mint sprigs (for garnish)

Combine water and honey in a small saucepan and boil 2 minutes. Remove from heat and let cool completely. Place all ingredients, including cooled syrup, in a blender or food processor, whirling until smooth. Freeze in ice cream maker according to manufacturer's directions. Or freeze in a metal pan until firm, then break into chunks and puree in a food processor. Garnish with mint sprigs. *MAKES: 1 quart or 8 servings*

Out-of-town students who came to Nancy's classes were treated to an evening at a Mexican restaurant by Nancy and her husband Frank. Often, local students or friends of the Parkers were included to make the party a bit more interesting. These evenings began with frozen margaritas in the Parker's beautiful back yard. It amazed everyone that, after a grueling day of demonstrations, Nancy could have the energy to fill that big punch bowl with what had to take hours to make. Then she shared the recipe and we learned the truth.

Frozen Margaritas For A Crowd

2 cups vodka
1 6-ounce can frozen limeade
¾ cup water
1 liter lemon-lime soda
Several drops green food coloring (for color)
Lime juice and salt
Lime slices for garnish

Combine first 5 ingredients. Pour into a large container allowing at least 2 inches at the top for expansion. Freeze until slushy. At serving time, spoon mixture into a punch bowl and break up any large chunks. Dip glasses into lime juice, then into salt, if desired. Garnish each serving with a lime slice. SERVES: 8

Perhaps Nancy's greatest creation was never served to her students. But everyone who took her classes has raved about this recipe. It is for a simple goop that, when used, will grease and flour a pan all at once. Nancy's Miracle Pan Preparation is aptly named.

Nancy Parker's Miracle Pan Preparation

1 cup cake flour
⅔ cup shortening
¼ cup corn oil

Combine all ingredients in a food processor or mix with a electric mixer, blending until smooth. Store, tightly covered, in the refrigerator. This will keep indefinitely. Use any time a recipe calls for a greased and floured pan. MAKES: 2 cups

Thanks to the influence of great cooks like Nancy Parker, Mary Koock, and Madalene Hill, Mother and I have both come to the conclusion that good cooks are developed over a lifetime of learning. The lessons may come quickly, but the experience does not. Each cook that crosses your path may give you one recipe, or a dozen. The real art is to take those friendships, lessons and recipes and make them a part of your life. Each time Mother or I cook a recipe given to us by someone, it brings back memories of that person and of the good times we've shared. Therefore, the real value of the cards in our recipe files is in the recollections.

"This time, you own the restaurant."

Chapter Five

The Puddin Hill Store

In 1975, the first of the really dramatic changes that would shape the future of Mary of Puddin Hill occurred — certainly the one that has brought us the most fun. That was the year Mother and Dad built and opened the Puddin Hill Store.

Before the store was opened, sales of the fruit cakes were conducted almost exclusively by mail order. There were a few local folks or travelers stopping off the highway who would come in the office door and purchase a cake. It just didn't seem like much, so those sales were largely ignored. A counter was set up to write orders, the fruit cakes and other products were displayed, and Dad's secretary would get up from her desk to help any customer who came in.

Then one day, Dad and Mother were visiting with their good friend and business adviser, Fred Allen. While looking at some financial numbers, the amount credited to sales from walk-in traffic leaped out. It was higher than anyone had anticipated. Fred suggested Mother and Dad give serious consideration to opening a retail store next to the bakery.

It sounded like a very good idea, so plans were drawn for a small store and workroom. That spring and summer my husband, Mike, and I spent every weekend in Greenville helping Mother and Dad design and decorate the store. We scoured the antique and junk shops around East Texas for memorabilia to hang on the walls. Antique store fixtures were bought and refinished to hold displays of candy, jellies, teas and gift items. Old lumber, doors and moldings, and bits of wooden gingerbread ornamentation were sought from buildings slated for destruction. As word got out around Greenville and Hunt County just what we were doing, folks began bringing us things that were of no more use, but just too good to throw away. We took everything offered, declaring that if we ran out of wall space, we'd just "hang it from the ceiling." We did.

Along the way, Dad got a good deal on a refrigerated deli case. He bought it, declaring we ought to serve coffee, soft drinks and dessert. That sounded agreeable, so we purchased a table and some chairs to put by the deli case.

The store opened in October of 1975. Folks who came to see it were delighted. Somehow, we had managed to create an atmosphere that was appealing and nostalgic. Everywhere there was something to see — from old pictures of early Greenville, to a collage of old farm implements, to the post office boxes and stamp window from an old general store.

Our merchandise mix was very simple in the first year. The main offerings were those products sold in our mail-order catalog — the fruit cakes and some candy items that were being made for us. We bought a few varieties of hard candy, some jellies and honey, plus teas, relishes and seasonings from Madaline Hill's Hilltop Herb Farm.

Mother decided that as long as we had a deli case, we might as well offer sandwiches in case someone stopped by off the interstate highway, which was situated about 100 yards off the front porch. But she decided that she didn't want an ordinary sandwich, and certainly not ordinary bread. After some experimentation, she presented her creation. It showed her culinary skills at their best — ham, jalapeño cheese, lettuce and tomato were rolled inside a large flour tortilla. She also created a spread that held the sandwich together while imparting a "what do you think is in this?" sort of taste. Mike christened it the "Tortilla Maria".

Tortilla Maria

Tortilla Maria Spread:
1 8-ounce package cream cheese, softened
1 tablespoon soy sauce
1 tablespoon sherry
¼ cup finely chopped green onion

Combine cream cheese, soy sauce and sherry in a food processor or mixing bowl and blend until smooth. Stir in chopped green onion. Store, covered, in the refrigerator, but allow sauce to come to room temperature before using or it will be too thick. *MAKES: 1½ cups*

For each sandwich:
1 10-inch flour tortilla
2 - 3 tablespoons Tortilla Maria Spread
4 ounces deli ham, sliced thin
½ cup shredded lettuce
¼ cup chopped tomato
⅓ cup grated jalapeño cheese

Spread tortilla generously with Tortilla Maria Spread, being sure to get as close to the edges of the tortilla as possible. Place ham slices in the center of the tortilla, then top with lettuce, tomato and cheese. Fold each side over to the center to form a long roll. Wrap the end in a napkin or waxed paper to catch any filling that might fall out. (It has been our experience that folding up the end of a tortilla that hasn't been heated will cause it to crack, which is why I recommend the wrapping.) *MAKES: 1 sandwich*

To Mother and Dad's surprise, the local folks began coming out for lunch. Since there was only one table, most of the business was take-out. But those who stayed to sit around the table and enjoy the ambience of the store seemed to have a very good time. Space was made for a second table by scooting one of the candy cases into the adjacent work room, inviting customers to step in there to continue shopping. Gradually, the working space got smaller and smaller while the sales and dining space got larger and larger.

Two years after it was opened, *Texas Highways* magazine ran a feature story on the Puddin Hill Store. As one would expect, the traffic in the store picked up noticeably. But what no one anticipated was the dramatic effect that the article would have on the mail-order end of the business. That fall reminded Mother and Dad of their third season in business, when sales had increased well beyond expectations. The efforts to keep up with the baking of 200,000 pounds of fruit cake, handling the mail orders efficiently, and keeping the shelves of the Puddin Hill Store stocked was hard work.

When the season ended, they realized that the next few years would take an all-out effort. Plans were made to expand the store and production facilities. A candy kitchen with a chocolate enrober was added, allowing them to make their own chocolates and other candies. Mother found herself posing for the cover of the catalog for the first time. The number of mailings increased. And it all worked. Mother and Dad were riding the crest of the mail-order boom in America and the craving for anything "Texan" as state pride blossomed.

Meanwhile, the restaurant-that-was-never-intended-to-be continued its stubborn efforts to be acknowledged. At Mother's suggestion, one of the store staff began making a pot of soup every day to offer with the sandwiches. Cynthia was a creative cook in her own right. She enjoyed varying the menu with a different soup every day. Some came from recipes her own family enjoyed, and others came from the collection of cookbooks and recipes that Mother had inherited from her cousin Stella. Before long, local customers were phoning the store to see what soup was on the stove that day. Others asked to be called when their favorite was being served.

Cynthia set down all her recipes in an old spiral-bound notebook. Each listed the ingredients needed to make enough soup to serve the growing crowds showing up for lunch. After two years, Cynthia left us to raise her family. We have had several "soup-makers" since, and each cook has added to the collection in the "soup book," now tattered and stained from rigorous daily use. The recipes we've selected to share from that volume are the favorites of our customers and the Puddin Hill family. We have cut the recipes down to eight servings, since most cooks don't make soup for up to a hundred hungry folks on a regular basis like we do.

Canadian-Style Bacon And Cheese Soup

6 – 8 strips bacon
2 tablespoons oil
½ cup finely chopped celery
2 tablespoons finely chopped green pepper
2 tablespoons finely chopped red pepper or pimiento
¼ cup finely chopped onion
¼ cup flour (Wondra, if possible)
4 cups milk
1 cup chicken broth
1 teaspoon garlic salt
1 teaspoon sugar
1 teaspoon liquid smoke
1 tablespoon parsley
¼ teaspoon tumeric
¼ teaspoon pepper
8 ounces American cheese, cubed (do not substitute)
8 ounces cream cheese, cubed

Cook bacon in a large pot until crisp. Drain bacon, crumble and set aside. Pour off all but 2 tablespoons of the bacon drippings; add oil. Sauté celery, green and red peppers and onion in mixture of drippings and oil over medium heat until soft — about 5 minutes. Sprinkle flour over vegetables and cook for 2 minutes, stirring constantly. Add milk, chicken broth and seasonings. Reduce heat and simmer for 15 minutes to blend flavors. Add cubed cheeses, stirring constantly until cheeses are melted. Do not allow soup to come to a boil. Serve in soup bowls and sprinkle with crumbled bacon. *SERVES: 8*

HINT: Wondra, the instant flour, is ideal for using to thicken soups, sauces and gravies because it dissolves without forming lumps.

Creamy Reuben Soup

1 14½-ounce can beef broth
1 14½-ounce can chicken broth
½ cup chopped celery
½ cup chopped onion
1 green pepper, seeded and chopped
2 tablespoons cornstarch
¼ cup water
1 12-ounce can corned beef, diced
2 cups sauerkraut, rinsed and drained
4 cups (1 quart) half and half
½ cup (1 stick) butter or margarine
3 cups (12 ounces) Swiss cheese, grated
Chopped parsley and croutons for garnish

Combine first 5 ingredients in a large pot and bring to a boil. Reduce heat and simmer until vegetables are tender, about 10 minutes. Stir cornstarch into water until smooth, then add to vegetables and simmer until mixture thickens, about 2 minutes. Add corned beef and sauerkraut, stirring gently to blend. Add half and half and butter. Simmer until butter has melted and soup is heated. Do not allow soup to boil. Remove from heat and add cheese, stirring until cheese has melted. Pour into soup bowls and garnish with chopped parsley and croutons. *SERVES: 8 – 10*

Cheese Chowder

⅔ cup chopped onion
2 cloves garlic, minced
1 cup chopped celery
1 cup chopped carrots
1 cup cubed potatoes
6 cups chicken broth
1 12-ounce can whole kernel corn, drained
⅓ cup butter or margarine
⅓ cup flour
3 cups milk
2 tablespoons prepared mustard
¾ teaspoon white pepper
1 teaspoon salt
½ teaspoon paprika
1 2-ounce jar pimiento, drained
3 cups (12 ounces) shredded Cheddar cheese

Combine first six ingredients in large pot over medium-high heat. Bring to a boil, reduce heat, cover and simmer 15 – 20 minutes or until potatoes are tender. Stir in corn and remove from heat. Melt butter in heavy saucepan. Stir in flour and cook 1 minute. Gradually add milk and cook, stirring constantly, until mixture thickens. Blend in remaining ingredients. When cheese melts, add to vegetable mixture, stirring until well-blended. Heat through, but do not allow to boil. *SERVES: 8*

French Onion Soup

SOUP:
- 3 tablespoons butter or margarine
- 2 tablespoons oil
- 6 large onions, peeled and thinly sliced
- 2 cloves garlic, minced
- 2 tablespoons flour
- ¼ teaspoon pepper
- ½ teaspoon salt
- 4 cups beef broth
- ½ cup Burgundy wine

BREAD TOPPING:
- 8 slices French bread, toasted or 4 English muffins, split and toasted
- ½ cup grated Parmesan cheese

In a large pot with a tight fitting lid, heat butter and oil over medium heat until butter is melted. Add onion and garlic; stir until wilted, about 5 minutes. Reduce heat to low. Cover onions with a piece of buttered waxed paper. Cover with lid and cook the onions for 20 minutes, keeping on very low heat. Remove lid and waxed paper. Sprinkle flour, pepper and salt over onions, stirring until blended — about 2 minutes. Add beef broth and wine. Simmer over low heat for 30 minutes. Serve soup topped with a slice of French bread or an English muffin half, sprinkled with 1 tablespoon of Parmesan cheese. *SERVES: 8*

HINT: Cooking the onions in the manner described in this recipe brings out the natural sweetness of the onions, cutting out the bitter taste. Use it whenever you need cooked onions (to top sandwiches, steaks, etc.)

Lucky Black-Eyed Pea Soup

- 2 16-ounce packages frozen black-eyed peas
- 8 strips bacon
- 1 onion, finely chopped
- 1 10-ounce can Ro-tel tomatoes
- 1 16-ounce can stewed tomatoes
- 1 15-ounce can beef broth
- 1 teaspoon salt
- ½ teaspoon pepper
- 1 cup (4 ounces) grated sharp Cheddar cheese

Cook the peas according to the directions on package; drain. Cook bacon until crisp. Remove, crumble and set aside. Sauté the onion in the bacon drippings until soft. Add the peas, tomatoes, broth, salt and pepper and cheese, simmering until cheese has melted. Pour into a blender and purée. Garnish with the crumbled bacon. *SERVES: 8*

Confetti Clam Chowder

2 tablespoons butter or margarine
2 medium onions, chopped
1½ cups chicken broth
2 large potatoes, cut in ½-inch cubes
1 bay leaf
¼ teaspoon celery salt
1 teaspoon Italian seasoning, crumbled
2 6½-ounce cans minced clams, drained, reserving liquid
2 15-ounce cans Mexicorn, drained
2 cups milk
2 cups half and half
1 teaspoon salt
½ teaspoon pepper

In large pot, melt butter over medium heat and sauté onions until soft. Add broth, potatoes, seasonings and clam liquid. Simmer 20 minutes or until potatoes are soft. Add clams and the remaining ingredients. Simmer another 10 minutes or until soup is heated. Do not allow soup to come to a boil. Remove bay leaf, taste and adjust seasonings.
SERVES: 8

Creamy Pecan Soup

2 cups diced potatoes
3 cups cauliflower flowerettes
½ cup thinly sliced carrots
5 cloves garlic, minced
1 onion, chopped
3 cups chicken broth
1 cup finely ground pecans
¾ cup heavy cream
1 cup (4 ounces) grated Swiss cheese
1 tablespoon cumin
¼ teaspoon ginger
½ teaspoon salt
¼ teaspoon pepper
Lemon slices for garnish

Combine potatoes, cauliflower, carrots, garlic, onions and broth in a large saucepan and bring to a boil. Reduce heat and simmer for 30 minutes. Place mixture in a blender and process until smooth. Return to pan and, over low heat, whisk in pecans, cream, grated cheese and seasonings. Do not allow soup to boil. Garnish each serving with a thin slice of lemon. SERVES: 8

Pud's Mushroom Soup

¼ cup butter or margarine
1 onion, finely chopped
1 pound mushrooms, sliced
2 tablespoons browning sauce (Kitchen Bouquet or B. V.)
¼ cup flour
8 cups (2 quarts) beef broth
1 teaspoon salt
½ teaspoon pepper
½ teaspoon nutmeg
1 cup heavy cream
Sliced mushrooms for garnish

Melt butter or margarine in a large pot over medium heat. Add onion and cook until translucent, about 5 minutes. Add sliced mushrooms and cook another 5 minutes, stirring constantly, until mushrooms are soft. Stir in browning sauce, blending well. Sprinkle flour over the mushroom mixture and cook, stirring constantly, for 2 minutes. Add beef broth and seasonings, reduce heat and simmer for 15 minutes. Stir in heavy cream and heat another 5 minutes. Do not allow soup to boil. Garnish each serving with a mushroom slice, if desired. *SERVES: 8*

HINT: A quick way to slice mushrooms is to use a hard cooked egg slicer. Place a mushroom on the base with the stem up, and press down with the top. Evenly sliced mushrooms in a flash!

Mad Mary's Chili

2 tablespoons chili powder
1 teaspoon salt
½ teaspoon black pepper
¼ cup butter or margarine
1 cup chopped onion
2 cups sliced fresh mushrooms
1 cup chopped celery
1 pound lean ground beef
1 cup water
2 28-ounce cans stewed tomatoes
1 teaspoon Worchestershire sauce
1 tablespoon sugar
1 15-ounce can pinto beans, drained
½ cup grated Cheddar cheese
½ cup sour cream

In small cup, combine chili powder, salt and pepper; set aside. Melt butter in large pot over medium heat. Sauté onion, mushrooms, and celery in butter until softened. Add ground beef, ¼ of the chili powder mixture and cook, breaking up meat until browned. Stir in remaining chili powder mixture, water, tomatoes, Worchestershire and sugar. Simmer for 15 minutes. Add beans and simmer another 10 minutes. Garnish each serving with cheese and sour cream. *SERVES: 8*

Zucchini And Swiss Cheese Soup

3 cups thinly sliced zucchini
2 teaspoons salt
¼ cup unsalted (sweet) butter
1 medium onion, finely chopped
½ clove garlic, minced
¼ teaspoon crumbled rosemary
⅛ teaspoon ground cardamon
½ teaspoon salt
¼ teaspoon white pepper
4 cups chicken broth
1 tablespoon lemon juice
½ cup dry white wine
¾ cup grated Swiss cheese
¼ cup dry Madeira
½ cup chopped raw zucchini for garnish
Freshly grated Parmesan cheese

Scrub and trim ends from zucchini, but don't peel. Slice thinly, place in a colander, sprinkle with salt and let stand 5 minutes to permit water to drain. Pat dry with paper towels. Melt butter over low heat in a large pot. Add onion and garlic. Cook 4 – 5 minutes, stirring often until limp but not brown. Stir in zucchini slices and cook 5 minutes or until zucchini deepens in color. Add seasonings, chicken broth, lemon juice and white wine. Simmer over low heat 20 minutes, stirring occasionally. Remove from heat. Purée soup in a food processor or blender or push through a strainer. Return soup to pot, add grated cheese and Madeira. Heat over low heat for 5 – 6 minutes, until warmed and cheese is melted. Ladle into soup bowls and garnish with chopped zucchini and Parmesan cheese. *SERVES: 6*

Gazpacho

1 46-ounce can V-8 juice
1 tablespoon sugar
1½ teaspoons salt
1 clove garlic, minced
1 tablespoon lemon juice
2 tablespoons white wine vinegar
½ teaspoon Tabasco
¼ cup olive oil
1 teaspoon Worcestershire sauce
1 small cucumber, pared, seeded and diced (about ¾ cup)
1 large or 2 small green peppers, diced (about ¾ cup)
1 cup diced celery
¼ cup chopped green onion
2 large tomatoes, seeded and diced

Combine V-8 juice, sugar, salt, garlic, lemon juice, vinegar, Tabasco, oil and Worcestershire in large bowl. Beat with a wire whisk to blend. Add the remaining ingredients; stir. Cover and chill several hours or overnight. *SERVES: 8*

Goulash!

1½ pounds chili grind beef (or coarsely ground beef)
2 medium onions, finely chopped
1 clove garlic, minced
3 tablespoons tomato paste
3 tablespoons paprika
1 tablespoon caraway seeds
1½ teaspoons marjoram
1 teaspoon grated lemon peel
¼ teaspoon Tabasco sauce
½ teaspoon sugar
2 teaspoons salt
½ teaspoon pepper
6 cups water
2 medium potatoes, peeled and cut into ½-inch cubes
Sour cream (for garnish)

Combine beef, onions and garlic in a large pot. Cook over medium-high heat until beef is browned and onions are soft. Pour off any excess fat. Add tomato paste and seasonings; stir to blend. Add water and stir well. Reduce heat and simmer for 1 hour on low heat. Add potatoes and cook another 20 minutes, or until the potatoes are soft. Serve in bowls, garnishing each with a generous dollop of sour cream. SERVES: 8

"Has Bean" Chowder

1½ pounds bulk pork sausage
1⅔ cups water
1 tablespoon tomato paste
1 15-ounce can kidney beans, undrained
1 16-ounce can whole tomatoes, whirled in blender
1 onion, finely chopped
1 large potato, cut in ½-inch cubes
½ cup finely chopped green pepper
1 bay leaf
½ teaspoon salt
½ teaspoon thyme
¼ teaspoon garlic powder
¼ teaspoon pepper
1 tablespoon onion soup mix
¼ teaspoon nutmeg

Brown sausage, stirring to crumble; drain. Add remaining ingredients and bring to a boil. Cover, reduce heat and simmer 45 minutes. Remove bay leaf before serving. SERVES: 6-8

Emerald Isle Soup

6 cups chicken broth
2 10½-ounce packages frozen green beans, thawed
4 potatoes, peeled and cubed
1 large onion, quartered
½ cup (1 stick) butter or margarine
4 teaspoons dill weed
2 cloves garlic, minced
1 teaspoon salt
½ teaspoon pepper, freshly ground
½ cup sour cream
2 tablespoons lemon juice

In a large saucepan, combine all ingredients except sour cream and lemon juice and bring to boil over high heat. Reduce heat, cover and simmer until vegetables are tender — about 20 – 25 minutes. Transfer soup to blender in batches and purée until smooth. Return to saucepan. Add sour cream and lemon juice and cook on low until heated through. Do not allow soup to boil. SERVES: 8

Wild Rice Pilaf Soup

½ pound bacon
2 cups finely chopped celery
2 cups finely chopped carrots
2 cups sliced mushrooms
1 cup chopped green onions
9 cups beef broth
4 cups V-8 juice
1 10-ounce package frozen English peas
1 package quick cooking wild and long grain rice mix
2 tablespoons tomato paste
2 teaspoons seasoned salt
2 teaspoons dried basil, crumbled
½ teaspoon pepper

Dice bacon and cook in a large saucepan or stockpot until crisp. Remove and set aside. Pour off all but ¼ cup of the bacon drippings from pan and add celery, carrots, mushrooms and onions. Cook, stirring constantly, over medium heat until vegetables begin to soften, about 10 minutes. Set aside ½ cup of bacon for garnish. Add remaining bacon and the rest of the ingredients and simmer over low heat for 25 – 30 minutes. Ladle into soup bowls and garnish with reserved bacon. SERVES: 8 – 12

The secret of The Puddin Hill Store's gumbo recipes lies in the roux, the blend of butter, oil or bacon drippings with flour. The color of the roux can range from blond to dark chocolate, depending on cooking time. Remember that the longer the roux cooks, the darker it turns and the thinner the gumbo will be. I suggest that you use a cast iron skillet to make your roux. Heat the oil, drippings or butter and slowly add the flour using a wire whisk to blend. When well blended, switch to a wooden spoon and stir constantly over medium heat until you reach the desired color. If little black flecks appear, dump the entire thing and start all over! That is burned flour and will adversely affect the flavor. The roux continues to darken as it cools, but the addition of onion, green pepper or celery stops the browning process and enhances the flavor. Roux can be made ahead and stored in the refrigerator. Before reheating, spoon off any excess fat.

East Texas Red Bean Gumbo

2 15-ounce cans pinto beans
1 10-ounce can Ro-tel tomatoes
6 tablespoons vegetable oil
6 tablespoons flour
2 medium onions, finely chopped
1 bell pepper, seeded and chopped fine
1 pound fully cooked smoked sausage, cut in ½-inch slices
1½ cups water
½ cup grated hot pepper cheese

Purée beans and their liquid in a blender or food processor; set aside. Repeat with tomatoes. In a large pot, heat the oil and slowly add flour, using a wire whisk to blend. When well-blended, switch to a wooden spoon and stir constantly until mixture has turned a light brown color. Add onions and cook, stirring constantly, until translucent. Add bell pepper and sliced sausage, stirring until sausage is browned and pepper is softened — about 5 minutes. Pour in puréed beans, tomatoes and water; bring to a boil. Reduce heat and simmer 30 – 40 minutes. Serve gumbo, garnishing each serving with 1 tablespoon grated pepper cheese. *SERVES: 8*

Chicken Gumbo

½ cup (1 stick) butter or margarine
½ cup flour
1 clove garlic, minced
2 cups finely chopped onion
2 cups chopped celery
2 cups seeded and chopped green pepper
½ cup chopped fresh parsley
1 cup chopped green onions (include tops)
6 – 7 cups chicken broth, heated
1 16-ounce bag frozen cut okra, thawed
1 28-ounce can tomatoes (if whole, whirl in blender or processor)
1 cup raw (not instant) rice
4 cups diced, cooked chicken
Salt and pepper to taste
V-8 juice and additional chicken broth for thinning

Begin the gumbo with a roux as follows: in a large cast iron skillet, heat butter and slowly add flour using a wire whisk to blend. When well blended, switch to a wooden spoon and stir constantly until the color of a copper penny, about 20 minutes. Sauté garlic, onion, celery, green pepper, parsley and green onions in roux. Gradually stir in heated broth. Add okra, tomatoes, rice and chicken. Add salt and pepper to taste. Simmer 20 – 30 minutes longer, until rice is tender. Adjust seasonings. If soup becomes too thick, thin with a mixture of half V-8 and half chicken broth.
SERVES: 10

As the Puddin Hill Deli's popularity has increased, so has the menu. In addition to the Tortilla Maria, other sandwiches are offered on the menu. In each case we have adhered to Mother's original concept that the sandwiches be hearty, but different from the fare served at other restaurants.

Effervescent Crescent

For each sandwich:
1 large croissant, split in half lengthwise
2 ounces thinly sliced deli ham
2 ounces thinly sliced deli turkey
2 ounces thinly sliced Swiss cheese
½ cup frozen chopped broccoli, thawed under hot water
¼ cup Hollandaise sauce (see page 264)

Preheat oven to 300°. Open the croissant and place one half on an ungreased baking sheet. Layer the ham, turkey and Swiss cheese on the croissant. Top with the broccoli and Hollandise sauce. Place the second half of the croissant over the sandwich and heat at 300° for 15 – 20 minutes, or until heated through. (You may also heat the sandwich in the microwave oven.) *MAKES: 1 sandwich*

Pocket Full O' Sandwich

CHICKEN SALAD
3 cups cooked, diced chicken
¼ cup chopped celery
¼ cup chopped onion
¼ cup chopped almonds
¼ cup chopped ripe olives
1 teaspoon tarragon
1½ teaspoons seasoned salt
1½ teaspoons Worcestershire
½ teaspoon Tabasco
1½ teaspoons lemon juice
⅓ cup mayonnaise

Combine all ingredients, stirring gently to blend. Chill.

AVOCADO SPREAD
2 avocados
1 ounce cream cheese, softened
1 tablespoon Worcestershire
1 tablespoon lemon juice
1 teaspoon Tabasco

Peel and quarter avocados. With electric mixer or food processor blend all ingredients until smooth.

6 – 8 pita bread rounds
2 – 3 cups shredded lettuce
1 medium tomato, chopped
1 cup alfalfa sprouts

Cut each pita in half and open pocket with fingers. Spread inside of pocket with avocado mixture. Fill ⅔ full with chicken salad. Top with lettuce, tomatoes and sprouts. *MAKES: 6 – 8 pitas*

NOTE: The chicken salad is absolutely delicious served alone, too.

For lighter appetites, the Puddin Hill Deli offers a salad samplin' of three different salads. The selection usually includes one main dish salad, one vegetable salad and one fruit salad, and varies from day to day.

Fried Chicken Salad

SALAD:
- 2 pounds frozen, breaded chicken or turkey nuggets, thawed and cooked according to package directions
- 1 cup whole kernel corn, drained
- 1 green pepper, chopped
- 1 2-ounce jar diced pimiento, drained
- 2 green onions and tops, chopped

DRESSING:
- 1 cup mayonnaise
- 2 teaspoons whole grain prepared mustard
- 2 tablespoons chopped parsley
- 1 tablespoon chopped green onion
- ½ cup heavy cream, whipped

Combine prepared nuggets with the remaining salad ingredients; set aside. For dressing, combine mayonnaise, mustard, parsley and green onion, stirring until smooth. Fold in whipped cream. Reserve ½ cup dressing, then toss remaining dressing with salad ingredients. Serve at once, garnishing each serving with a dollop of reserved dressing. SERVES: 6 - 8

NOTE: This salad may be made several hours ahead and refrigerated until serving time. Do not make the day before, because the nuggets will get soggy.

Strawberries Framboise

- 6 tablespoons raspberry vinegar
- 6 tablespoons granulated sugar
- 1 tablespoon raspberry liqueur (optional)
- 2 pints fresh strawberries, washed and hulled

Stir vinegar and sugar over low heat until sugar dissolves. Let cool. Stir in liqueur. Pour over berries and refrigerate for 1 hour. Drain berries and serve as a fruit salad or as a tart and refreshing dessert. SERVES: 6 - 8

NOTE: Liquid drained from strawberries may be re-used to marinate more berries, if desired. Refrigerate until needed.

Puddin Hill Store's Tortellini Salad

SALAD:
- 1 pound cheese-filled tortellini, cooked and drained
- ½ cup chopped celery
- 1 red bell pepper, chopped (or 2-ounce jar diced pimiento, drained)
- ¼ cup sliced green onion
- 1 cup fresh broccoli flowerettes
- 1 small zucchini, thinly sliced

DRESSING:
- 1 envelope ranch-style salad dressing mix
- 1 cup sour cream
- ½ cup mayonnaise (not salad dressing)

Combine salad ingredients in a large bowl. In a separate bowl, combine dressing ingredients and blend with a wire whisk. Pour over salad and gently toss to blend. Chill several hours before serving. *SERVES: 8*

Reuben Salad

DRESSING:
- ⅓ cup mayonnaise
- ¼ cup drained sweet pickle relish
- 1 tablespoon Dijon mustard
- 1 tablespoon prepared horseradish
- 1 teaspoon Worcestershire sauce
- 1 tablespoon catsup

SALAD:
- 1 16-ounce can sauerkraut, rinsed and drained well
- 1½ cups cooked corned beef, cubed
- 1½ cups Swiss cheese, cubed
- 2 cups rye bread croutons

Blend ingredients for dressing in a small bowl; set aside. In a large bowl, combine salad ingredients. Add dressing, tossing gently until well-coated; chill. Top with rye croutons. *SERVES: 8*

RYE BREAD CROUTONS:
Cut 4 slices rye bread into 1-inch cubes. Melt ½ cup butter or margarine in a large skillet over medium heat. Add bread cubes and toss until toasted. Drain on paper towels.

Fruited Chicken-Pecan Salad

SALAD:
- 2½ cups diced cooked chicken
- 1 cup seedless grapes
- 1 cup chopped pecans or almonds
- 1 teaspoon minced onion
- ½ cup pineapple chunks, drained
- ½ cup sliced black olives
- ½ cup sweet gherkins, thinly sliced

DRESSING:
- ½ cup mayonnaise
- ¼ cup Poppy Seed Dressing (see page 91)
- 1 teaspoon salt
- ½ cup heavy cream, whipped

Combine the salad ingredients in a large bowl. In a separate bowl, thoroughly blend mayonnaise, Poppy Seed Dressing and salt. Fold in whipped cream. Add to chicken mixture and toss to coat. Chill 2 – 3 hours before serving. (Commercial Poppy Seed Dressing may be used.) *SERVES: 8*

Marinated Brussels Sprouts

VEGETABLES:
- 1 20-ounce package frozen Brussels sprouts
- 1 8-ounce jar button mushrooms, drained
- 1 2-ounce jar diced pimiento, drained

MARINADE:
- ¾ cup salad oil
- ½ cup lemon juice
- 1 tablespoon sugar
- 2 teaspoons salt
- 1 teaspoon dry mustard
- ½ teaspoon pepper
- ½ teaspoon basil
- 1 small garlic clove, crushed
- 1 tablespoon minced fresh parsley

Cook Brussels sprouts according to package directions. Drain and combine with mushrooms and pimiento. Blend marinade ingredients in a small bowl, using a wire whisk, until smooth. Pour over warm sprouts mixture. Cover and chill several hours or overnight. *SERVES: 8*

Japanese Chicken Salad

SALAD:
- 3 cups shredded green cabbage
- 1 cup shredded red cabbage
- ¼ cup chopped green onion
- ½ cup chopped almonds
- 1 6-ounce package frozen pea pods, thawed
- 2 cups diced chicken
- 1 3-ounce package Ramen Soup Noodles

DRESSING:
- ½ cup vegetable oil
- ¼ cup sesame oil
- ½ cup vinegar
- 2 tablespoons soy sauce
- 1 teaspoon grated fresh ginger

Combine salad ingredients and set aside. In a separate bowl, blend dressing ingredients with a wire whisk until smooth. Pour over salad, toss lightly to mix and refrigerate for at least 1 hour to allow flavors to blend. *SERVES: 8*

Oriental Chicken Salad

SALAD:
- 3 cups diced cooked chicken
- 1 6-ounce package frozen pea pods, thawed
- 1 8-ounce can bamboo shoots, drained
- 1 5-ounce can water chestnuts, drained
- ½ bell pepper cut into thin strips
- ½ cup toasted almonds
- 1 tablespoon finely chopped candied ginger (optional)
- 2 3-ounce cans Chow Mein noodles

DRESSING:
- ⅔ cup vegetable oil
- ¼ cup sesame oil
- ¼ cup soy sauce

Combine all salad ingredients except Chow Mein noodles. Set aside. In a separate bowl, blend dressing ingredients with a wire whisk until smooth. Pour over salad, toss lightly and refrigerate several hours. At serving time, add the Chow Mein noodles and toss again. *SERVES: 8*

Creamy Lemon Fruit Salad

1 16-ounce bag whole frozen strawberries
1 16-ounce bag frozen sliced peaches
1 11-ounce can Mandarin oranges, drained
1 8-ounce can pineapple chunks, drained
1 3½-ounce package instant lemon-flavor pudding and pie filling mix
1 banana, sliced
2 kiwi fruit, peeled and sliced

Combine strawberries, peaches, oranges and pineapple in a large mixing bowl. Sprinkle dry pudding mix over fruit and gently stir until all are coated. Let stand until serving time to allow frozen fruits to thaw. Just before serving, add banana and kiwi, stirring carefully so they aren't crushed. SERVES: 8

Tuna Hula Salad

1 13-ounce can chunk light chunk tuna, drained and flaked
1 cup chopped celery
1 bell pepper, chopped
¾ cup cubed Cheddar cheese
½ cup cashews or almonds, chopped
1 8-ounce can pineapple chunks, drained
¾ cup mayonnaise
1 teaspoon curry powder
2 tablespoons chopped parsley

In a large bowl, combine first 6 ingredients; set aside. Blend mayonnaise, curry and parsley until smooth. Add to tuna mixture, toss gently and chill several hours before serving. SERVES: 6 – 8

Puddin Hill Store's Fruit Salad Dressing

1 16-ounce can cream of coconut
1 14-ounce can sweetened condensed milk

Combine ingredients and stir until smooth. Serve over any combination of fresh fruit. MAKES: 2½ cups

NOTE: This dressing also makes an excellent dip to place in the center of a fresh fruit platter.

In spite of all the discussion about the soups, sandwiches and salads, dessert is still the culinary superstar in the

Puddin Hill Store. The selection includes the cakes and pies offered through our Mary of Puddin Hill catalog. But there is also a selection of desserts created especially for the Puddin Hill Store. Most of these are made by Novelle "Jackie" Murphy, a wonderful woman who singlehandedly turns out six cakes a day, if necessary. She created the Carrot Cake we serve in the Puddin Hill Deli and has steadfastly guarded the recipe, refusing to yield even to the pressure of her family and friends. "I told them all that one day Pud would write a cookbook," she says, "and, as far as I'm concerned, they can wait to get the recipe!"

Eve's Temptation

¼ cup butter or margarine, melted
⅔ cup pecan pieces
⅔ cup firmly packed brown sugar
6 cups pared, cored, and sliced apples
2 tablespoons lemon juice
⅓ cup firmly packed brown sugar
1 tablespoon flour
½ teaspoon ground cinnamon
½ teaspoon ground nutmeg
¼ teaspoon salt
Your favorite pie crust recipe for a two crust pie

Preheat oven to 450°. Pour melted butter in the bottom of a 9-inch round layer cake pan. Swirl to coat bottom evenly. Spread pecan pieces on top of butter, then top with ⅔ cup brown sugar. Press sugar down firmly over pecans and butter. Set aside. Prepare pie crust and divide into two balls — one smaller and one larger. Roll out the larger ball to a circle about 13 inches in diameter. Fit over pecan layer in cake pan, pressing down to cover bottom. Dough should hang over the rim of pan. Combine apples and lemon juice in a bowl. In a separate bowl, blend remaining brown sugar, flour, cinnamon, nutmeg, and salt. Add to apples, gently mixing until they are evenly coated. Spoon into crust. Roll remaining pastry into a 9-inch round. Fit over apples and fold bottom crust over the top one, crimping the edges well. Bake at 450° for 10 minutes then lower heat to 350° and bake 30 minutes longer or until top curst is browned. Remove from oven, and as soon as syrup stops bubbling, place serving plate over cake pan and invert out onto plate. Serve hot or at room temperature. *SERVES: 8*

Puddin Hill Store's Carrot Cake

2 cups sugar
1½ cups vegetable oil
4 eggs
2 teaspoons vanilla
2¼ cups all-purpose flour
2 teaspoons cinnamon
2 teaspoons baking soda

1 teaspoon salt
2 cups shredded carrots
2 cups flaked sweetened
   coconut
1 8-ounce can crushed
   pineapple, drained
1 cup chopped walnuts

Preheat oven to 350°. Generously grease 3 8-inch cake pans. Cover the bottom of each pan with a piece of waxed paper cut to fit. Grease waxed paper circles. Combine sugar, oil, eggs and vanilla in a large bowl and blend. Combine flour, cinnamon, soda and salt in a separate bowl, then gradually add to sugar mixture. Fold in carrots, coconut, pineapple and walnuts. Divide batter among prepared pans. Bake at 350° for 50 – 55 minutes, or until toothpick inserted in center of each cake comes out clean. Cool in pans 5 minutes, then invert onto rack, remove pans, and let cool. When cool, remove waxed paper from each layer and frost with the following frosting:

FROSTING:
1 8-ounce package cream
   cheese, softened
⅔ cup melted butter or
   margarine
⅓ cup milk

1 tablespoon vanilla
¼ teaspoon salt
3½ – 4 cups powdered
   sugar
½ cup walnuts

Combine cheese, butter, milk, vanilla and salt in a large bowl and beat well, using an electric mixer. Beat in enough powdered sugar to make mixture spreadable. Use about ⅔ cup of frosting between each layer, then frost top and sides with remaining icing. Gently pat walnuts onto top of cake for garnish. *SERVES: 8 – 12*

Peanut Butter Pie

- 1 8-ounce package cream cheese, softened
- 1 cup chunky peanut butter
- ⅔ cup powdered sugar
- ⅓ cup half and half
- 1 8-ounce container whipped topping (Cool Whip)
- 1 prepared graham cracker crust

WHIPPED CREAM TOPPING:
- ½ cup heavy cream
- 1 tablespoon powdered sugar

Beat cream cheese, peanut butter and powdered sugar together until smooth. Gradually add half and half, beating until well blended. Stir in whipped topping. Spoon into graham cracker crust. Whip cream, gradually adding powdered sugar until soft peaks form. Spoon or pipe around the edge of pie. Freeze pie, and slice while frozen. Let stand 20 minutes before serving. *SERVES: 8*

Entice-Mint Pie

- 8 ounces white or pastel "chocolate" mint wafers
- 1 8-ounce package cream cheese, softened
- ½ cup powdered sugar
- 3 tablespoons half and half
- 1 8-ounce container whipped topping (Cool Whip)
- 1 prepared graham cracker crust

TOPPING:
- ⅔ cup sour cream
- 2 teaspoons sugar
- 8 mint wafers for garnish

Melt mint wafers in the top of a double boiler over simmering water. Combine cream cheese, melted mint wafers, and powdered sugar in a mixing bowl and beat with an electric mixer until smooth. Gradually add half and half, beating until well blended. Stir in whipped topping. Spoon into graham cracker crust. Blend the sour cream and sugar together and spread over pie. Garnish with 8 mints on top. Refrigerate several hours before serving. This pie may also be frozen. *SERVES: 8*

Harvest Pie

PRALINE PIE SHELL

⅓ cup butter or margarine
⅓ cup sugar
½ cup chopped pecans
1 baked 9-inch pie shell (deep dish-type if using a commercial crust)

Preheat oven to 425°. Combine butter and sugar in saucepan. Cook on medium heat, stirring constantly until sugar melts and bubbles vigorously. Remove from heat and stir in pecans. Spread in baked pie shell and bake at 425° for 5 minutes.

FILLING:

1 4½-ounce package of egg custard mix
1 cup canned pumpkin
1 cup apple butter
⅓ cup firmly packed brown sugar
⅔ cup evaporated milk
2 eggs, separated
2 tablespoons pumpkin pie spice
2 tablespoons sugar

Combine custard mix, pumpkin, apple butter, sugar, milk, egg yolks and spice in a large saucepan. Beat with an electric mixer until smooth. Place saucepan over medium heat and bring mixture to a boil, stirring constantly, until thickened. Beat egg whites, gradually adding the sugar, until stiff. Remove mixture from heat and fold in egg whites. Pour into prepared crust and chill several hours, until mixture is set. Just before serving, top with whipped cream topping.

TOPPING:

½ cup heavy cream
2 tablespoons powdered sugar

Whip cream, gradually adding powdered sugar, until soft peaks form. Spoon or pipe around edge of pie. *SERVES: 8*

One of my favorite aspects of the Puddin Hill Store is the opportunity to experiment with lots of new recipes. That challenge is not limited to the deli. Frequently, a customer will ask us to suggest some way to prepare or serve a dish using one of the gourmet products on our shelves. Often, that is enough inspiration, and I'm off to the kitchen. Although many of the recipes are developed with a specific brand of seasoning or condiment in mind, some of the best are not.

This dish was developed after Mother and Dad visited a restaurant in Scottsdale, Arizona. The chef layered ingredients, pizza-style, onto Armenian cracker bread, known as lahvosh.

We sell the bread in our store, so, with Mother's help, this version was developed. We jokingly decided that it was actually closer to the Mexican nacho than to pizza, since there was no tomato sauce, so we christened our version "Armenian Nachos".

Armenian Nachos

- 1 large (about 12-inch) lavosh (Armenian cracker bread found in gourmet food shops)
- 6 ounces very thinly sliced Dofino, Mozzarella, Havarti or any mild-flavored white cheese
- ½ cup finely diced ham
- ½ cup finely diced summer sausage, pepperoni, or salami
- ½ cup chopped green pepper
- ¼ cup sliced ripe olives
- ¼ cup sliced green olives
- ½ cup chopped fresh mushrooms
- 2 tablespoons chopped chives (optional, but delicious)

Preheat oven to 350°. Place lavosh on a baking sheet or pizza pan — it won't lie flat, so don't press it or it will break. Cover the lavosh with sliced cheese so that no cracker shows. Scatter the remaining ingredients in order listed evenly over the surface, being careful not to let any pile up too much anywhere or the cheese will not melt. Try to cover the entire area — have patience with the lumps and bumps. Bake in a 350° oven for 20 minutes until the cheese is melted and bubbly and the lavosh has flattened out. Cut with a pizza cutter and serve. This is delightful if served with a tossed green salad and wine. *SERVES: 4*

Chocolate Mint Mystery Cookies

1 cup butter or margarine, softened
1 cup granulated sugar
½ cup brown sugar
2 teaspoons vanilla
2 eggs
3 cups flour
1 teaspoon baking soda
¼ teaspoon salt
2 tablespoons water
1 pound milk chocolate mint wafers
Pecan halves, for garnish (optional)

Cream butter and sugars together until mixture is fluffy. Add vanilla and blend. Add eggs one at a time, beating well after each addition. Sift flour, soda and salt together and add to butter mixture, alternating with water. Mix until well blended. Chill dough several hours. To form cookies, enclose each wafer in about 1 tablespoon of chilled dough. If desired, you may top each cookie with a pecan half. Place on ungreased baking sheets, about 2 inches apart. Bake at 350° until cookies are browned — about 12 – 15 minutes. *MAKES: 4 – 5 dozen*

Occasionally, those experimentations lead to something too good to simply put on a recipe sheet. Such is the case with Hocus Pecos Dip. It was developed as a serving suggestion for a cumin-flavored seasoning we had on our shelves. The result was so good we began selling the dip ready-made in the store. It has a unique Southwest-style flavor, and is always the first to go when served at a party.

Hocus Pecos Dip

2 8-ounce packages cream cheese, softened
1 cup Picante sauce
1 bunch green onions, finely chopped (about 1 cup)
1 2-ounce jar dried beef, finely chopped
1 teaspoon cumin
½ teaspoon oregano
½ teaspoon salt

Place cream cheese in a mixing bowl or food processor and beat until smooth. Add Picante sauce and beat until no lumps of cream cheese remain. Stir in onions, beef and seasonings. Chill. Serve with tortilla chips. *SERVES: 12*

Whole Wheat Gems are among the best cookies I have ever eaten. The recipe came from Jacquelyn Smyers, an expert on serving tea. She visited the Puddin Hill Store to promote her cookbook, *Come For Tea*, and served this delightful cookie. Walnuts and whole wheat flour are combined to produce a nutty, not-too-sweet taste.

Whole Wheat Gems

½ cup butter or
   margarine, softened
⅓ cup sugar
1 egg
½ teaspoon vanilla

1 cup whole wheat flour
1 cup finely chopped
   walnuts
Jam or jelly

Preheat oven to 350°. Cream butter and sugar together until fluffy. Add egg and vanilla and blend until smooth. Stir in whole wheat flour and walnuts. (This can be made in the food processor in a snap!) Form dough into balls about 1 inch in diameter. Place 2 inches apart on baking sheets. Make a depression in the center of each cookie using your finger, or the handle of a wooden spoon. Bake at 350° for 12–15 minutes. Remove from oven and cool. At serving time, fill the center of each cookie with jam or jelly. MAKES: 4 dozen

HINT: *If you have lots of cookies to fill, try putting the jelly in a squeeze bottle like those used to serve mustard or ketchup — makes it easy!*

While at the Puddin Hill Store, Jacquelyn offered this advice on serving hot tea successfully at a party.

Serving Tea To A Crowd

Make a strong brew of tea (2 tablespoons of loose tea with 1½ cups of boiling water — steep for 5 minutes) and pour it into something that can keep your concentrate warm for a while (a teapot set over a candle warmer or a thermos pot). Have additional hot water ready in another pot or a large coffee-maker. To serve, pour a slosh of tea concentrate into each cup and add hot water until the desired strength is reached. Each cup of tea is then prepared fresh and as your guest likes it — not too strong or too cold!

Several years ago Mother began to make and serve a wonderful dip loaded with chili powder, ground beef and cheese. Later, Dad worked with a spice company to develop a package of the seasonings in order to make preparation easier. It is now a best-seller in our store. Since Dad did the leg-work, he got to have his name put on the package — and now claims the original recipe.

Sam Lauderdale's Original Chili Dip

3 pounds lean ground beef
2 tablespoons bacon fat or vegetable oil
½ cup flour
3 medium onions, finely chopped
1 14½-ounce can beef broth
1 8-ounce can tomato sauce
6 tablespoons chili powder
1 teaspoon cumin
½ teaspoon oregano
1 teaspoon salt
1 2-pound box American cheese, grated

In a large pot, brown ground beef over medium heat, stirring constantly. Add bacon fat or oil, then sprinkle flour over beef and stir until blended. Add onions, beef broth, tomato sauce and seasonings. Simmer for 30 minutes, stirring often, until mixture thickens. Reduce heat to very low, and add grated cheese, stirring until cheese is melted. (Do not substitute another type of cheese for the American cheese, or the dip will get stringy and greasy.) Serve dip hot with tortilla chips. Dip may be prepared ahead, omitting the cheese, and frozen. Add cheese before serving. SERVES: 20 – 25

HINT: *Leftover chili dip makes a great taco salad! Reheat dip and pour over shredded lettuce. Top with chopped tomatoes, avocado slices, black olives, sour cream and grated cheese. Serve with tortilla chips.*

The Puddin Hill Store, like the rest of Mary of Puddin Hill, is busiest during the months of October, November and December. There is a permanent staff of about 50 people throughout the company. During the fall the ranks swell to about 180, as the part-time seasonal helpers begin working. The peak of the seasonal rush comes in late November and early December. During that time, the hours are often long and the demands exhausting. After Christmas, however, things slow down so much that some employees are looking for things to do. In an effort to keep some of our staff busy, we began baking breads to sell in the store three days a week. Since we like to offer unique products, we took care to come up with a selection of breads that would be special. Now, from January to July, the smell of homemade bread drives everyone crazy. I have adapted our most popular bread so it can be made using frozen bread dough.

Cobblestone Breads

ITALIAN COBBLESTONE BREAD:
1 1-pound loaf frozen bread dough, thawed
1 egg
2 teaspoons Italian seasoning

CHEESE COBBLESTONE BREAD:
1 1-pound loaf frozen bread dough, thawed
1 egg
½ cup grated Cheddar or Swiss cheese

BUTTER AND EGG COBBLESTONE BREAD
1 1-pound loaf frozen bread dough, thawed
1 egg
2 tablespoons butter or margarine, softened

JALAPEÑO COBBLESTONE BREAD
1 1-pound loaf frozen bread dough, thawed
1 egg
¼ cup Mexicorn, drained
2 tablespoons buttermilk
2 tablespoons dry Taco mix
2 tablespoons chopped jalapeños or green chilies

PECAN COBBLESTONE BREAD
1 1-pound loaf frozen bread dough, thawed
1 egg
⅔ cup chopped pecans

General Instructions:
Place thawed bread dough on a tray with a rim. (I use an inexpensive plastic tray.) Make a well in the center of the dough and pour egg into it. Top with remaining ingredients. Using a dough cutter or a large knife, cut through the dough repeatedly until the bits are about the size of marbles. Use the blade of the knife or a spatula to scoop the bread mixture back on top of itself, mixing thoroughly. Pour mixture into a greased 9×5×3-inch loaf pan. Cover and let rise in a warm draft-free place until doubled in bulk, about 45 minutes. Bake at 350° for 30 – 35 minutes, until browned and loaf sounds hollow when tapped. Let cool in pan 5 minutes, then turn out and serve hot or let cool. *MAKES: 1 loaf each*

NOTE: All cobblestone breads make good sandwiches. The Pecan Cobblestone Bread and the Cheese Cobblestone Bread also make delicious toast for breakfast.

Once a month, we bake a wonderful whole wheat bread. I first tasted this bread while on the faculty at Stephens College in Columbia, Missouri. Its slightly sweet taste makes sandwiches or toast extra special. The bread was so popular with the students that white sandwich bread was only offered as a courtesy. When I left the college to return to Greenville, I wanted the recipe for that bread. The baker refused to give it to me at first, but thanks to the efforts of the secretary to the director of food service for the college, he finally capitulated. Thinking he would discourage me from ever trying to make the bread, he wrote out a recipe that would make twelve loaves at a time — exactly what I wanted! Since then, Stephens College Whole Wheat Bread has had loyal fans lined up in the Puddin Hill Store whenever we make it. I have reduced the recipe to make 2 loaves, a much more practical number for home baking.

Puddin Hill Store (and Stephens College) Whole Wheat Bread

2 packages dry yeast
1 cup warm water
  (105° – 110°)
1 tablespoon shortening
3 tablespoons sugar
1½ teaspoons salt
3 tablespoons molasses
2 cups whole wheat flour
1¼ – 1½ cups all-purpose flour

Dissolve yeast in warm water and let stand about 5 minutes. In a large mixing bowl, combine remaining ingredients. Add dissolved yeast, mixing to make a stiff dough. Turn out onto a floured board. Knead, adding more all-purpose flour if necessary, until dough is smooth and elastic — about 10 minutes. Put dough into a well-oiled bowl and turn, so that oiled surface is on top. Cover and let rise in a warm, draft-free place until doubled in bulk, about 30 – 40 minutes. Punch dough down and knead briefly, 5 or 6 times. Return to bowl and let rise again. Punch down after second rising, then let dough rest for 15 minutes. Make into 2 loaves and put into greased 8½ × 4½ × 2¾-inch loaf pans. Cover and let rise until doubled. Bake at 350° for 30 minutes or until loaves sound hollow when tapped. Remove from oven and brush tops with melted butter, if desired. *MAKES: 2 loaves or 20 – 24 rolls*

NOTE: This also makes excellent rolls. Pinch off balls about the size of an egg, and place in a well-greased pan or individual muffin tins. Let rise and bake 20 – 25 minutes.

Mother and Dad are frequently on hand in the store to visit with customers. It is not uncommon to find Mother with an iced tea pitcher or coffee pot in her hand offering refills to her guests. She says she spent a lifetime with a crowd around for the noon meal, so this isn't any different. Dad is usually helping the staff clear the dishes from the tables. His business card says, "Sam Lauderdale: Owner, President and Janitor," so he is simply living up to one of his titles. On one particularly crowded day, Mother looked across the store to see Dad juggling a load of dishes as the next wave of diners searched for places to sit. She remarked, "Sam Lauderdale, when I met you, you were busing tables at Tommy Knight's Restaurant in Austin. About the only thing that has changed is, this time, you own the restaurant!" They say everything comes full circle. I guess it's true.

*"I've always said Mother and Dad
had two children...
one was a fruit cake and one was me."*

Chapter Six

Pud and Mike
The inmates take over the asylum

To be honest, when Mike Kearns and I married, the thought of being in business with Sam and Mary Lauderdale was the farthest thing from our minds. We had great dreams of careers of our own, and that great big world beyond Greenville, Texas, beckoned. But life seldom goes as first planned, so when the opportunity to carry on the Puddin Hill tradition came, we took it.

Of course, I was raised at Mary of Puddin Hill, so it was simply part of my life from the very beginning. I have said for many years that Mother and Dad had two children — one was a fruit cake and the other was me. (Lots of my friends said that they could not tell the difference.) I got my nickname "Pud" from the company, too. The name on my birth certificate is Mary Jane, which is also Mother's name. Grandmother's first name was Mary, too, although she went by Gertrude. She began a tradition of giving her daughters first names that could be passed on to each succeeding generation. Mary was chosen for Mother, because it had a double tie to her family — not only was it a name that had been in Grandmother's family for several generations, but Pop's grandmother had also been named Mary — Mary Horton, the first Mary on Puddin Hill.

The Christmas before I was born, one of the young men working in the Puddin Hill warehouse began a joke that would eventually give me my nickname. He began teasing Mother and Dad about how "Little Pud" would be into everything the next season. Soon, Mother and Dad — and everyone else — were referring to me as "Little Pud." When I was born, the nickname continued. A nurse at the hospital got wind of the joke and put "Little Pud" on my identification bracelet. Although they continued to call me by that name, Mother stopped short of putting it on the birth certificate. And she insists that, had I been a boy, the name would never have been allowed to stick!

Growing up with the name "Pud" (it was later shortened — when I started to grow) turned out to be a mixed blessing. On one hand, it was unique enough that I was never confused with another classmate in school. But it also meant that I received some teasing when I was young. I tried going by Mary in school for about six months, but gave it up. I had never learned to answer to that name, and found the teachers losing patience when they tried to call on me in class.

As an adult, I now realize that giving me the name "Pud" was the greatest present Mother and Dad have ever given me. Because it is so unique, people rarely forget my name. And it makes a natural ice-breaker when meeting someone new. After all, when the response to, "And where did you get such an unusual name?" is "Oh, I was named after a fruit cake," folks just seem to want to know more.

I grew up with the company, and from the time I was small I can remember wanting to be part of Puddin Hill. As a youngster, I could help with small tasks like counting out labels or sorting letters by zip codes. It was fun, and an important way to be of "help" to Mother and Dad.

My career plans were directed toward fashion design, though. Grandmother, remembering her own days as a children's wear designer, was eager to encourage my interests. The world was changing dramatically from her days as a young woman. I suppose she saw the chance to live out her dreams of a real career in fashion design through me. She spent many hours training me to see design elements in clothing and to draw inspiration from the world around me.

With the enthusiastic support of Grandmother and, of course, Mother and Dad, I began to study fashion design at Texas Christian University in Fort Worth, Texas. During freshman orientation on the campus, I met an engaging senior named Mike Kearns. I was thrilled by the attention he gave me, and came home excitedly telling my parents how wonderful college was going to be. "Watch out for those seniors," Mother warned. "I'll bet he was only scouting the incoming crop of girls. If I were you, I wouldn't expect to see him again when I got back to campus in the fall." Fortunately for me, in this case Mother was wrong, and she's had to live it down ever since. When we met, Mike actually had more experience in cooking than I did. Mamie had done most of the day-to-day cooking at our house because the company's demands on Mother increased every year. Mamie was reluctant to teach me the basics. For one thing, I am left-handed and she is right-handed. She could never get used to the idea of my doing everything backwards, especially when it came to using sharp knives. I got a few lessons in breakfast making from Dad and lots of ideas on entertaining from Grandmother and Mother. And Grandmother had taught me a little about making bread. But when it came to the basics of preparing a meal, I was not very skilled.

Mike, on the other hand, had a father who was a chef. Bob Kearns had studied restaurant and hotel management during the Depression, and had managed several restaurants before Mike was born. Then Jo, Mike's mother, told Bob he could either be a chef or a father because, in her opinion, it was impossible to successfully do both. Bob concurred and moved into sales of restaurant equipment. He satisfied his need to get in the kitchen by serving as chief cook at church functions or helping Jo in the kitchen. Mike says that his mother was not often pleased to have Bob as her kitchen assistant. It seems that he could not cook for less than twelve, and it took every pot in the kitchen for him to make macaroni and cheese.

Mike developed an interest in food and its preparation from both his mother and father. Jo Kearns was determined to raise a son who could be independent in terms of cooking and housekeeping. And Mike often accompanied his dad into restaurant kitchens to check on equipment. When we met, he was enrolled in a gourmet cooking class at Texas Christian University, just for the fun of it.

Mike had no plans to go into the restaurant business, however. His sights were set on a career in church business administration. Upon graduation, he enrolled in Brite Divinity School on the TCU campus.

Almost three years after we met, we were married. As a new bride, I was anxious to prepare dishes that my rail-thin husband would enjoy. I remembered seeing Mother, Grandmother and Mamie cook in what appeared to be an effortless manner. They didn't even seem to use recipes! "I can do that, too," I thought. But, oh, was I mistaken. About half of the dishes I tried to throw together were thrown out! Mike told me that I cooked by the "dump" method . . . dump a little of this in . . . dump a little of that in . . . and if it doesn't work, just dump the whole mess out.

While trying to learn to cook, I was also trying to learn to be a fashion designer. I had gone to work for a children's wear company in Fort Worth as assistant to a very talented designer, Irene Stewart. Her mind was filled with wonderful ideas for little girls' party dresses, but Parkinson's Disease had attacked her body, making the simple acts of sketching and cutting fabric exhausting efforts for her. The company hired me to be her hands so that her designs could be executed. The opportunity was too good to pass up, so I talked my parents into letting me quit college and work with Irene. I'd go back to school later, I promised.

Mike was in seminary during this time. He was studying and serving as student minister in various churches, trying to get experience and bring in a few dollars where he could. Combining his income and mine, we managed to get by pretty well . . . as long as I didn't keep experimenting in the kitchen. Fortunately, Mother came through with a copy of the cookbook Grandmother had helped to write for her church. *Crestview Culinary Collections* put me on the right track in the cooking department. I learned to read a recipe and follow it step by step. Jo Kearns was a real help, too, sharing some of Mike's favorite recipes with me. When she sent me a stack of recipe cards, Mike saw the recipe for a cheesecake on top of the stack. He asked me to try and make it for him. At the time, the ingredients needed to make the cake seemed very costly, especially to a beginning designer and a graduate student. When the next payday came, I splurged and bought everything needed to make Mike's favorite cake. To my utter amazement, it turned out perfect — my first real cooking success. After that, whenever we felt we could afford it, I baked this cheesecake. We named Jo's recipe Payday Cheesecake. Ironically, I now realize that, as cheesecakes go, this one is a real bargain to make. And it's still our favorite.

Payday Cheesecake

1½ cups graham cracker crumbs
⅓ cup brown sugar
½ teaspoon cinnamon
⅓ cup melted butter or margarine
1½ cups creamed cottage cheese

1 8-ounce package cream cheese, softened
2 eggs, beaten
½ cup sugar
½ teaspoon vanilla
1 cup sour cream

Preheat oven to 325°. Combine crumbs, brown sugar, cinnamon, and butter until crumbly. Press in an even layer over bottom and sides of an 8-inch springform or cake pan. Puree cottage cheese in a blender or food processor, then blend in cream cheese. Add eggs, sugar and vanilla and blend until smooth. Pour into crumb-lined pan and bake at 325° for 35 minutes. Spread with sour cream while still hot. Cool, then chill. *SERVES: 10*

Gradually my confidence began to build and, as it did, cooking became fun. I tried a few more recipes in the stack that Jo had sent, and had a few more successes. Because they were Mike's favorite dishes, he was delighted with my growing culinary prowess. Two of the most often requested were dishes Mike had enjoyed as a child. When I asked Jo about them, I discovered that they were recipes her mother had often prepared. Barbecued Steakers was at the head of the list. It's simply small hamburger patties simmered in a barbecue sauce, but to kids, it's the best supper known. The secret is having scads of mashed potatoes on the side to douse with the extra sauce.

Barbecued Steakers

2 pounds ground beef
1 teaspoon salt
½ teaspoon pepper
1 teaspoon onion powder

2 cups catsup
4 tablespoons brown sugar
2 tablespoons Worcestershire sauce

Combine ground beef, salt, pepper and onion powder, blending well. Form into flattened balls about 2 inches in diameter. Brown steakers on both sides in a large skillet over medium heat. Remove steakers and drain excess fat from the skillet. Return steakers to the skillet. Combine the remaining ingredients together and pour over steakers. Bring to a boil, reduce heat and simmer, uncovered, 10 minutes. Serve with mashed potatoes, pouring extra sauce over both meat and potatoes. *SERVES: 6 - 8*

Jo also sent me her recipe for Spiced Apples. It was one she had copied from her mother's collection. On the recipe card her mother had "one 29-cent package red hots" in the list of required ingredients. After some discussion, Jo and I decided that, in today's terms, that package must contain about one-half cup... and cost about a dollar!

Spiced Apples

10 – 12 small apples
3 cups water
3 cups sugar
½ cup red hot (cinnamon) candies
½ teaspoon red food coloring (optional)

Peel, core and slice apples about ¼-inch thick. Set aside. In a large saucepan, bring remaining ingredients to a boil and cook until red hots are dissolved. Add sliced apples, reduce heat and cook until apples are tender and have become translucent, and syrup has thickened, about 45 – 50 minutes. Cool, then refrigerate apples and syrup. The apples make a delightful side dish or garnish for any meal, from sandwiches to steaks. *MAKES: About 6 cups*

Mother's help was especially valuable, because she offered some recipes that were just right for entertaining. She and Dad always enjoyed having guests for dinner, and encouraged me to invite friends over, too. Mother said that, thanks to television, my generation thought that the house had to be spotless, the food nothing short of gourmet, and the hostess calm and collected before company could set foot inside the front door. She stressed that nothing was as important as the simple act of getting together and sharing good times. But good food sure could add to the success of an evening!

Chicken Molé Frijolé

8 chicken breast halves
2 – 3 tablespoons vegetable oil
1 teaspoon salt
2 16-ounce cans pinto beans
½ cup chopped onion
1 clove garlic, minced
½ cup tomato sauce
½ cup dry red wine
½ ounce semi-sweet baking chocolate
½ cup chopped blanched almonds

Heat oil in heavy frying pan over medium heat. Slowly brown chicken breasts, sprinkling with salt as they brown; set aside. Drain beans, reserving liquid. Pour off all but 1 tablespoon drippings. Add onion and garlic, cooking until golden brown. Mix in bean liquid, tomato sauce and wine. Simmer about 10 minutes. Stir chocolate into sauce, simmering until chocolate is melted. Pour beans into a buttered 13×9-inch baking dish. Top with chicken breasts. Pour the sauce over all and sprinkle with almonds. Cover and bake at 350° for about 40 minutes. Remove cover, continuing to bake another 20 – 25 minutes or until almonds are toasted. If you are not ready to serve the casserole, reduce heat to 225° to keep warm. *SERVES: 6 – 8*

Green Enchilada Sauce For Beef, Chicken Or Cheese Enchiladas

SAUCE:
1 10½-ounce can cream of mushroom soup
1 4-ounce can green chilies
½ cup chopped onion
3 cloves garlic, minced
½ cup chicken broth

Place all ingredients in blender and blend until smooth. Pour into saucepan and simmer 10 minutes to blend flavors. *MAKES: 2½ cups*

Beef, Chicken Or Cheese Enchiladas

BEEF ENCHILADA
1 pound ground beef
¼ cup finely chopped onion
2½ cups Green Enchilada Sauce (see preceding recipe)
10 8-inch flour tortillas
1 cup (4 ounces) grated sharp Cheddar cheese

Preheat oven to 350°. Brown ground beef and onion; drain any excess fat. Add 1 cup of Green Enchilada Sauce and simmer 10 minutes. Soften tortillas in hot oil or the microwave. Place ¼ cup of meat in each tortilla and roll. Place seam side down in a greased 11×7-inch baking dish. Top with remaining sauce and cheese and bake in a 350° oven for 20 minutes or until cheese has melted.

CHICKEN ENCHILADAS
3 cups cooked, diced or shredded chicken
2½ cups Green Enchilada Sauce (see preceding recipe)
12 corn tortillas
1 cup sour cream
1 cup grated (4 ounces) Monterrey Jack cheese

Preheat oven to 350°. Combine 3 cups chicken and ½ cup Green Enchilada Sauce. Soften tortillas in hot oil or the microwave. Fill and roll each tortilla with 2 tablespoons chicken mixture. Place seam side down in a greased 11×7-inch baking dish. Blend 1 cup sour cream into 2 cups sauce and pour over enchiladas. Top with cheese and bake at 350° for 25 minutes.

CHEESE ENCHILADAS
3 cups (12 ounces) grated Monterrey Jack cheese or sharp Cheddar cheese
¼ cup finely chopped onion
2½ cups Green Enchilada Sauce (see preceding recipe)
12 corn tortillas

Preheat oven to 350°. Combine 2 cups grated Monterrey Jack cheese with onion. Soften tortillas in hot oil or the microwave. Fill and roll each tortilla with about 2 tablespoons cheese mixture and 1 tablespoon Green Enchilada Sauce. Place enchiladas seam side down in a greased 11×7-inch baking dish. Pour remaining sauce over the enchiladas, top with 1 cup cheese and bake in a 350° oven 20 minutes or until cheese melts.

Mother gave me a recipe for a rich, hearty spaghetti sauce. Unlike most conventional sauces, it called for more than just tomatoes and oregano. Over the years, with patience and practice, I have learned to successfully add to, or change recipes. The adaptations I have made to this spaghetti sauce have helped make it one of my biggest culinary successes. I also use the spaghetti sauce as the topping for polenta casserole, an Italian-style dish using cooked cornmeal as a replacement for lasagna noodles.

Pud's Spaghetti Sauce

1 pound fully cooked smoked sausage
¼ cup olive oil
2 cloves garlic, minced
1 medium onion, finely chopped
1 green pepper, finely chopped
1 red bell pepper, finely chopped (optional)
2 stalks celery, chopped
1 carrot, finely chopped
½ cup chopped parsley
1 pound ground Italian sausage, ground beef or ground turkey
2 6-ounce cans tomato paste
1 28-ounce can tomatoes or 4 cups fresh tomatoes, peeled, seeded and chopped (reserve liquid)
1 teaspoon beef bouillon granules (or 1 cube)
1 teaspoon oregano
1 teaspoon basil
¼ teaspoon cumin
¼ teaspoon thyme
2 cups red wine (more may be added)
Parmesan cheese, freshly grated

Slice smoked sausage into quarters lengthwise, then in small pieces about ½ inch thick; set aside. Heat olive oil in a large pot over medium heat. Sauté vegetables and parsley until soft. Add ground sausage, cooking until browned. Drain off excess fat. Add sausage pieces and cook about 5 minutes. Add tomato paste, tomatoes and liquid, bouillon granules, seasonings and red wine. Simmer on low, uncovered, for 1 hour, stirring occasionally. Add more red wine if necessary. Serve over freshly cooked spaghetti with lots of grated Parmesan cheese. *SERVES: 8*

Polenta Casserole

1½ cups enriched yellow cornmeal
1½ cups cold water
2 teaspoons salt
4½ cups boiling water
6 cups Pud's Spaghetti Sauce (or other hearty spaghetti sauce)

2 cups (8 ounces) shredded Mozzarella cheese
½ cup (3 ounces) freshly grated Parmesan cheese

To make polenta, combine cornmeal, cold water and salt in a small bowl. In a large, heavy saucepan, bring 4½ cups water to a rapid boil. Slowly add cornmeal mixture, stirring constantly until thickened. Cover and continue to cook over very low heat for 15 minutes, stirring occasionally. Pour hot cornmeal mixture into ungreased 15 × 10 × 1-inch jelly roll pan. Refrigerate about 1 hour or until firm. Preheat oven to 350°. Cut chilled polenta into 16 pieces. Place 8 polenta slices onto bottom of ungreased 13 × 9-inch baking dish. Spoon half of the spaghetti sauce over and around polenta. Sprinkle with 1 cup Mozzarella cheese and ¼ cup Parmesan cheese. Place remaining polenta slices over cheese. Spoon remaining sauce over and around polenta, sprinkle with remaining cheeses and bake in a 350° oven about 30 – 35 minutes. Let stand about 5 minutes before serving. Cut into squares to serve.
SERVES: 8

Success in fashion design also came my way. I moved from children's clothing into the trendier junior market, designing for a company selling fashions to the large chain stores. It was really fun to have the chance to study the latest "ins and outs," interpreting them for the young, stylish teens who bought my designs.

Mike's career was finally getting on track, too. He graduated from seminary and was offered a position with the Missouri Regional Offices of the Christian Church (Disciples of Christ). It would mean a move to Jefferson City, Missouri, if he accepted the job. It would also mean an indefinite hold on my career in fashion design.

After lots of soul-searching, we decided that the chance was too important for Mike to pass up, and he took the job. But Mike displayed a special concern for my feelings when he headed to Missouri. Remembering I had promised Mother and Dad several years before that I would finish my college education, and understanding what a difficult move this would be for me, Mike enrolled me at Stephens College in nearby Columbia.

He had all the paperwork completed before I even finished my work in Dallas and joined him.

The move to Missouri followed a devastating loss for me. About a month before we headed north, Grandmother was tragically killed in an automobile accident. Not only was I facing a great change in my life, but it would be made without the moral support of one who had influenced and encouraged me so very much. While we were going through Grandmother's house, someone came across her recipes — twenty-one file card boxes worth! She had dreamed of writing a cookbook of her own one day, but just never got around to doing it. Mother wisely decided I might need something more than college classes to help me adjust to the move. She suggested that I take on the project of going through Grandmother's recipes and cookbook collection to find the best. Then, someday there might be the chance to compile them into a cookbook.

I leaped at the chance. The number of recipes in the boxes was staggering, but I slowly sorted through them. Mother and Mary Koock taught me how to read and write recipes, making sure all instructions were written clearly. Nancy Parker's cooking classes supplied instruction in basic techniques. Cooking became the creative outlet that fashion design had once been. We found it easy to make friends in our new home by inviting them over for supper. I cooked furiously and, armed with a stack of reference cookbooks, learned something new about cooking every day. Some pretty good recipes came out of those efforts.

Sweet And Sour Baked Fish

2 envelopes powdered vegetable stock
2 cups water
4 tablespoons flour
1 tablespoon ground ginger
¼ teaspoon nutmeg
¼ teaspoon cinnamon
¼ teaspoon mace
1 bay leaf
¼ cup molasses
¼ cup honey
¼ cup cider vinegar
1 large onion, finely chopped
¼ cup golden raisins
¼ cup slivered blanched almonds
¼ cup sesame seeds
2 pounds fish fillets (sole, turbot, orange roughy or any other mild white fish)

In a medium saucepan, combine all ingredients except fish and bring to a boil over medium heat. Reduce heat, cover and simmer 15 minutes. Place fish in a buttered 13×9-inch baking dish. Pour sauce over fish and bake for 20 minutes at 350°, or until fish flakes easily. *SERVES: 6*

Chioppino

- ½ cup olive oil
- ½ cup finely chopped onion
- 1 tablespoon (5 – 6 cloves) finely minced garlic
- ¼ cup chopped fresh parsley
- 1 tablespoon finely chopped celery
- 1 tablespoon finely chopped green pepper
- 1 28-ounce can whole tomatoes
- 1 6-ounce can tomato paste
- 2 teaspoons salt
- 1 tablespoon paprika
- ¼ teaspoon pepper
- 2 teaspoons basil
- ½ cup dry sherry
- 2 cups water
- ½ pound firm-fleshed white fish, cubed
- ½ pound uncooked shrimp, peeled and deveined
- ½ pound scallops
- 12 clams in shell, well scrubbed (optional)
- 12 mussels in shell, well scrubbed (optional)
- 8 thick slices French or sourdough bread, buttered and toasted

Heat olive oil in a large pan over medium heat. Add onion, garlic, parsley, celery and green pepper. Sauté until vegetables are soft. Purée tomatoes and their liquid in blender or food processor. Add puréed tomatoes, tomato paste, salt, paprika, pepper, basil and sherry. Bring to a boil, reduce heat and simmer 15 minutes. Add water and simmer for 1 hour. Add fish, shrimp and scallops, cover and simmer 5 minutes. If using clams or mussels, add to soup, cover and cook 8 – 10 minutes until fish is firm and shells have opened. Ladle into large soup bowls and top with a slice of toasted bread. *SERVES: 8*

> HINT: *To hold your clams and mussels until cooking time, put them into a large container filled with water and salt (¼ cup salt to 1 gallon water). Add a handful of flour or cornmeal and let them sit until cooking time, then scrub well and cook as instructed.*

Kraut-Stuffed Chops

½ cup (1 stick) butter or margarine, divided
4 loin pork chops, 1½ inches thick — have butcher cut a pocket in each chop
1 green pepper, finely chopped
½ cup chopped onion
1 pound carrots, peeled and shredded
1½ teaspoons salt
¼ teaspoon pepper
¼ teaspoon thyme
1 tablespoon sugar
1 16-ounce can sauerkraut, drained

Preheat oven to 350°. Lightly grease a 3-quart baking dish with a lid. In a large skillet, melt 4 tablespoons of the butter over medium heat and brown chops on both sides. Remove chops and set aside. Add remaining butter to drippings in skillet and sauté pepper and onion until tender. Stir in carrots and sauté one minute. Remove from heat. Add salt, pepper, thyme, sugar and sauerkraut. Toss until combined. Stuff mixture into pocket of each chop and secure with toothpicks. Spoon remaining mixture into prepared dish and place stuffed chops on top. Cover and bake at 350° for 45 minutes. Remove lid and continue baking another 40 minutes. *SERVES: 4*

Baked Chicken German Style

½ cup (1 stick) butter or margarine
½ cup all-purpose flour
2 cups chicken broth
1½ cups milk
2 teaspoons fresh lemon juice
½ teaspoon salt
½ teaspoon freshly ground pepper
¼ teaspoon nutmeg
8 ounces egg noodles, cooked and drained
3 cups cooked, diced chicken
⅔ cup freshly grated Parmesan cheese
2 teaspoons paprika

Preheat oven to 350°. Melt butter in large saucepan over medium low heat. Whisk in flour and stir 3 minutes. Gradually whisk in broth and milk. Reduce heat, simmering until thick — about 10 minutes. Blend in lemon juice and seasonings. Combine cooked noodles and half the sauce, tossing gently to blend. Place in the bottom of a buttered 2-quart casserole. Top with chicken and remaining sauce. Combine Parmesan cheese and paprika, sprinkle over casserole. Bake until bubbling and golden brown — about 30 minutes. Serve hot. *SERVES: 6-8*

My final semester of classes at Stephens saw another opportunity come my way. Five weeks into the term, one of the faculty members in the fashion department became ill. Someone was needed to cover one of her classes, and another instructor mentioned my name. Before I had time to think, I was facing a classroom of first-year design students, trying to make what I thought was at least a one-hour lecture last fifteen minutes! Somehow, I survived that semester, and was offered a full-time teaching position upon graduation. The experiences gained in my time at Stephens made me realize that life never offers a simple, straightforward existence. Opportunities with choices to be made, and catastrophes beyond one's control are factors which one faces throughout life's journey. I came to realize that teaching was probably only the second career in whatever lay ahead. Grandmother had moved from interest to interest in what had sometimes seemed to be capriciousness. Perhaps, in reality, it was only her way of adapting to the elements both in and out of her control.

The cookbook plans were put on hold during the time I taught at Stephens. But the interest in cooking and collecting new recipes didn't abate. I loved the lazy Missouri summers when classes were out. I had the time to pursue cooking as that creative outlet I needed. Baking bread brought back fond memories of Grandmother. And the produce available at the local farmer's market offered additional inspiration.

Deep-Fried Baby New Potatoes

2 pounds tiny new potatoes (about 1 – 2 inches in diameter)
Oil for deep-frying
Garlic salt

Scrub potatoes thoroughly, but do not peel. Cook potatoes in enough water to cover for 10 minutes. Drain thoroughly and pat dry. Heat oil in a large skillet or deep-fat fryer to 360° – 370°. Fry potatoes, a few at a time, until skins become brown and crisp. Drain potatoes on paper towels, then place in a paper bag. Sprinkle generously with garlic salt, close bag and shake to coat potatoes. Serve at once.
SERVES: 6 – 8

Pud's Blackberry Cobbler

PASTRY:
- 4 cups flour
- 1 tablespoon sugar
- 2 teaspoons salt
- 1¾ cups shortening
- 1 tablespoon raspberry vinegar
- 1 egg, beaten
- ½ cup cold water

Combine flour, sugar and salt in a mixing bowl or the work bowl of a food processor. Add the shortening and blend until the mixture resembles cornmeal. Combine the vinegar, egg and water and mix together. Add to the flour mixture and stir or process until mixture will pack together into a ball — more water may need to be added. If not using a food processor, knead on a lightly floured surface a few times. Wrap dough in waxed paper and chill 1 hour.

FILLING:
- 6 cups fresh or frozen blackberries (thawed)
- 1½ cups sugar
- 3 tablespoons raspberry vinegar
- ½ cup flour
- 4 tablespoons butter or margarine

Preheat oven to 450°. Combine the blackberries, sugar and vinegar. Sprinkle the flour over the mixture a little at a time and stir in. Set aside while lining pan with pastry. Divide pastry into two balls, one slightly larger than the other. Roll out larger ball on a floured surface into a 15×20-inch rectangle. Gently lift pastry and line a greased 13×9-inch pan, allowing dough to fall over the edges. Fill with blackberry mixture, and dot with 4 tablespoons butter. Roll out remaining ball of pastry into a 13×9-inch rectangle. Place on filling and seal and crimp edges. Make about 8 small slashes in the crust to allow steam to escape. Place pan on a cookie sheet to catch any drips. Bake 15 minutes at 450°, then reduce heat to 350° and bake until crust is browned — about 40 – 45 minutes. Remove from oven and let stand for 10 – 15 minutes if you wish to serve it hot, or allow to cool and serve at room temperature. Good with a scoop of ice cream! *SERVES: 12 – 16*

NOTE: There doesn't seem to be enough raspberry vinegar in this to have an effect on the flavor, but, oh, it does!

Everybody's Favorite Poppy Seed Bread

BREAD:
- 3 cups flour
- 1½ teaspoons salt
- 1½ teaspoons baking powder
- 2¼ cups sugar
- 3 eggs
- 1 cup plus 2 tablespoons vegetable oil
- 1½ cups milk
- 1½ tablespoons poppy seed
- 1½ teaspoons vanilla
- 1½ teaspoons almond flavoring
- 1½ teaspoons butter flavoring

GLAZE:
- ¼ cup orange juice
- ¾ cup sugar
- ½ teaspoon butter flavoring
- ½ teaspoon almond flavoring
- ½ teaspoon vanilla

For bread, preheat oven to 350°. Grease two 8½ × 4½ × 2 ¾-inch loaf pans. Combine all bread ingredients in a large mixing bowl and beat until smooth. Pour into prepared pans. Bake 1 hour at 350° or until tester inserted in center comes out clean. (Crack down center is characteristic.) Cool in pans 5 minutes; remove from pans. While loaves are cooling, combine glaze ingredients in a small saucepan; bring to a boil. Remove from heat and brush loaves with glaze, generously covering both top and sides.
MAKES: 2 loaves

Whole Wheat Zucchini Bread

- 3 eggs
- 1¾ cups sugar
- 1 cup vegetable oil
- 3 teaspoons vanilla
- 2 cups grated unpeeled raw zucchini
- 2 tablespoons grated orange peel
- 1 teaspoon salt
- ¼ teaspoon baking powder
- 1 teaspoon baking soda
- 2 teaspoons cinnamon
- 1½ cups whole wheat flour
- 1½ cups all-purpose flour
- ½ cup raisins
- 1 cup pecans or walnuts

Preheat oven to 325°. Grease 2 9×5-inch loaf pans. Beat eggs until light and fluffy. Add sugar and mix well. Stir in oil, vanilla, zucchini and orange peel. Sift dry ingredients together and add to zucchini mixture, mixing until well-blended. Stir in raisins and nuts. Divide mixture between prepared pans. Bake at 325° for 50–55 minutes until browned. Cool in pans about 10 minutes, then remove and cool completely before slicing. This recipe also makes good muffins. MAKES: 2 loaves or 20–24 muffins

The next crook in the road over which Mike and I were journeying led us back to Greenville. During the four years that we had been in Missouri, Mary of Puddin Hill had grown beyond all expectations. Mail order was becoming a way of life for the American public. As one of the older companies in the business, Puddin Hill was in a position to grow quickly. It was no longer the "little place on the highway" that it had been for so many years. That growth brought a whole new set of problems for Mother and Dad, not the least of which concerned the future of the company — their master creation — with regard to their only child. And Mike and I, realizing that we needed to make decisions about what lay ahead for us, felt it was time to learn enough about Mary of Puddin Hill to make an informed decision. We also came to the understanding that both the Christian Church and Stephens College would go on without us. Mary of Puddin Hill, as we knew it, would not.

In 1982, we decided to redirect our career plans and move to Greenville. Mother and Dad alternated between being thrilled and apprehensive. What would the future hold?

Fortunately, the transition from two decision-makers to four has gone as smoothly as could be expected. Mike and I have found our own niches in areas that needed more attention than Mother or Dad could effectively give them, so there has been little competition or rivalry. And Mother and Dad are extraordinary people, willing to encourage the gradual transition of leadership from one generation to the next.

Our first child was born shortly after we returned to Greenville. Robert Michael Kearns entered the world in June of 1982. Because Mike was an only child, Jo asked if she could come and be "Grandma" when our baby came.

When Mike called to tell his parents that we were heading for the hospital, Jo couldn't stand to sit home and wait. She headed for the nearest shopping mall to start buying baby clothes. In fact, she was out shopping when we called to tell her she had a grandson. She immediately went out again and purchased the blue items needed to complete the layette. Armed with enough clothes for two babies, and a stack of recipes to try out on us, she headed north from Corpus Christi.

Jo had been saving her favorite recipes for this occasion. Of course, she cooked Barbecued Steakers and Cinnamon Apples for Mike. But there were lots of new recipes for us to taste, too. It was so nice not to have to worry about cooking while adjusting to a new baby. Earlier that spring, Bob had planted a garden. Thanks to the warmer climate of South Texas, he was already harvesting vegetables. The space in their car not taken up with Jo's purchases was filled with Bob's produce. We ate like royalty.

Crustless Quiche

10 slices bacon
1 cup (4 ounces) grated Swiss cheese
¼ cup minced green onion
4 eggs
1 12-ounce can evaporated milk
½ teaspoon salt
¼ teaspoon sugar
⅛ teaspoon cayenne pepper
⅛ teaspoon nutmeg

Preheat oven to 350°. Cook bacon until crisp, then drain and crumble. In an ungreased 10-inch pie plate, layer crumbled bacon, cheese, and green onion. Blend remaining ingredients in a blender or with a wire whisk and pour over cheese mixture. Bake 30 – 35 minutes at 350°. Remove from oven and let quiche stand 10 minutes before serving. SERVES: 6

HINT: *To cook bacon without the bother of crumbling, cut each strip into pieces about ½-inch square. Cook as you would bacon strips, stirring constantly if cooking in a skillet. In a microwave, try shorter cooking times so the bacon does not burn.*

Summer's Bounty Casserole

4 cups sliced zucchini (about 5 large)
½ cup chopped onion
1 17-ounce can cream-style corn
1 8-ounce package cream cheese, cubed
1 4-ounce can chopped green chilies, undrained
½ teaspoon salt
¼ teaspoon pepper
1 cup soft bread crumbs
2 tablespoons butter or margarine

Cook zucchini and onion in boiling water to cover until tender, about 10 minutes. Drain well. Preheat oven to 350°. In a large mixing bowl combine corn and cream cheese with hot squash and onion. Add chilies, salt and pepper, blending thoroughly. Pour into a buttered 2-quart flat baking dish. Combine bread crumbs and melted butter and sprinkle over casserole. Bake at 350° for 40 – 45 minutes, until browned and bubbly. If it is browning too quickly, cover loosely with a piece of aluminum foil. SERVES: 8

Buttermilk Pie

½ cup flour
3¾ cups sugar
1 teaspoon salt
6 eggs
1 cup (2 sticks) butter or margarine, melted
1 cup buttermilk
1 teaspoon vanilla
2 9-inch unbaked pie crusts (deep-dish type if using a commercial crust)

Preheat oven to 350°. In a large mixing bowl, combine flour, sugar and salt. In another bowl, beat eggs until light, then add butter, buttermilk and vanilla, stirring to blend. Slowly add liquid to dry ingredients, beating until smooth. Divide batter between the two unbaked pie crusts. Bake at 350° for 50 – 60 minutes, until center is set. Cover tops loosely with foil if browning too quickly. Cool.
SERVES: 12 – 16

Mediterranean Tomatoes

4 large tomatoes, peeled and cut into wedges
¼ cup sliced pimiento-stuffed olives
¼ cup chopped green onion

MARINADE:
½ cup olive oil
¼ cup red wine vinegar
¼ cup lemon juice
1 teaspoon dried basil, crumbled (or 1 tablespoon fresh basil, chopped fine)

1 cup sliced mushrooms (optional)
2 avocados, cubed (optional)

1 clove garlic, minced
¼ teaspoon thyme
½ teaspoon salt
½ teaspoon pepper

In a large bowl, place a layer of tomatoes. Sprinkle with half the olives and onions, then add a layer of mushrooms and avocado. Repeat layers, ending with a layer of tomatoes. Combine marinade ingredients in a small bowl, blending with a wire whisk. Pour over tomatoes, cover and refrigerate several hours or overnight. SERVES: 8 – 10

Bob's Cookie Jar Gingersnaps

2 cups sifted flour
1 tablespoon ginger
2 teaspoons baking soda
1 teaspoon cinnamon
½ teaspoon salt
¾ cup butter or
   margarine, softened
1 cup sugar
1 egg
¼ cup molasses
Sugar

Preheat oven to 350°. Sift the flour, ginger, soda, cinnamon and salt together twice. Cream the butter in a bowl and add the sugar gradually, beating until well blended. Beat in the egg and molasses. Add flour mixture and blend well. Shape into balls using 1 teaspoon dough for each and roll in additional sugar to coat. Place 2 inches apart on ungreased cookie sheets. Bake at 350° for 12 – 15 minutes or until lightly browned and cracked. *MAKES: 3 – 4 dozen*

When I returned to Puddin Hill and my roots, my interest in using all the recipes I had sorted through was rekindled. The cookbook slowly got back on track again. I also took over the development of new products for the bakery and chocolate kitchen.

In the past few years at Puddin Hill, I have added another son (Richard Sample Kearns), six new baked products for the catalog, seven new chocolates, over three hundred recipes for this book, and more pounds than I care to mention! What a transition — from a young bride who could barely get a meal onto the table to a cook confident enough to take a crack at a recipe that makes 20 cakes at a time.

These recipes are some of my own favorites. There is probably some deep-seated meaning to presenting several healthy, low calorie recipes, followed by my favorite sinfully rich dessert. But I'm the type who checks out the dessert offerings on a restaurant menu before ordering the entree.

Perfect-Every-Time Baked Fish

Ingredients are given for 1 serving. Recipe may be increased for the number of servings required.

6 – 8 ounces fish for each serving (snapper, orange roughy, sole, swordfish or any mild fish can be used)	1 tablespoon butter or margarine, melted 1 teaspoon fresh lemon juice Paprika

Preheat oven to 500°. Lightly oil a baking dish large enough to hold the fish in a single layer. Combine butter or margarine and lemon juice. Pour over fish, sprinkling generously with paprika. Bake at 500° for 8 – 10 minutes, until fish is tender and flakes easily with a fork. If the fish is thick, more baking time may be needed.

NOTE: For a Southwestern flavor, substitute lime juice for the lemon juice and sprinkle with a bit of chili powder added to the paprika.

Pud's Granola

4 cups uncooked quick rolled oats	2 tablespoons vegetable oil
½ cup wheat germ	2 tablespoons vanilla
½ cup fresh coconut, grated (frozen or unsweetened may be used)	2 teaspoons cinnamon
	2 tablespoons honey
	6 packages artificial sweetener (or 6 tablespoons brown sugar)
½ cup sesame seeds	
½ cup sunflower seeds (unsalted, if possible)	1 cup raisins
½ cup chopped pecans	1 cup dried apricots, snipped (or dried fruit mix)
½ cup slivered almonds	
¾ cup water	

Preheat oven to 325°. Combine first 7 ingredients in a large bowl and toss to blend. In another bowl, combine water, oil, vanilla, cinnamon, honey and artificial sweetener and beat with a wire whisk to blend. Pour over oat mixture and stir until dry ingredients are thoroughly coated. Spread onto 2 15×10×1-inch non-stick jellyroll pans. Bake at 325° for 20 – 25 minutes, stirring every 10 minutes. Return cooked granola to large bowl and stir in raisins and apricots. Cool, then store in an airtight container *MAKES: 9 cups*

Chicken with Mushrooms and Vermouth

4 chicken breast halves, skinned, boned and cut into 1-inch wide strips
¼ cup butter or margarine
1 clove garlic, minced
1 teaspoon salt
¼ teaspoon pepper
1 tablespoon lemon juice
½ pound fresh mushrooms, sliced
¾ cup dry vermouth
¼ cup chopped fresh parsley

Melt butter in a large saucepan over medium heat and brown chicken strips. Add garlic, salt, pepper and lemon juice. Heap mushrooms on top, pour on vermouth, cover and cook for 15 minutes or until chicken is fork tender. Sprinkle with parsley just before serving. This is delicious served alone or over rice or noodles. *SERVES: 4*

Heavenly Brulee

4 egg yolks
⅓ cup sugar
2 cups half and half
1 teaspoon vanilla
½ cup firmly packed dark brown sugar

Preheat oven to 325°. Beat egg yolks until lemon colored with a wire whip, then gradually add sugar, beating until smooth. Heat half and half in a small saucepan over low heat until just warm. Remove from heat and slowly pour into egg yolk mixture, stirring with whip until blended. Stir in vanilla. Divide mixture between 6 4-ounce ramekins or pour into a 9-inch glass pie plate. Set into a larger pan with deep sides, and pour boiling water into pan until it comes halfway up the sides of the dishes. Bake at 325° for 30 – 40 minutes until custard is just barely set. Remove from water and refrigerate for several hours until custard is cold. When cold, gently spread a thin layer of brown sugar over the top of the custard. Preheat broiler and broil each custard briefly until sugar has melted. Watch carefully, as the sugar can burn! Serve immediately or return to refrigerator and chill until topping is cold. *SERVES: 6*

Mike and I have never looked back on the careers we both left. The opportunities and catastrophes come on a daily basis now, but the freedom to choose the future course of both our lives and that of the company has been wonderful. Besides, who wouldn't want to live in a chocolate-lover's paradise?

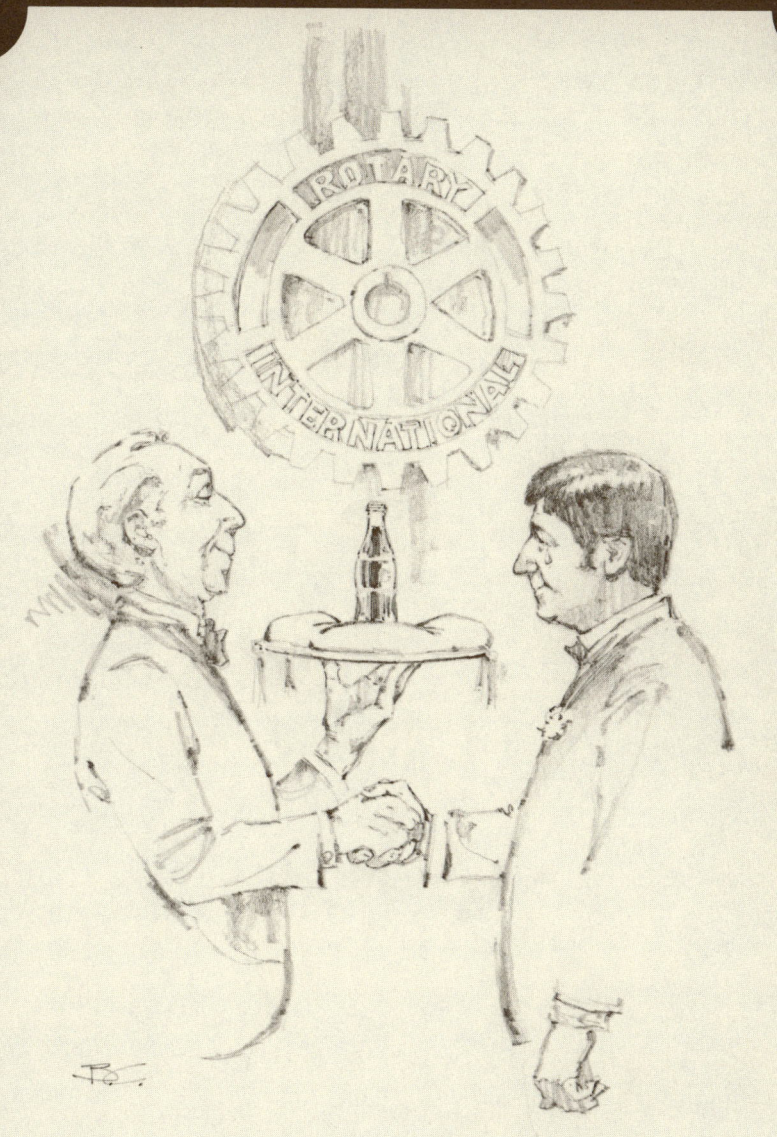

"The bottling plant presented him with
their first bottle of Coca-Cola Classic
in a ceremony at the Rotary Club."

Chapter Seven

Weddings to Wakes
(Parties and Covered Dish Meals)

Any celebration is an excuse for good food, as far as my family is concerned. It doesn't necessarily matter whether there is a real event, such as a wedding or an anniversary to acknowledge, or some "notable date" manufactured just for the occasion. Parties are times for sharing lots of good times and delicious food.

James and Mary Horton established the family tradition of entertaining friends and family over a hundred years ago when they hosted a Fourth of July celebration on Puddin Hill. In Mary's memoirs, she said that over 100 people attended, some coming by wagon from as far as fifty miles away. Most of the folks camped around the Horton's home and stayed for several days, since it was such a distance to come. There is no doubt that Mary was proud of her cooking, because her memories of that event dwell as much on the food she prepared and served as they do on the activities of the guests who came to the celebration.

Likewise, Grandmother and Mother have shared lots of memories of parties or family gatherings and meals. People have always played an important role in the life of my family, and sharing special times with them makes up a large portion of the memories. Grandmother often spoke of the pleasure she took in preparing meals for special guests. Although she was a master at the art of entertaining a few, it was in the party category where Grandmother could really show her talents. She loved orchestrating all the details, from the invitations to the table settings to the beautiful garnishes on the food. And her parties were memorable events for every guest, because she knew how to make everyone think she had slaved for hours over each and every little aspect, especially the food she served them.

Mother learned the art of giving parties from Grandmother and, in turn, taught some of those skills to me. At most of the parties or celebrations she and I have planned, lots of creative thinking is put into the food we will be serving. Often a theme is selected and dishes are chosen to compliment that theme. On other occasions, it is the food that determines the theme for the party. A good example of a party theme worked around the menu is the Chocolate Celebration that Mother and I hosted for a close friend just before she was to be married. Our friend Linda dearly loved chocolate, and since chocolate is considered one of the ultimate romantic foods, it was a natural pairing. The invitation read, "If chocolate is the food of love . . . then let us be like lovers!" Guests were invited to a champagne and chocolate dessert party, and what a feast awaited them!

Mother and I searched through our very best chocolate dessert recipes, and selected those which would provide an assortment to tempt everyone. We gave extra consideration to recipes that could be prepared ahead of time, in order to cut down on the confusion of last minute work that some dishes require. Finally, we chose an assortment of cakes, pies, candies, and cookies. Then we threw in a couple of really unique recipes that would get the guests talking — always good as icebreakers when folks don't know one another.

When it was spread out on the table, the assortment was a spectacular sight!

Menu for Chocolate Celebration
Texas Big Mouth Cookies
White Chocolate Truffles
Southern Chocolate Delights
Chocolate and White Chocolate Dessert Spreads with Assorted Fresh Fruits and Cookies
Chocolate Truffles
Chocolate Amaretto Cheesecake
Black Bottom Pie
Fabulous Party Cake
Rocky Road Torte
Mary's Brownies
Chocolate-covered Fresh Strawberries
Chocolate-covered Sweet Pickles

Hot Chocolate on Ice
Champagne, Coffee and Liqueurs

The real fun of a party like this is that all the guests are awed by the display of so much chocolate. Chocolate seems to bring out the kid in all of us, and everyone is eager for a taste of everything. Most guests will take a small sample, so you don't need to allow a full serving of each item for everyone. And, of course, if there are favorite chocolate recipes of your own, you can certainly make additions or substitutions to this menu. All the recipes can easily be reduced in quantity to serve a smaller crowd, or increased along with the guest list.

We planned to serve about 50 guests, so two of each cake and the cheesecake were prepared, and each was cut into small slices. I made four pies, because they are not as easy to slice and serve as cakes. Double recipes were made of each candy, the brownies and the cookies. We took care not to make the cookies or truffles much more than bite-sized pieces. Because we knew that the guests would love them, we allowed two strawberries and one pickle per person. Of course, everyone had to try a pickle! The Hot Chocolate on Ice was a frozen beverage offered for those who did not want champagne (but everyone was intrigued by the name, and wanted a taste).

Because most of the desserts were variations on the colors brown and white, we felt that some sort of signs would be necessary to let guests know what each tray offered. But we didn't want ordinary signs. Small chocolate place cards were set beside the trays. On each card was the name of one of the items on the tray, written in white chocolate. The cards were really easy to make, and were the talk of the party.

Texas Big Mouth Cookies

½ cup (1 stick) butter or margarine, softened
1 12-ounce jar chunky peanut butter
1 cup brown sugar
1 cup granulated sugar
1 teaspoon vanilla
3 eggs
1 teaspoon light corn syrup
2 teaspoons baking powder
3½ cups uncooked quick rolled oats
½ cup semi-sweet chocolate chips
½ cup M & M's
½ cup raisins
½ cup pecans or walnuts

Preheat oven to 350°. In a large mixing bowl, cream butter, peanut butter and both sugars together until smooth. Add vanilla, eggs and corn syrup and beat well. Stir in remaining ingredients, working dough until well-blended. Drop 2 tablespoons of dough onto greased cookie sheets, spacing about 2½ inches apart. Bake at 350° for 12 – 15 minutes, until browned. *MAKES: 3 dozen*

White Chocolate Truffles

- 12 ounces white chocolate
- ⅔ cup whipping cream
- 3 tablespoons unsalted (sweet) butter (at room temperature)
- 1 tablespoon lemon juice, amaretto, brandy, or other flavoring (less for extracts)
- ½ – 1 cup ground nuts, sprinkles or powdered sugar

Break the white chocolate into marble-sized chunks. Place chunks in the work bowl of a food processor fitted with a steel blade. Process until the white chocolate is about the size of very coarsely ground cornmeal. Heat the cream in a saucepan until almost boiling, stirring so a skin does not form on the top. When cream has tiny bubbles around the edge of the saucepan, remove from heat. Immediately turn the food processor on and pour the cream down the feed tube in a slow steady stream. Process about another 30 seconds after the cream has been added in order to melt every bit of the white chocolate. Cut the butter into chunks and, with the machine running, drop them down the feed tube. Process about 30 seconds, or until no bits of butter are visible. Add the lemon juice or liqueur and pulse the machine just to blend. Pour white chocolate mixture into an 8-inch cake pan and chill in the refrigerator or freezer until it is quite firm. Use a spoon, melon baller or #100 ice cream scoop to roll the cold, firm mixture into ¾-inch diameter balls. Roll each ball in finely ground nuts, sprinkles or powdered sugar. Store in an airtight container in the refrigerator or freezer. *MAKES: about 3 dozen*

Southern Chocolate Delights

- 6 ounces semi-sweet chocolate
- ½ cup Southern Comfort (or bourbon)
- 3 tablespoons light corn syrup
- 2½ cups vanilla wafer crumbs
- 1 cup powdered sugar, divided
- 1 cup chopped pecans
- ¼ cup cocoa

Melt chocolate in the top of a double boiler over simmering water. Remove from heat and stir in Southern Comfort and corn syrup. In another bowl, combine vanilla wafer crumbs, ½ cup powdered sugar and pecans. Add chocolate mixture and stir well. Let stand for 30 minutes. Combine remaining powdered sugar and cocoa. Form chocolate mixture into 1-inch balls and roll in sugar-cocoa mixture. Store in an airtight container in the refrigerator. *MAKES: About 5 Dozen*

Chocolate Dessert Spread

FOR DARK CHOCOLATE SPREAD

12 ounces semisweet chocolate
1⅔ cups heavy cream
5 tablespoons unsalted (sweet) butter
2 tablespoons liqueur (brandy, amaretto, cognac, Kahlua, etc.)

FOR WHITE CHOCOLATE SPREAD

12 ounces white chocolate
1½ cups heavy cream
4 tablespoons unsalted (sweet) butter
1½ teaspoons lemon juice

PROCEDURE FOR EITHER SPREAD

Break chocolate into marble-sized chunks. Place chunks in the work bowl of a food processor fitted with a steel blade. Process until chocolate is about the size of very coarsely ground corn meal. Heat the cream in a sauce pan until almost boiling, stirring so a skin does not form on the top. When cream has tiny bubbles around the edge of the sauce pan, remove from heat. Immediately turn the food processor on and pour the cream down the feed tube in a slow steady stream. Process about another 30 seconds after the cream has been added in order to melt every bit of the chocolate. Cut the butter into chunks and, with the machine running, drop them down the feed tube. Process about 30 seconds, or until no bits of butter are visible. Add the liqueur or lemon juice and pulse the machine just to blend.

Pour mixture into a 3-cup serving bowl. Place a piece of plastic wrap over the surface so that a skin will not form. Chill the spread to firm it up — several hours.

At least one hour before serving, set the spread out to come to room temperature. Serve with a platter of fresh fruit and simple cookies (ginger snaps, shortbread wafers, vanilla wafers, Bordeaux cookies, etc.). Use butter spreaders for guests to serve themselves. *MAKES: 3 cups of either spread.*

Chocolate Truffles

- 12 ounces semi-sweet chocolate
- 1 cup whipping cream
- 4 tablespoons unsalted (sweet) butter (at room temperature)
- 1 tablespoon cognac, brandy, amaretto, rum or other flavoring (less for extracts)
- ½ – 1 cup ground nuts, cocoa, powdered sugar or sprinkles

Break chocolate into marble-sized chunks. Place chunks in the work bowl of a food processor fitted with a steel blade. Process until chocolate is about the size of very coarsely ground cornmeal. Heat the cream in a saucepan until almost boiling, stirring so a skin does not form on the top. When cream has tiny bubbles around the edge of the saucepan, remove from heat. Immediately turn the food processor on and pour the cream down the feed tube in a slow steady stream. Process about another 30 seconds after the cream has been added in order to melt every bit of the chocolate. Cut the butter into chunks and, with the machine running, drop them down the feed tube. Process about 30 seconds, or until no bits of butter are visible. Add the liqueur or flavoring and pulse the machine just to blend. Pour chocolate mixture into an 8-inch cake pan and chill in the refrigerator or freezer until it is quite firm. Use a spoon, melon baller or #100 ice cream scoop to roll the cold, firm mixture into ¾-inch diameter balls. Roll each ball in finely ground nuts, cocoa, powdered sugar or sprinkles. (I like to make several flavors, rolling one in cocoa, one in powdered sugar and one in a blend of equal amounts of cocoa and powdered sugar.) Store in an airtight container in the refrigerator or freezer. *MAKES: 3 – 4 dozen*

Chocolate Amaretto Cheesecake

CRUST:
- 2 cups chocolate wafer cookie crumbs
- ⅓ cup unsalted (sweet) butter, melted

FILLING:
- ½ cup almond paste
- 1½ cups sugar
- 3 8-ounce packages cream cheese
- 4 eggs
- 6 ounces milk chocolate, melted
- 1 teaspoon vanilla
- ¼ cup Amaretto
- 2 teaspoons almond extract

TOPPING:
- 1 cup sour cream
- 2 teaspoons almond extract
- 2 tablespoons sugar
- 16 chocolate-covered almonds, for garnish

Combine crumbs and butter until well-blended. Press onto bottom and sides of a 9½-inch pan with removable bottom (cheesecake or springform-type pan). Combine almond paste and sugar, beating until smooth. Add cream cheese and then eggs one at a time, beating after each addition until smooth. Add melted chocolate, vanilla, Amaretto and almond extract. Pour filling into prepared crust. Bake at 350° for 45–50 minutes. While cake is baking, prepare topping. Mix sour cream, almond extract and sugar together until smooth. Remove cake from oven and top with sour cream mixture. Return to oven and bake 10 more minutes. Allow cheesecake to cool at least 1 hour, then chill until serving time (at least 4 hours). Remove sides of pan and cut into 16 slices, garnishing each slice with a chocolate-covered almond. *SERVES: 16*

Black Bottom Pie

Prepare a Gingersnap Crust (see following recipe).

BASIC FILLING:
1¾ cups milk
½ cup sugar
1 tablespoon cornstarch
Pinch salt
4 egg yolks, beaten

Heat milk in the top of a double boiler set over hot water until bubbles form around edges. Mix sugar, cornstarch and salt together, then stir into milk. Add about ½ cup of the milk mixture into the beaten egg yolks to warm them, and add warmed yolks to milk mixture. Cook, stirring constantly, until custard thickens and will coat the back of the spoon. Divide custard in half.

FOR CHOCOLATE LAYER:
2 ounces unsweetened chocolate
1 ounce semi-sweet chocolate
1 teaspoon vanilla

To one half of the custard, add the chocolates and the vanilla, stirring until chocolate is melted. Slowly pour into the Gingersnap crust, being careful not to disturb crust.

FOR RUM-FLAVORED LAYER:
1 envelope gelatin
¼ cup cold water
4 egg whites
½ teaspoon cream of tartar
½ cup sugar
3 tablespoons light rum

Soak gelatin in cold water. Stir softened gelatin into the remaining half of the custard while it is still warm, making sure gelatin is completely dissolved. Let cool. Beat the egg whites and cream of tartar, adding ½ cup sugar slowly; beat until stiff. Fold egg whites into the cooled custard; stir in rum. Spread carefully over the chocolate layer. Chill several hours or overnight. Before serving, spread topping on pie.

TOPPING:
1 cup heavy cream
2 tablespoons powdered sugar
Grated bitter or semi-sweet chocolate

Combine the cream and powdered sugar, beating until soft peaks form. Spread over pie. Sprinkle with grated bitter or semi-sweet chocolate. Refrigerate again, if necessary. (Whipped cream will only hold an hour or two, so don't put it on the pie too far ahead of serving.) *SERVES: 8*

Gingersnap Crust

1½ cups gingersnap cookie crumbs

5 tablespoons butter or margarine, melted

Preheat oven to 325°. Mix crushed cookies and melted butter. Line a 9-inch pie plate covering both sides and bottom with the buttered crumbs, pressing flat and firm. Bake 10 minutes at 325° to set. *MAKES: 1 crust*

NOTE: This crust is good as a base for custard or fruit pies, especially chocolate or peach. Or try with ice cream (butter pecan is good) or canned pumpkin pie filling.

Fabulous Party Cake

1 cup milk
7 ounces unsweetened chocolate
2 egg yolks, slightly beaten
1¼ cups sugar
4 cups flour
4 teaspoons baking powder
½ teaspoon baking soda
1 teaspoon salt

1 cup (2 sticks) unsalted (sweet) butter, softened
⅔ cup almond paste
1 tablespoon vanilla
1¼ cups firmly packed brown sugar
4 eggs, separated
½ cup water
¼ cup milk
½ cup sugar

Grease the bottoms only of 3 11×7×1½-inch cake pans. Line with waxed paper and grease the waxed paper; set aside. Heat milk and chocolate in the top of a double boiler over simmering water, stirring vigorously as mixture will be very thick. Stir about ¼ cup of the mixture into the two egg yolks to warm them, then blend into mixture in double boiler. Cook 2 minutes, stirring constantly. Add sugar and stir until dissolved — mixture will thin out with this addition. Remove from heat and let cool. While mixture cools, sift together flour, baking powder, soda and salt; set aside. In a large mixing bowl, cream butter or margarine, almond paste and vanilla until well-blended. Gradually add brown sugar and beat well. Add the four egg yolks and beat again. Blend in the cooled chocolate mixture. Combine water and milk in a measuring cup and add to batter along with dry ingredients in thirds, beating until smooth after each addition. In a separate bowl, beat egg whites until frothy. Gradually add remaining sugar, and beat until stiff. Carefully fold egg whites into batter. Divide batter among prepared pans and tap to release air bubbles. Bake cakes at 375° for 20–25 minutes. Cool 10 minutes in pans, then remove from pans and cool completely. When cool, frost with Mocha Almond Paste Frosting.

Mocha Almond Paste Frosting

3 egg whites
1¾ cups sugar
½ cup water
1½ cups unsalted (sweet) butter, softened
½ cup almond paste
1 tablespoon cocoa
1 tablespoon instant coffee crystals, crushed to a fine powder

Beat egg whites until stiff; set aside. Combine sugar and water in a saucepan and bring to a boil. Cook until mixture reaches a temperature of 238° on a candy thermometer. Pour mixture into stiffly beaten egg whites in a very thin stream, and beat until egg whites are thick. Cool. Cream butter and almond paste until well-blended. Add cocoa and coffee and beat until smooth. Gently fold egg white mixture into butter mixture. (In warm weather it may be necessary to chill the frosting to get a good spreadable consistency) Spread frosting on cooled cake, allowing about ½ cup between layers, and using remaining frosting to cover outside and top of cake. Refrigerate cake until serving time. This cake freezes beautifully. *SERVES: 12 - 16*

NOTE: Mother often makes this cake more spectacular by splitting each layer horizontally and using additional frosting as filling (she makes a double batch). We also use the frosting recipe to frost any plain chocolate cake — it adds a delicious touch.

Rocky Road Torte

1 cup (2 sticks) unsalted (sweet) butter
4 tablespoons cocoa
4 eggs, beaten
2 cups sugar
1½ cups flour
⅛ teaspoon salt
2 teaspoons vanilla
1 cup chopped pecans
1 6-ounce package semi-sweet chocolate chips
1½ cups miniature marshmallows

Preheat oven to 350°. Generously grease 2 8-inch cake pans. Melt butter and cocoa together. Set aside to cool before proceeding. When cool, beat in eggs and sugar, then add flour, salt and vanilla, blending well. Stir in pecans and ½ cup of the chocolate chips. Divide batter between cake pans. Bake at 350° for 25 – 30 minutes. Cool in pans for 5 minutes, then turn one layer out onto serving plate. Sprinkle chocolate chips and marshmallows over the top of the layer, then top with the second layer. Allow cake to cool, then frost with the following frosting:

ROCKY ROAD FROSTING
½ cup (1 stick) unsalted (sweet) butter
4 tablespoons cocoa
1 teaspoon vanilla
½ cup milk
4 – 5 cups powdered sugar
1½ cups miniature marshmallows
½ cup finely chopped pecans

Melt butter and cocoa together over low heat. Remove from heat and add vanilla and milk. Beat in enough powdered sugar to get a good spreadable consistency. Frost the sides of the cake, then add marshmallows to the remaining frosting and pile onto the top of the cake. Sprinkle top with chopped pecans. *SERVES: 8-12*

Mary's Brownies

4 ounces unsweetened chocolate
1 cup (2 sticks) unsalted (sweet) butter
1 heaping cup flour
2 cups sugar
½ teaspoon baking powder
½ teaspoon salt
4 eggs
2 teaspoons vanilla
1 cup pecans

Preheat oven to 350°. Grease a 13×9-inch cake pan; set aside. Melt chocolate and butter together in top of double boiler set over hot water. Sift flour, sugar, baking powder and salt together. Add the chocolate mixture and then beat in eggs one at a time. Add the vanilla and the pecans. Pour into prepared pan and bake at 350° for 30 minutes. Cool, then spread with frosting.

FROSTING:
½ cup (1 stick) unsalted (sweet) butter
2 squares unsweetened chocolate
2 tablespoons water
¼ cup sugar
2½ cups powdered sugar
1 egg

Melt the butter and chocolate together in top of double boiler set over hot water. In another pan, boil sugar and water 1 minute. Stir into butter-chocolate mixture; let cool. Beat powdered sugar and egg, then blend with cooled chocolate mixture. Beat until smooth and creamy. Spread over brownies. Allow frosting to set, then cut into small squares. *MAKES: about 36 brownies*

Hot Chocolate On Ice

¼ cup unsweetened cocoa
¼ cup sugar
3 cups milk
⅛ teaspoon salt
1 teaspoon vanilla

In saucepan stir cocoa, sugar, milk and salt over moderate heat until sugar is dissolved. Add vanilla. Pour into an 8×8 metal pan and freeze. Before serving, remove from freezer and let stand 20 minutes. Break up and stir with electric mixer until thick and creamy and full of ice crystals. Serve in 4 chilled glasses. *SERVES: 4*

Chocolate is probably one of the most fickle ingredients used in cooking, which is why few cooks try to make chocolate-dipped candies at home. If chocolate is not melted properly (a very complicated process of melting and cooling called tempering) the cocoa butter will rise to the surface, causing a white film to appear on the surface — known as bloom. Although bloom does not affect the taste or texture of the chocolate, it is not attractive. Because tempering at home is quite difficult, I have suggested an alternate method for dipping the strawberries and pickles using a blend of chocolate and unsalted butter. The taste will not be affected, and it is quite easy to do. Just be sure the strawberries and pickles are absolutely dry, because a small drop of water can make the chocolate thicken and become grainy.

Chocolate-Covered Strawberries and Sweet Pickles

2 pints fresh strawberries
1 cup small sweet pickles (or sweet gherkins)
1 pound milk chocolate
¼ cup unsalted (sweet) butter

Select whole strawberries that are firm and blemish-free. Carefully rinse in cool water to remove the sand that might be clinging to them. Try to rub or handle the strawberries as little as possible, because too much pressure might cause the berries to bruise and release moisture. Spread the berries out on paper towels to dry for at least 2 hours, turning occasionally to make sure that every side is dry. Drain the pickles and spread them out on a towel to dry for at least 2 hours, turning occasionally.

Melt the chocolate and butter together in the top of a double boiler set over gently simmering water. (The water must NOT be boiling and the pot must NOT be touching the water or the chocolate might scorch.) While chocolate is melting, line several cookie sheets or trays with waxed paper; set aside. When the chocolate is about half-melted, remove from heat and stir constantly until the remaining chocolate has melted and the mixture is smooth. Holding each strawberry by the stem, dip about three-fourths of each berry in the chocolate. Allow the excess to drip off and lay on waxed paper. Repeat with remaining berries. When a tray is full, place it in the refrigerator. Drop pickles into chocolate, one at a time and use a fork to gently turn each over until it is completely coated. Remove pickle and shake off excess chocolate. Lay each pickle onto waxed paper. Refrigerate until serving time. *The strawberries are very fragile, and must be eaten the same day.* SERVES: 12

NOTE: This method can also be used to dip other fresh fruit. Try thin slices of orange or lemon (leave the peel on), bananas, grapes or blueberries.

Chocolate Place Cards

Probably the best material to use to make placecards is chocolate-colored compound coating, as working with pure chocolate for molding is quite difficult for the novice. Compound coating is available at many cake or craft supply stores. It is usually sold in small disc shapes in 1-pound bags, and is available in pastel colors and white as well as chocolate color. Melt the coating in the top of a double boiler over simmering water until just melted and smooth. Use a shiny, scratch-free cookie sheet as a mold, and pour a layer about ¼-inch thick. Allow to cool and harden (compound coating will set up at room temperature), and unmold the slab carefully. Use a sharp knife and a ruler as a guide and straight edge to score the slab into strips about 2-inches wide (or size of your choice). You will find that, if the knife will not penetrate the chocolate completely, repeated scoring will work. Cut each strip into rectangles about 2½-inches long. Using any remaining chocolate strips, cut triangles (cut 1-inch squares diagonally for easy triangles) for the stands. You may either attach the backs before decorating the place cards or decorate the cards while they are laying flat, then attach the backs. To attach, lay the rectangles face down on waxed paper and use a little additional melted coating to spread on one edge of the triangle. Attach at the center of the rectangle and toward the lower edge so that it will stand up. Let the coating get firm before attempting to stand the cards upright. You may decorate the cards in any way desired. Royal icing (decorator's icing) works beautifully and may be tinted any color. Ready-made purchased decorations may also be attached, using a dab of melted coating. These are often available at cake or craft supply stores. If you wish to use more coating to decorate the place cards, melt white or colored coating, using decorator's tubes to apply the coating. It is thinner in consistency than Royal or Buttercream icing, so practice on waxed paper first to get the feel of it. Once you are comfortable working with melted coating, you can pipe a border, write names and even create figures and shapes on the cards. For further assistance, *Chocolate Artistry*, by Elaine Gonzales is THE book on working with chocolate or compound coating to create place cards, figures, molds and anything else you can imagine. It is published by Contemporary Books, Inc., 180 North Michigan Avenue, Chicago, IL 60601, and is readily available at book stores. I can't recommend this book enough!

Please don't wait to have a chocolate party to try any of these desserts. Believe me, each one is delicious by itself.

In summer, the Texas heat makes a chocolate party almost impossible to attempt. But, since everyone likes dessert, Mother and I have found that an Old-Fashioned Ice Cream Social is a great summertime get-together. And when the temperature rises, something cooling is often a better choice for guests. This is another party that can be easy to prepare, yet fun for everyone. Guests create their own sundaes, each an individual masterpiece.

I like to have this party outside, with a garden theme. Although homemade ice cream would be a nice touch, I purchase a five-gallon barrel of vanilla ice cream from the local dairy store. In keeping with the garden theme, I clean up my old wheelbarrow, line it with a plastic sheet, and fill it with ice. This keeps the ice cream cold and makes a clever serving stand.

I purchase fifteen to twenty plain four-inch terra cotta pots from the dime store and line each with a plastic beverage cup. (Mother has a collection of lovely ceramic cache-pots that she uses.) Each cup is filled with one of the toppings for the ice cream, with a spoon added for serving. Twelve-inch terra cotta pot saucers lined with a circle of foil serve as cake plates. A large pot lined with plastic and filled with ice holds aerosol cans of whipped cream. I fill a few pots with blooming plants to add color to the table, too.

As for the toppings, it's fun to let your imagination run wild! We always have a good chocolate fudge sauce and peanut butter sauce. Sliced fresh strawberries or peaches, with a light dusting of sugar are good offerings, as are creme de menthe and coffee liqueur. Mother likes to buy a jar of a fruit conserve — peach or plum are her favorites — and stir in ¼ cup brandy or rum for each cup of conserve. An assortment of toppings to sprinkle over the sauces might include chopped pecans, cocktail peanuts (the salt blends very well with the ice cream), Grape-Nuts, coconut, slivered almonds, and chocolate chips. And, of course, whipped cream and cherries finish off each sundae.

A simple, unadorned cake goes best with the ice cream. Nothing beats a good pound cake or an angel food cake (purchased or homemade). An assortment of cookies or Mary's Brownies (see page 179) are also delicious to serve.

Menu for Old Fashioned Ice Cream Social
*Vanilla Ice Cream with Assorted Toppings
Fudge Sauce
Peanut Butter Sauce
Sliced Fresh Strawberries
Sliced Fresh Peaches
Creme De Menthe
Coffee Liqueur
Plum Conserve with Brandy
Chopped Pecans
Salted Cocktail Peanuts
Grape Nuts
Coconut
Chocolate Chips
Whipped Cream
Maraschino Cherries*

*Perfect Pound Cake
Coffee Angel Food Cake*

Fudge Sauce

4 ounces unsweetened chocolate
½ cup (1 stick) unsalted (sweet) butter
3 cups sugar
1 12-ounce can evaporated milk
Dash salt

Melt chocolate and butter in the top of double boiler set over hot water. Add sugar a little at a time until it is completely blended with the chocolate-butter mixture. (This will be very thick). Gradually add evaporated milk and a dash of salt, stirring until mixture is smooth. Serve hot over ice cream or cake. This can be stored in a covered jar in the refrigerator and reheated as needed. *MAKES: 3 cups*

Peanut Butter Sauce

1 cup sugar
1 tablespoon light corn syrup
¼ teaspoon salt
¾ cups milk

6 tablespoons peanut butter (smooth or chunky)
¼ teaspoon vanilla

Mix sugar, corn syrup, salt and milk in a medium saucepan and cook over low heat until thickened, stirring constantly. Add peanut butter and blend. Remove from heat, cool and add vanilla. Chill until serving time. Store any leftover sauce in a covered container in the refrigerator. *MAKES: 2 cups*

Perfect Pound Cake

1 cup (2 sticks) unsalted (sweet) butter, softened
1⅔ cups sugar
5 eggs, at room temperature

2 cups flour
1 teaspoon vanilla or almond extract

Preheat oven to 275°. Grease a 10-inch tube or bundt pan. In a large mixing bowl, cream butter and sugar together until light and fluffy. Add eggs one at a time, beating well after each addition. Add flour and vanilla or almond extract, beating to form a smooth batter. Pour into prepared pan and bake at 275° for 1 hour and 30 minutes, until tester inserted in the center comes out clean. Cool in pan 15 – 20 minutes, then remove from pan and cool. (This cake is also delicious sliced right after removing from pan, buttering each slice generously and spreading with peach or plum jelly.) *MAKES: 1 10-inch cake*

Coffee Angel Food Cake

1 package Angel Food Cake Mix

2 tablespoons powdered instant coffee

Prepare cake according to package directions, dissolving instant coffee in water required for beating powdered egg whites. Bake and cool according to package directions. Frost with Coffee Buttercream Frosting, if desired, or serve plain with ice cream.

COFFEE BUTTERCREAM FROSTING:

½ cup (1 stick) unsalted (sweet) butter, softened
¼ teaspoon salt
1 teaspoon vanilla
2 tablespoons powdered instant coffee
2½ cups powdered sugar
3 – 4 tablespoons milk or cream
¼ pound chocolate coffee beans for garnish

Cream butter with salt, vanilla and coffee until smooth (if you are using coffee crystals, you will have better results if you whirl them in a blender or food processor until finely powdered). Add powdered sugar and beat until blended. Add milk a tablespoon at a time until a smooth spreadable consistency is reached. Trim any uneven areas from top of cake, invert onto serving plate, then frost top and sides. Garnish with chocolate coffee beans, if desired. *SERVES: 12 – 16*

NOTE: Try this frosting on any white or chocolate cake or on brownies.

This party is easy and impressive even if you don't cook! In fact, there are really very few items Mother and I serve at our ice cream socials that don't come straight out of a package, can or jar. Guests can come very casual for a fun, relaxed event that's easy on the host or hostess.

A more elegant party is found in the menu that Grandmother and Mother served at the bridal luncheons they gave when each of my cousins married. The selection was inspired by the soup and assorted tea sandwiches offered on the menu at the Zodiac Restaurant at Neiman-Marcus. Grandmother always admired the way the food was presented on the plate there. It served as a model for her own combination of flavors. Each plate held a cup of soup, fruit salad with poppy seed dressing and four sandwiches carefully chosen to offer a variety of tastes. Each sandwich was a quarter of a whole one, cut diagonally to create a triangle shape. The sandwiches were placed side by side with the longest part of the triangle standing on the plate, so that each revealed its filling. White and whole wheat breads offered contrast as well.

Grandmother also discovered that everything could be prepared ahead of time and the plates partially assembled. At serving time, only the cup of soup had to be added to each plate. She could join her guests instead of fussing in the kitchen. Her choice of dessert was a light grape sherbet. She made the recipe twice — once using white grape juice and the second time using purple grape juice. A scoop of each was served, garnished with a mint sprig or a few whole grapes, and Lemon-Almond Cookies (page 47) and Alexandrites (page 44) were passed around.

Mother has continued to rely on variations of this menu for luncheons. She has added a few new sandwich fillings inspired by those she has enjoyed while traveling. In her search for new ideas for the Puddin Hill Store's Deli menu, Mother loves to see what other regions of the country have to offer. She brings the ideas home to her own kitchen as well as the one in the store.

Menu for Soup and Sandwich Luncheon
Shrimp Bisque Au Rhum

*Assorted Sandwich Quarters
Egg Salad with Green Chilies
Pecan Pâté
Swiss Cheese and Thousand Island Dressing
Pork and Pineapple*

*Grape Sherbet
Cookies*

Shrimp Bisque Au Rhum

1 pound cooked shrimp, coarsely chopped
2 10-ounce cans tomato soup
2 10-ounce cans split pea soup
3 cups half and half
½ cup light rum
½ cup heavy cream, whipped (for garnish)

Reserve ½ cup of the shrimp for garnish. Combine both soups with half and half in the top of a double boiler set over hot water. Stir until smooth and heated through. Add shrimp and heat for 2 minutes. Remove from heat and stir in rum. Garnish each serving with a spoonful of whipped cream and reserved shrimp. *SERVES: 8*

Egg Salad With Green Chilies Sandwiches

12 hard cooked eggs, peeled
1 4-ounce can chopped green chilies, drained
¼ – ⅓ cup mayonnaise
2 teaspoons prepared mustard
½ teaspoon salt
16 slices whole wheat bread

Chop eggs coarsely and combine with remaining ingredients, except bread, adding mayonnaise as necessary to reach a spreadable consistency. Spread on 8 slices bread, top with remaining slices. Trim crusts, then cut each sandwich into quarters. *SERVES: 8*

NOTE: For a more Southwestern flavor, try spreading egg salad on flour tortillas. Roll and eat like a burrito.

Pecan Paté Sandwiches

1 cup (4-ounces) grated American cheese
1½ cups ground pecans
½ cup chili sauce
⅓ cup salad dressing (not mayonnaise)
16 slices whole wheat bread
Additional salad dressing

Combine all ingredients, except bread, in a mixing bowl and blend until smooth. Spread bread with salad dressing. Spread 8 slices with pecan mixture; top with remaining bread. Trim crusts, then cut each sandwich into quarters. *SERVES: 8*

Swiss Cheese and Thousand Island Dressing Sandwiches

3 cups (12-ounces) coarsely grated Swiss cheese
¾ cup Thousand Island Dressing

16 slices bread
Additional Thousand Island dressing

Combine cheese and Thousand Island dressing until thoroughly mixed. Spread each slice of bread with additional dressing. Spread cheese mixture on 8 slices bread. Top with remaining slices. Trim crusts, then cut each sandwich into quarters. *SERVES: 8*

NOTE: This spread is better blended in a mixing bowl than in a food processor.

Pork and Pineapple Sandwiches

2 cups roast pork, coarsely ground or chopped
1 15-ounce can crushed pineapple, drained
½ cup mayonnaise
2 tablespoons sweetened condensed milk

½ teaspoon dry mustard
¼ teaspoon onion juice
½ teaspoon poultry seasoning
16 slices bread
Additional mayonnaise (optional)

Combine all ingredients except bread in a mixing bowl and blend thoroughly. Spread on 8 slices bread (spread bread with additional mayonnaise, if desired), top with remaining slices. Trim crusts, then cut each sandwich into quarters. *SERVES: 8*

NOTE: You may grind or chop the pork in a food processor, but do not use it to blend all ingredients — the mixture will turn to mush.

Grape Sherbet

20 large marshmallows
½ cup sugar
¼ cup water
1 cup white grape juice
3 tablespoons lemon juice
1 cup heavy cream, whipped
Additional whipped cream and grapes for garnish, if desired

In a medium saucepan, combine marshmallows, sugar and water; cook over medium heat, stirring constantly, until marshmallows have melted. Remove from heat; add grape juice and lemon juice. Cool slightly, then fold in whipped cream. Pour into an 8-inch square pan and freeze 4 – 5 hours or overnight. (You can also pour this in an ice cream maker and freeze according to the manufacturer's directions.) Cut into squares and garnish each serving with a dollop of whipped cream and a grape. *SERVES: 8*

NOTE: This is especially effective if you make a second batch of sherbet using purple grape juice. Serve a scoop of each to your guests.

One of the more unusual parties I've ever given was for my husband, Mike, to celebrate one of the more important moments in his life — the return of real Coca-Cola. Mike, you see, is well-known around Greenville for his love of the beverage. Early each morning, I drink my cup of coffee and shudder in amazement as he sips a cold Coke. When we travel, the first thing he does in the hotel is check out the vending machine. If it doesn't offer "the real thing," he immediately gets directions to the nearest convenience store.

When "New Coke" was introduced and the Coca-Cola Company took away his lifelong drinking companion, Mike was distraught. He stocked up on the old formula, but his supply soon ran out. He was forced to take desperate actions, occasionally stopping by our local bottling plant, where the owners knew him well. He'd stand around, looking lost, until they would finally take pity, offering him a 6½-ounce bottle of the original formula they had stashed away for themselves.

Public outcry over Coca-Cola's decision finally brought back the old formula, under the name "Coca-Cola Classic," and Mike was a grateful man. His friends at the bottling plant presented him with the first bottle of Coca-Cola Classic off the bottling line in a ceremony at the local Rotary Club. That's when I hatched the idea of throwing a celebration marking the occasion.

The key to the party turned out to be a fajita recipe that I had seen about a year before in a Southwest Airlines in-flight magazine. I was intrigued by the fact that the beef was marinated for twenty-four hours in Coca-Cola. Thinking it would be fun to surprise Mike with it sometime, I studied the recipe intently. In the confusion at the airport, I left the magazine on the plane and had to rely on my memory to make it. My version turned out to be very good, and it has become the standard way most of our friends prepare fajitas.

Wouldn't it be fun, I thought, to come up with a party for Mike where every dish served had some Coca-Cola in it? A little research, a little creativity, and some help from Mike's friends at the bottling company, meant that soon his Coke Party invitations were in the mail.

All the guests came dressed in red and white for the occasion. Some even had managed to find tee shirts or hats with the Coca-Cola logo on them. One guest strung bottle caps together to make a necklace and dangled more from her ears. The owners of the bottling company offered banners and promotional material for decorations. They were also the guests of honor.

We offered a real variety of drinks — 6½-ounce bottles, 10-ounce bottles, 12-ounce cans and 2-liter bottles — Coca-Cola only. Rum and bourbon were available for mixing, if the guests so desired. The only other beverage option was water.

The one dish on the menu that did not have Coke in it was the Guacamole I served with fajitas. When one of the guests discovered that, he splashed about a teaspoon or so into the bowl and stirred it in, declaring proudly that now everything had been made with a little Coca-Cola.

Menu for Coca-Cola Party
Zippy Cheese Crackers
Coca-Cola Queso
Coca-Cola Fajitas
Pico de Gallo and condiments
Guacamole*
Coca-Cola Salad
Coca-Cola Cake
Coke Floats

*see index for recipe

Zippy Cheese Crackers

1 pound sharp Cheddar cheese, grated
1 cup (2 sticks) butter or margarine, softened
¼ cup flour
¾ cup yellow cornmeal
2 teaspoons taco or picante sauce
1 teaspoon Coca-Cola (optional)
2 teaspoons dry mustard
½ teaspoon salt
¼ teaspoon pepper
⅛ teaspoon cayenne pepper
Jalapeño nacho slices (optional)

Blend cheese with butter. Add flour, cornmeal, taco sauce, Coca-Cola and seasonings and beat until a smooth dough is formed. (This can be made in a food processor.) Divide dough in half, and shape each half into a cylinder about 2 inches in diameter. Roll in waxed paper and chill several hours or overnight. (Rolls can be frozen at this point for later use.) At baking time, preheat oven to 325°. Slice cylinders ¼-inch thick and arrange about 2 inches apart on ungreased baking sheets. Top each cracker with a jalapeño slice, if desired. Bake at 325° for 7 – 10 minutes, or until golden. Serve hot, or cool crackers on waxed paper. This makes a spicy accompaniment for soups and salads, or a good appetizer. *MAKES: 4 dozen*

Coca-Cola® Queso

2 tablespoons vegetable oil
1 cup chopped marinated onions (reserved from fajitas)
1 cup chopped marinated green peppers (reserved from fajitas)
2 9-ounce cans Nacho Cheese dip
1 15-ounce can Chili con Carne without beans
2 tablespoons Coca-Cola

Heat oil in a large saucepan over medium heat and sauté onions and peppers until tender. Add cheese, chili, Coca-Cola, cooking over low heat until heated through. Serve hot, with tortilla chips for dipping. *SERVES: 8*

COCA-COLA IS A REGISTERED TRADE MARK OF THE COCA-COLA COMPANY, ATLANTA, GA.

Coca-Cola® Fajitas

2 pounds skirt steak
Creole or Cajun seasoning
Garlic salt
¼ cup soy sauce
¼ cup sherry
2 onions, thinly sliced
2 green peppers, thinly sliced
4 limes, halved
1 2-liter bottle Coca-Cola

2 – 3 dozen flour tortillas (allow at least 2 per person)
Sour cream
Pico de Gallo (recipe follows)
Guacamole (see index)
Grated cheese
Shredded lettuce
Chopped tomatoes

Sprinkle the meat on both sides with Creole or Cajun seasoning and garlic salt — be very generous with both. Mix the soy sauce and the sherry together and rub the mixture over the meat on both sides. In a deep pot (I use my Dutch oven) put a layer of meat, a layer of onion and pepper slices then squeeze the juice of 1 lime over all — throw the lime in too. Repeat 3 more times. Pour enough Coca-Cola over the meat to completely cover. MARINATE AT LEAST 24 HOURS. Drain off marinade. Wrap peppers and onions in foil (save 1 cup of each if you plan to make the Coca-Cola Queso). Cook meat and vegetables on a grill to desired doneness. Thinly slice meat across the grain. Serve sliced meat on hot flour tortillas, topped with your favorite combination of sour cream, Pico de Gallo, guacamole, grilled onions and peppers, grated cheese, lettuce and tomatoes. Roll up and eat with fingers. *SERVES: 6 – 8*

COCA-COLA IS A REGISTERED TRADE MARK OF THE COCA-COLA COMPANY, ATLANTA, GA.

Pico De Gallo

2 tomatoes, coarsely chopped
1 onion, finely chopped
1 – 4 jalapeños, seeded and minced very fine

¼ cup chopped cilantro
1 teaspoon salt

Combine all ingredients and chill until serving time. Serve as a condiment for fajitas or other Mexican food or as a dip with tortilla chips. *MAKES: about 2 cups*

NOTE: If jalapeños are too hot for your taste, substitute canned chopped green chilies to taste.

Coca-Cola® Salad

- 1 16-ounce can pitted dark sweet cherries
- 1 15-ounce can crushed pineapple
- 1 6-ounce box cherry flavored gelatin
- 1 3-ounce package cream cheese, softened
- 1 6½-ounce bottle Coca-Cola (or ¾ cup)
- 1 cup pecans
- 1 cup sour cream
- Pecan halves for garnish (optional)

Drain the juice from both the cherries and pineapple and combine in a large saucepan; bring to a boil. Remove from heat and add gelatin, stirring until dissolved. Add cream cheese and stir until cheese has melted. Stir in Coca-Cola, cherries, pineapple and pecans and pour into a 8-inch square baking dish. Chill until set. Spread with sour cream and cut into squares, garnishing each serving with a pecan half, if desired. *SERVES: 8*

COCA-COLA IS A REGISTERED TRADE MARK OF THE COCA-COLA COMPANY, ATLANTA, GA.

Coca-Cola® Cake

- 1 teaspoon baking soda
- ½ cup buttermilk
- 2 cups flour
- 2 cups sugar
- 1 cup (2 sticks) butter or margarine
- 1 cup Coca-Cola
- 3 tablespoons cocoa
- 2 eggs, beaten
- 1 teaspoon vanilla
- 2 cups miniature marshmallows

Preheat oven to 350°. Grease a 13×9-inch cake pan. Stir soda into the buttermilk; set aside. Combine flour and sugar, mixing well. Heat butter, Coca-Cola and cocoa, and bring to a boil. Pour over flour and sugar, and stir well. Add buttermilk, eggs, and vanilla, beating to make a smooth batter. Stir in marshmallows and pour into prepared pan. Bake for 30 – 35 minutes at 350°. The marshmallows will rise to the top during the baking. Cool in pan, then frost with the following:

ICING:
- ½ cup (1 stick) butter or margarine, softened
- 6 tablespoons Coca-Cola
- 3½ cups powdered sugar
- 1 teaspoon vanilla
- 3 tablespoons cocoa
- 1 cup pecans

Cream butter. Add remaining ingredients and beat until smooth. Pour over cake while still in the pan. Cool, then cut into squares to serve. *SERVES: 12 – 16*

COCA-COLA IS A REGISTERED TRADE MARK OF THE COCA-COLA COMPANY, ATLANTA, GA.

Of course, not all memories associated with food recall good times. In the small towns of East Texas and throughout the South, family and friends rally whenever there is a death in the family. Within hours of the loss of a loved one, dishes of food begin to appear at the homes of grieving relatives. Caring friends and neighbors come to cook and clean and, in general, relieve the family of mundane tasks in their time of sorrow. This practice dates back to the early settlers of the region, and is one of the nicest customs retained from those days. Otherwise, of course, the mourning period and traditions have changed greatly, even though the grief felt by family members is still just as real.

My family remembers my great-great-grandmother as a lady who was always in mourning for someone. Considering the circumstances of her life, this was an understandable description of Mary Jane Dyer. Born in Canton, Mississippi, she married during the Civil War siege of nearby Vicksburg, and raised her family during the difficult Reconstruction years. Mary Jane found that life was not easy, especially for members of aristocratic Southern families who had lost almost everything except pride and a sense of propriety. She married young and was widowed a few years later with two small daughters in her care. She never remarried, saying that she would devote her life to seeing that her daughters were comfortably married.

It was Mary Jane Dyer who brought her two daughters to Texas when the boyfriend of the older girl moved west. Mary Jane must have felt that life would be better in East Texas and, certainly the prospect of eligible bachelors would be vastly improved.

Grandmother always felt that "Grandma Chicago," as Mary Jane Dyer came to be known because of her frequent train trips to Chicago to visit family members, secretly preferred the role of "stately widow in mourning" to that of wife, which another marriage would bring. Perhaps her role model was Queen Victoria of England who mourned the loss of her husband, Prince Albert, for the rest of her life, never remarrying either. And, since Grandma Chicago was a proper lady, she probably studied the best etiquette books of the period, which carefully outlined the correct practices for those in mourning to follow.

Whatever her reasons, Grandma Chicago kept a wardrobe of mourning clothes ready for any occasion. Sometimes the mourning periods were brief, other times they occupied several months. The "proper" period of time was determined by how closely the deceased was related. And, of course, by the time that the period of mourning had ended for one, another death sent her back to the wardrobe and into her dark clothes again.

Although Grandma Chicago would probably find today's customs somewhat disconcerting, especially for a true Southern lady, she would more than likely appreciate the food that caring friends still bring. Most of the good cooks I know in this area keep a selection of recipes they can pull out and prepare with some ease for these occasions. Casseroles, vegetables and desserts seem to be the most popular dishes, because they can hold a long time and are relatively easy to reheat and serve.

The same qualities of ease in preparation, heating and serving make these recipes good contributions for "covered dish" meals like church suppers, neighborhood picnics, and "potluck" occasions as well. Covered dish lunches are held regularly by the family and employees at Puddin Hill to mark birthdays and special occasions. Everyone brings something, even if it is a can of dip and package of chips. Many members of the "Puddin Hill Family" relish these meals because of the wonderful food that always appears. Some are expected to bring a certain item considered to be their specialty, and loud protests are heard if it isn't on the table. The highlight of every year is the annual Thanksgiving dinner. The dishes and platters of heavenly smelling fare are spread over four long tables, and everyone leaves the kitchen with plates piled high.

Jalapeño Dip

1 pound Velveeta cheese
2 cups mayonnaise
2 pickled jalapeño peppers, seeded and chopped very fine
1 teaspoon juice from jalapeños (more if you like it hot)
1 large onion, chopped very fine

Chill cheese for several hours until cold enough to grate, then grate as fine as possible. Stir in mayonnaise, chopped jalapeño, juice and onion. Stir until well blended and smooth. Heat in the top of a double boiler over hot water, then serve hot with tortilla chips. *SERVES: 12*

NOTE: This can be made in a food processor quickly and easily. Grate the cheese with the grating attachment, then blend all ingredients until smooth using the steel blade attachment.

Cheesy Chicken Lasagna

- 3 tablespoons butter or margarine
- ½ cup chopped green pepper
- ½ cup chopped red pepper (substitute 1 4-ounce jar diced pimiento, drained, if needed)
- ½ cup chopped onion
- ½ pound sliced fresh mushrooms
- 1 10-ounce can condensed cream of chicken soup
- ½ teaspoon basil
- 1 8-ounce package lasagna noodles
- 2 cups cooked, diced chicken
- 1½ cups cream-style cottage cheese
- 1½ cups grated Mozzarella cheese
- ¾ cups grated Parmesan cheese

Melt butter in a large skillet over medium heat. Sauté green and red peppers and onion until softened. Add mushrooms and cook until they are wilted. Stir in undiluted soup and basil and simmer about 5 minutes. Remove from heat and set aside. Cook lasagna noodles until tender; drain. In a buttered 11×7-inch baking dish, layer the ingredients in the following order, using ⅓ of each with every layer: noodles, chicken, mushroom sauce mixture, cottage cheese, Mozzarella cheese, and Parmesan cheese. Repeat three times, ending with Parmesan cheese sprinkled over the top. Bake at 350° for about 30 minutes, or until cheese has melted and casserole is bubbly.

SERVES: 8

Deluxe Limas

- 1 10-ounce package frozen lima beans
- 3 strips bacon
- 1 medium onion, finely chopped
- 1 rib celery, finely chopped
- 1 green pepper, finely chopped
- 2 tablespoons chopped parsley
- ¼ teaspoon salt
- ¼ teaspoon pepper
- 3 tablespoons butter or margarine, melted

Preheat oven to 350°. Cook frozen limas in 4 cups boiling water for 7 minutes. Drain and set aside. While beans are cooking, fry bacon until crisp; crumble and reserve. Sauté onion, celery and green pepper in bacon drippings until soft — about 3 minutes. Combine with reserved bacon, beans, parsley and salt and pepper. Pour into a 1-quart baking dish, drizzle with melted butter, cover and bake at 350° for 30 minutes. This can be made ahead and refrigerated before baking. Add 5 minutes to baking time.

SERVES: 8

Spinach Aspic

1 10-ounce package frozen chopped spinach
2 envelopes unflavored gelatin
¾ cup water
2 chicken bouillon cubes
1½ cups cottage cheese
2 tablespoons lemon juice
½ cup sour cream
½ cup chopped celery
⅓ cup chopped green pepper
2 tablespoons minced green onion
3 hard cooked eggs, peeled

Cook spinach according to package directions and drain, reserving ½ cup liquid. In a saucepan, soften gelatin in water. Add bouillon cubes and heat until dissolved. Remove from heat and add spinach liquid. In blender or food processor whirl cottage cheese until creamy, add spinach, lemon juice, sour cream and gelatin mixture. Pour into a large mixing bowl and fold in chopped vegetables. Place in a 6-cup mold and chill until set. Remove from mold and serve, garnished with hard-boiled egg daisy. (Use mashed egg yolks mixed with mayonnaise and a drop of yellow food coloring for center of daisy and egg whites cut into fourths for the petals.) *SERVES: 8 – 12*

Baked Mustard Potatoes

6 medium potatoes
½ cup (1 stick) butter or margarine
¼ cup flour
3 cups milk
1 teaspoon salt
1 teaspoon white pepper
1 tablespoon dry mustard
1 cup (4 ounces) grated Cheddar cheese

Boil potatoes in their jackets until tender, 20 – 25 minutes. Drain and cool potatoes until they can be handled. While potatoes are cooling, prepare sauce. Melt butter in a large saucepan over medium heat. Add flour and cook 2 minutes, stirring constantly. Stir in milk. Reduce heat and simmer, stirring occasionally, until thickened and smooth — about 10 minutes. Season with salt and pepper; set aside. Preheat oven to 300°. Slice cooked and cooled potatoes into ½-inch slices and place in a buttered 2-quart baking dish. Pour sauce over potatoes and sprinkle with dry mustard. (You may use more mustard, if desired.) Top potatoes with grated cheese and bake uncovered for 45 minutes or until bubbly and lightly browned on top. *SERVES: 8*

Johnnie Bazzeti

- 3 tablespoons vegetable oil
- 2 large onions, chopped
- 1 clove garlic, minced
- 1 large green pepper, chopped
- 2 carrots, thinly sliced
- 2 cups chopped celery,
- 1½ pounds ground beef
- 1 15-ounce can whole tomatoes
- 1 6-ounce can tomato paste
- 2 teaspoons chili powder — (more to taste)
- 1 teaspoon salt
- 1 tablespoon Worcestershire sauce
- 1 17-ounce can whole corn, drained
- 1 17-ounce can green peas, drained
- ½ teaspoon rosemary
- 1 4-ounce can mushrooms, drained
- 1 3-ounce jar sliced stuffed olives, drained
- 1 cup pecan pieces
- 1 12-ounce package noodles, cooked and drained
- 1 cup (4 ounces) grated Cheddar cheese

In a large heavy sauce pan, heat oil and sauté onion, garlic, green pepper, carrots and celery until tender. Add ground beef, cooking until browned. Drain off excess fat. Add tomatoes, tomato paste, chili powder, salt and Worcestershire. Simmer for 5 minutes, stirring occasionally. Add corn, peas, rosemary, mushrooms and olives and cook for 10 minutes. Add pecans and cooked noodles, simmering until heated through. Serve, sprinkled with grated Cheddar cheese. *SERVES: 8*

Chocolate Nut Slices

- 1 cup firmly packed brown sugar
- ¼ cup evaporated milk
- ¼ cup light corn syrup
- 6 ounces semi-sweet chocolate
- 1 teaspoon vanilla
- 1½ cups pecan pieces

Combine brown sugar, evaporated milk and corn syrup in a medium saucepan and bring to a rolling boil. Let boil for 2 minutes. Remove from heat and add chocolate, stirring until melted. Add vanilla and pecan pieces. Stir constantly until mixture thickens and leaves the sides of the pan, 5 – 10 minutes. Spoon out onto a piece of waxed paper in a long, thin strip. With the aid of the waxed paper, form into a roll about 2 inches in diameter. Chill several hours, or until candy is firm. Remove waxed paper and cut into ½-inch thick slices. Store slices in an airtight container with waxed paper between each layer of candy. *MAKES: 3 dozen*

Chocolate Pie

1 cup sugar
¼ cup corn starch
¼ teaspoon salt
2 cups milk, divided
3 egg yolks
¼ cup cocoa
2 ounces semi-sweet chocolate, cut up in small chunks
1 tablespoon unsalted (sweet) butter
1 teaspoon vanilla
1 9-inch pie crust, baked and cooled (deep-dish type if using a commercial crust)
Meringue or toffee topping

Combine sugar, corn starch, salt and ¼ cup milk in a small mixing bowl. Blend in egg yolks. In the top of double boiler set over hot water, heat 1½ cups milk until bubbles form around the edges. Add about ½ cup of the hot milk to the egg yolk mixture, stirring until blended. Pour egg yolk mixture into hot milk, stirring with a wire whip or an electric mixer until smooth. Cook mixture over hot water, stirring frequently, until thickened. Stir cocoa and remaining ¼ cup milk together to form a smooth paste, then add to hot mixture. Add chocolate chunks, and stir until chocolate is melted and mixture is smooth. (An electric mixer will smooth out any lumps the mixture might have.) Remove mixture from heat, and add butter and vanilla, stirring until butter is melted. Turn mixture into a baked pie shell, and cover with waxed paper. Select either of the following toppings. Proceed at once with the meringue topping. Chill pie before adding toffee topping.

MERINGUE
3 egg whites
¼ teaspoon cream of tartar
4 tablespoons sugar
½ teaspoon vanilla

Preheat oven to 350°. Beat egg whites and cream of tartar until soft peaks form. Add sugar 1 tablespoon at a time until stiff peaks form. Remove waxed paper from pie filling and spread meringue over filling. Be sure to check the edges to see that they are completely sealed. Bake at 350° for 12 minutes, until meringue is lightly browned.

TOFFEE TOPPING
½ cup whipping cream
2 tablespoons powdered sugar
3 chocolate/toffee bars, crushed into fine bits (Heath bars)

Beat whipping cream until foamy, then add powdered sugar, beating until soft peaks form. Remove waxed paper from chilled pie and spoon or pipe whipped cream around the edge. Just before serving, sprinkle crushed toffee over both chocolate filling and whipped cream. *SERVES: 8*

I feel I must explain the unusual title of this next dish. When Grandmother died, the members of my family were the recipients of all the kindness and caring that could possibly be shown by friends. As we passed the day of the funeral in a numbed state, we were so grateful for all the food which had been brought to us. It helped feed the many people who had come from out of town to pay their respects. One casserole had been prepared by Mrs. Clark, a good friend of Grandmother's. She was a good cook, and we all knew that whatever she had made would be as delicious as it looked. On the top of the casserole cheese was sprinkled over what appeared to be sour cream. There were no serving instructions, so Mother added it to the rest of the food heating in the oven. At lunchtime, everyone wanted to try a bite of Mrs. Clark's casserole. It looked like one of the best, as well as one of the most intriguing. There appeared to be spinach in the mixture beneath the sour cream layer. After taking a taste, Mother's sister Sarah said, "Mary, I think this was one of those twenty-four hour salads that got heated by mistake." On closer inspection, we discovered that she was right. But most amazing was the fact that it tasted quite good served hot. After all, the ingredients are commonly found in casseroles. My family renamed Mrs. Clark's salad "Twenty-four Hour Salad Plus Thirty Minutes at 350°."

Twenty-Four Hour Salad Plus Thirty Minutes At 350°

SALAD:
- 1 10-ounce bag fresh spinach (about 4 cups)
- ½ cup chopped green onion
- 2 cups chopped celery
- 1 10-ounce package frozen English peas, thawed

ADD AT LEAST 4 OF THE FOLLOWING:
- 1 6-ounce package cooked frozen shrimp, thawed
- 1 cup cooked chicken, diced
- 1 cup (4 ounces) grated Swiss cheese
- 6 hard boiled eggs, sliced
- 12 slices bacon, cooked crisp and crumbled
- 1 small zucchini squash, thinly sliced
- 2 small yellow squash, thinly sliced
- 1 cup shredded carrots

DRESSING:
- 2 cups mayonnaise (not salad dressing)
- 2 cups sour cream
- 1 package original Ranch-Style dressing mix
- 1 tablespoon paprika
- 2 cups (8 ounces) grated Swiss cheese

Wash spinach and drain well. Remove stems and tear into small pieces. Combine spinach with remaining salad ingredients and toss. Put into a large salad bowl; set aside. Combine dressing ingredients, except Swiss cheese, stirring until well-blended. Carefully spread dressing over salad. Be sure to smooth dressing to the edges of the salad bowl to seal. Sprinkle with cheese. Cover with plastic wrap and refrigerate for about 24 hours.

To Prepare As a Casserole: Prepare salad as directed, dividing between two 11½×7½-inch glass baking dishes. Carefully pour 2 cups dressing over the salad in each baking dish, spreading to cover. Sprinkle 1 cup cheese over each dish. Cover with plastic wrap and refrigerate about 24 hours. Bake at 350° for about 30 minutes or until heated through and bubbly. *SERVES: 12 – 15 (Salad) or 20 – 24 (Casserole)*

HINT: *The salad dressing used for this dish is delicious served over any combination of fresh salad greens. In fact, it's Mother's favorite. Omit the Swiss cheese when using the dressing on another salad.*

"They called themselves the 'Bottle Scarred Veterans.'"

Chapter Eight

Good Times at Club Lake

One of the greatest joys of my life — and the lives of the two generations before me — has been the time spent at Club Lake. This is a small lake about 15 miles outside of Greenville where we've had rustic cabins for years. Officially, the title of the place is "Greenville Lake and Water Company," but, to my knowledge, no one has ever used that name. It's always been known as Club Lake.

When the lake was built in 1921, Pop furnished the feed for the mules used to haul the earth for the dam. Several years later, he and Grandmother bought a big two-story cabin with screened-in porches facing the lake. Each year, as soon as school was out, Grandmother loaded up Hal, Sarah, Jack, Mother, the cow, the chickens and Pop, and moved the whole bunch to the lake for three months. The kids could swim, fish, wander through the woods, or just be lazy. It was close enough that Pop could drive back and forth to town every day. Grandmother tended her garden, worked on one or more of her many projects, or enjoyed just sitting on the porch in the breeze, taking in the peaceful sights around her.

When Hal, Sarah, Jack and Mother grew up, each acquired a cabin on the lake for their families. In fact, Hal bought the cabin on one side of Grandmother and Pop's place and Mother and Dad bought the one on the other side. Just across the road, close friends Bobbie and Forest Lake had a place, and other good friends and neighbors from Greenville were neighbors at the lake as well. Club Lake is small enough that only two roads, one on each side of the lake (known as the "East Beach" and "West Beach") provide access to the ninety-some-odd cabins situated around the lake. It's an easy walk or bicycle ride from one cabin to another.

Today, there are a number of families in my generation who are still enjoying the lake. Few families get to spend the entire summer there, because more and more mothers are working, and the summer activities and recreational programs for the kids keep them in town during the week. But on the weekends, the lake is a busy place again, with lots of boating, fishing and water skiing taking place.

It means a lot to me to see my sons now growing up in the same place Mother and I roamed when we were young. Many families are now into the third or fourth generation at the lake. Although most of the rustic places have been rebuilt or greatly improved (we tore down the old shack several years ago and now stay in a "cabin" with central air conditioning, a television, microwave oven and three bathrooms), the lake itself remains much the same as it was over sixty years ago.

A typical day at Club Lake begins early. The birds and squirrels are out and it's fun to get up and watch them. Because there's plenty of time, breakfast is often a leisurely affair. The grown-ups have a cup of coffee on the porch or the deck while the kids put on their swimsuits and wander off to see who else is up and ready to play. Then, about the time everyone is getting hungry, someone gathers enough energy to go inside and fix something to eat. Or, even better, some early riser has prepared an easy coffee cake and the oven timer is announcing that it's ready.

Banana-Stuffed French Toast

2 bananas
1 large loaf French or Italian bread
2 eggs
1 cup milk
1 teaspoon vanilla
2 teaspoons honey
¼ cup butter or margarine
Powdered sugar
Maple syrup

Peel bananas and cut each in half. Carefully slice each half lengthwise into ¼-inch thick slices. Slice bread into 1-inch slices. Cut a pocket in each slice of bread, being careful not to cut the slice completely in half. Slide two or three of the banana slices into each pocket; set aside. Beat eggs, milk, vanilla and honey together until well blended; pour into a shallow dish. In a large skillet, melt two tablespoons of the butter or margarine over medium heat. Dip each slice of bread into the egg mixture, turning once to coat both sides. Fry bread slices in melted butter until golden brown on one side. Turn and cook until second side is browned. Sprinkle with powdered sugar. Repeat with remaining slices, adding more butter to the skillet as needed. Serve hot with additional powdered sugar or maple syrup.
SERVES: 4

Graham Cracker Coffee Cake

½ cup flour
1 teaspoon baking powder
½ teaspoon baking soda
½ teaspoon salt
1½ cups graham cracker crumbs (about 10 whole crackers)
½ cup (1 stick) butter or margarine, softened
⅔ cup granulated sugar
⅔ cup brown sugar, firmly packed
3 eggs
1 teaspoon vanilla
1 cup buttermilk
1 cup pecan pieces or walnuts
Butter

Preheat oven to 350°. Lightly grease an 8-inch square cake pan. Stir together flour, baking powder, soda, salt and graham cracker crumbs; set aside. Cream butter and sugars until fluffy. Add eggs one at a time, beating well after each addition. Blend in vanilla. Add dry ingredients and buttermilk alternately to egg mixture until blended. Stir in pecans and pour into prepared pan. Bake at 350° for 40 – 45 minutes, or until cake tester inserted in the center comes out clean. Serve hot with lots of butter. *SERVES: 8*

Grapes In Sour Cream

1 cup (8-ounces) sour cream
¼ cup firmly packed brown sugar
1 pound seedless grapes, washed and pulled from stems

Mix sour cream and brown sugar together until well blended and sugar has dissolved. Pour over grapes and toss gently to coat well. Chill before serving. Serve as a fruit with breakfast or brunch, or as a light dessert. *SERVES: 4*

NOTE: I like to place the grapes in the freezer about 30 minutes before serving to get them good and cold. The grapes look lovely served in champagne glasses or crystal bowls.

Blueberry Muffins With Lemon Honey Butter

MUFFINS:

2 cups sifted all-purpose flour
⅓ cup sugar
3 teaspoons baking powder
1 teaspoon salt
1 egg, well beaten
1 cup milk
¼ cup butter or margarine, melted and cooled
1 cup fresh or frozen blueberries, thawed
1 tablespoon sugar
1 teaspoon grated lemon rind

Preheat oven to 425°. Grease a 12-cup muffin tin or line with paper liners. Sift flour, sugar, baking powder and salt into a large bowl. In a separate bowl, mix egg, milk and melted butter. Add all at once to flour mixture, stirring lightly with a fork until just blended — batter will be lumpy. Fold in blueberries. Spoon into prepared muffin pan, filling each cup ⅔ full. Combine the remaining tablespoon sugar and lemon rind; sprinkle over muffins. Bake at 425° for 20 minutes or until golden. Allow muffins to stand in pan 5 minutes, then remove. Serve hot with Lemon Honey Butter. *MAKES: 1 dozen*

LEMON HONEY BUTTER

6 tablespoons butter or margarine, softened
6 tablespoons honey
¾ teaspoon grated lemon peel

Cream all ingredients together with a fork or electric mixer until well blended. *MAKES: ⅔ cup butter*

The rest of the morning is spent in a variety of ways. The kids take a walk in the woods or explore the shoreline to see what surprises might have washed up since their last survey. Around noon they take a dip in the lake, then sit on the pier until the sun has dried their hair and swimsuits. Adults have another cup of coffee and perhaps read the newspaper if someone has made a run into town or to the store that's about two miles away. Then a little cleanup is done before it's time to sit on the shore and watch the kids swim.

Lunch is always sandwiches made of cold cuts and sweet red tomatoes bought from the roadside stand between the lake and town. Bobbie Lake brings a container of pimento cheese — her specialty — and a sack of crisp, ice-cold celery to spread it on. Everyone gets a plastic cup for tea or lemonade. By the stack of cups is a big, felt-tip marker, put there so that each person can write his or her name on a cup. With all the activity going on in the summer, it's easy to go through dozens of cups each day, so Bobbie instituted the cup-marking system. Even the toddlers learn to recognize their name or special mark on a cup.

After lunch, the daily run to the dump ground is made. For some reason, this open stretch of dirt with piles of rubble has lured three generations of children, including me. Whoever is making the first trip to the dump understands that an escort of two to seven children will go along. While the trash is being disposed of, the kids wander among the discarded items, looking for any treasure that might be found. Those prizes are brought back to furnish a clubhouse or hideout in the woods.

Even the breeze off the lake can't compete with the hot afternoons in July and August. That's nap time. Everyone comes in for a while. The children rest, read books or work jigsaw puzzles. The grownups read for a while until they doze off. The only sounds are the song of the cicadas in the trees and the occasional drone of a motorboat as a skier whizzes by.

Finally, about four-thirty, the kids are ready to hit the water again. There is a good stretch of beach that runs in front of Grandmother's old cabin (now owned by Mother's brother Jack). Everyone congregates there for the next three hours. While the kids play in the water or water ski, the adults sit in the shade and visit, occasionally taking a dip to cool off. The conversation tends to lean towards important subjects like where the fish are biting and who has been spotted driving a boat recklessly. When I was a child, Mother and Bobbie appointed themselves the guardians of the boating rules and regulations on the lake. They were familiar with every boat and driver, as well as most of the water skiers. If someone was not driving in accordance with the rules, Mother and Bobbie noted who it was. Soon others on the lake began calling them for information, and this notorious duo became known around Club Lake as the "East Beach Biddies." It was a title they embraced and proudly emblazoned on a banner which flew from the pier whenever the "Biddies" took to the beach.

Mother and Bobbie both believe their practices should be continued. They see real potential for another generation of Biddies, so they're working very hard at training Bobbie's daughters, me, and several friends during the afternoon swim period.

After an hour or so of swimming and skiing, everyone begins to get hungry and thirsty. A trip is made back to each cabin for beverages and snacks. It has become a ritual each summer for Mother to make an enormous bowl of Guacamole Dip for everyone to enjoy. The tradition began over twenty-five years ago when Mary of Puddin Hill's supplier of dates for the fruit cakes would send Mother and Dad a "lug" of California avocados as a thank-you gift. This was in the days before avocados were available at the supermarket year round at the price of four for a dollar. A lug consisted of twenty-five to thirty avocados, all ripening within a day or two of one another! Mother would make guacamole every night for as long as the avocados lasted. Bobbie's son, Robert, dearly loved guacamole. He still remembers those days as the only time in his life when his mother didn't scold him for eating too much. Nowadays, with avocados easily obtainable, we make guacamole each summer and laugh about those days.

Guacamole

4 avocados, peeled and seeded
2 tablespoons finely chopped onion
1 tomato, seeded and chopped
¼ – ½ teaspoon Tabasco sauce
1 teaspoon garlic salt
2 teaspoons lemon juice

Mash avocados with a fork until softened. Add remaining ingredients and stir until well blended. Taste and adjust seasoning, if necessary. Serve with tortilla chips, as a salad, or as an accompaniment to Mexican dishes, especially fajitas. *MAKES: 2 cups*

HINT: *Many avocados will come loose from their peels very easily with the following technique: cut avocado in half, remove seed, then cut each half again lengthwise. Grasp a quarter avocado and, with other hand, gently pull the peel away from the flesh. Peel should come off in one piece. If not, then peel with knife or vegetable peeler.*

Another favorite dip for those summer afternoons is the one we simply call "Dip From The Store Down The Road." The store in question, known as Eakins' Store, sells all the necessities of lake life from candy bars to minnows to gasoline. Once, when company showed up just as the last of the guacamole disappeared, I made a mad dash to Eakins' Store to see what they might have that I could offer my guests. They stocked the food every fisherman or camper needed — chips, canned dips, and cans of chili. With a few purchases, I was soon able to serve a dip that everyone enjoyed. Since then, there have been many trips to the store down the road for dip fixin's.

Dip From The Store Down The Road

1 12-ounce can chili without beans
1 9-ounce can bean dip
1 9-ounce can nacho cheese dip

Tortilla chips or corn chips

Combine chili and dips in a medium saucepan, stirring until well blended. Heat over medium heat, stirring constantly, until heated through. Serve hot with chips for dipping. *SERVES: 8*

NOTE: This may also be made in the microwave. Put all ingredients into a microwave-safe container and cook at full power for 2 minutes. Stir and cook another 2 minutes at full power. Continue cooking and stirring until dip is heated to your satisfaction.

Just about dark, it's time to think about supper. While the skiers are making that last trip round the lake, the rest of the group heads back to the cabins to change out of swimsuits. Many evenings, everyone will get together again for supper — sometimes as many as fifteen or so. Mother likes to have lots of hamburger patties in the freezer. When the group heads down to the beach for swimming, she sets plenty out to thaw. Then when everyone hits the cabin with a ravenous appetite, the patties are ready to cook on the grill. Mother has never been one to believe in an ordinary hamburger, so she offers her own "special sauce" for guests to enjoy.

Ambrosia Hamburger Sauce

¼ cup Worcestershire sauce
1 cup mayonnaise
½ teaspoon Tabasco sauce
½ teaspoon oregano or thyme
½ cup catsup
¼ teaspoon pepper
¼ teaspoon garlic salt
¼ teaspoon celery salt

Mix all ingredients together to make smooth sauce. Spread on cooked hamburger patties served on toasted, buttered buns. *MAKES: 1¾ cups*

Somehow the amount of hamburgers or hot dogs and the respective buns never seems to come out equal. That problem can be easily solved by turning the leftover buns into breadsticks. The resulting crunchy sticks are wonderful with salads, spaghetti or all by themselves. I've listed some variations on the recipe using other types of breads. It's well worth making these breadsticks, even if you have to buy a package of hot dog buns.

Gone-In-A-Minute Bread Sticks

1 package hot dog buns (day old buns are great for this)
½ cup (1 stick) butter or margarine
1 tablespoon Worcestershire sauce
1 teaspoon seasoned salt
1 clove garlic, crushed (optional)
2 tablespoons poppy or sesame seeds (optional)

Preheat oven to 200°. Open hot dog buns and separate at seam. Cut each section in half lengthwise. Place strips onto an ungreased baking sheet. Melt butter in a saucepan over medium heat. Stir in Worcestershire sauce, seasoned salt and crushed garlic. Brush each stick generously with seasoned butter and sprinkle with poppy or sesame seeds. Place pan in a 200° oven and toast slowly — about 1 hour — so that the sticks will dry out and become crusty and crunchy. Let cool, then store in plastic bags.
MAKES: 32 sticks

HINT: *This recipe works just as well with other kinds of bread: Hamburger buns make party-size sticks — cut each half in fourths or fifths. English muffins are great with brunch dishes — slice each half horizontally into thin rounds, about ¼-inch thick. Pita Bread makes good dippers with appetizers — cut each into four or six wedges, then separate with fingers along pocket into two pieces. Bagels can be made into the popular bagel chips – prepare as for English muffins. Submarine loaves are large enough to use as pushers for spaghetti – cut in half lengthwise, then cut each half crosswise.*

Fish has always been a family favorite, especially at the lake. Mother began preparing this fish recipe years ago, and I still make it often. We take the electric skillet or deep fryer out onto the deck. This way we can visit and cook at the same time. The children love to "help" me make the coating for the fish by crushing the potato chips. I've also found that it is usually necessary to plan to make a few extra pieces as "food inspectors" are always around to sample. Cabbage salad (page 63) and bread sticks can be made earlier in the day to round out this meal.

Chipper Fried Fish

3 pounds firm-fleshed white fish (cod, catfish or whitefish are good)
1½ cups complete pancake mix
1 cup water
½ teaspoon Tabasco sauce
1 15-ounce package potato chips
Hot vegetable oil for frying

Rinse fish, then pat with paper towels until thoroughly dried. Cut into serving-size pieces and set aside. In a large mixing bowl, combine pancake mix, water and Tabasco until well blended and smooth. More water may be added as necessary to make a smooth batter. With a knife, pierce several very small holes in the potato chip package, then crush the chips inside with a rolling pin. Pour finely crushed chips into a pie plate or other flat dish. Heat oil in a large skillet until it is about 360° – 370°. Dip each piece of fish in the pancake batter, shaking off the excess, then roll in the crushed potato chips. Fry in hot oil until browned on one side, then turn and brown on the other (about 4 minutes per side). Drain on paper towels and keep warm while cooking remaining fish. Serve with cocktail sauce, tartar sauce or catsup. *SERVES: 8*

NOTE: This batter also makes a delicious coating for shrimp, scallops or oysters.

After a little more visiting, a card game or some further work on the jigsaw puzzle, it's bedtime for everyone.

Summertime at the lake was — and is — filled with many days similar to the one I've just described. That's part of the appeal of the place. But the Fourth of July has always been an extra special day. It's the kind of holiday that was meant to be spent at a spot like Club Lake.

When Mother was a girl, the Fourth of July meant that Pop hosted a reunion for his World War I company at the lake. They called themselves the "Bottle-Scarred Veterans," and spent the afternoon reminiscing about their days in France. Grandmother kept the big barbecue pit in back of the cabin under siege as she cooked dozens of chickens. She made her own barbecue sauce, which she brushed on the chickens while they cooked. She also simmered wieners in the same sauce, making lots of hot dogs for the kids to enjoy.

Barbecue Sauce for Chicken, Brisket or Wieners

2 tablespoons vegetable oil
1 medium onion, chopped
2 tablespoons vinegar
2 tablespoons brown sugar
¼ cup lemon juice
1 cup catsup
1 heaping teaspoon prepared mustard
1 cup water
½ cup chopped celery
1 teaspoon salt
¼ teaspoon cayenne pepper
3 tablespoons Worcestershire sauce

Heat oil in a medium saucepan and sauté onion until translucent. Add remaining ingredients and simmer for 30 minutes. Use as a barbecue sauce to baste chicken pieces or beef brisket while cooking on a grill or baking in the oven. To make barbecued wieners, place a package of wieners in a deep casserole and pour the sauce over them. Bake, uncovered, at 325° for one hour. Serve on hot dog buns. *MAKES: 3 – 4 cups sauce*

Pop insisted on Peach Ice Cream every Fourth of July. But Grandmother couldn't use just any peaches for her creamy blend. They had to come from Graham's Peach Orchard over on the other side of the lake. Grandmother made the custard the day before and let it get good and cold. Then, about mid-afternoon, Pop called all the kids together and lined them up. Grandmother brought out the freezer and, while Pop and his friends cranked, the kids took turns sitting on a newspaper on top of the ice cream freezer to hold it steady. It was the second coolest place around. (The coolest, of course, was in the water.) When the ice cream was ready to pack and get firm, the scramble was on to see who was lucky enough to get the dasher — the best part of homemade ice cream.

Jack's wife, Joyce, still makes the peach ice cream every year, and the old hand-cranked freezer is pulled out for that occasion. We all have electric freezers now, but somehow tradition prevails on the Fourth of July.

Peach Ice Cream

I recommend that you make the custard the day before you plan to freeze it.

½ gallon milk	2 tablespoons vanilla
6 eggs	8 very ripe peaches, peeled and mashed
½ teaspoon salt	
2 cups sugar	⅓ – ½ cup sugar, (more or less to taste)
2 tablespoons flour or cornstarch	3 – 4 cups half and half

Heat milk in a large heavy-bottomed saucepan until bubbles appear around edge. Remove from heat. In a mixing bowl, beat eggs; add salt, sugar and flour. Add egg mixture to milk and beat until well blended. Return to heat and cook over low heat until mixture coats a wooden spoon. The mixture scorches easily, so stir constantly. Remove from heat and add vanilla. Chill mixture. Just before freezing, prepare peaches, adding sugar to taste. Set aside to let the peaches become syrupy. Fill freezer container half full of chilled custard, adding half and half as necessary. Freeze according to ice cream maker's instructions until mushy. Add peaches and continue freezing until firm. Pack or freeze according to ice cream maker's instructions. *MAKES: 1 gallon*

HINT: Store any leftover ice cream in 8-ounce styrofoam cups, covering each with foil or plastic wrap secured with a rubber band. Homemade ice cream doesn't get as icy this way. Allow to thaw about 10 minutes before eating.

The holiday always ends on a beautiful note. A group of men shoot fireworks from a barge anchored in the middle of the lake to the oohs and ahhs of everyone on shore. Up and down the lake, Roman candles and bottle rockets are shot from every pier, their brilliant flashes reflecting in the water. All the children join in the fun with sparklers, writing their names and drawing pictures in the air with showers of light.

Fishing is a favorite pastime at Club Lake. Everyone has a preferred method — trot lines, rod and reel, or cane pole, to name a few — claiming theirs is the only way to catch the big ones. The same is true about the baits and lures used. Most folks take their fishing quite seriously, but Mother's sister Sarah tells of a Club Lake neighbor who would sit on the end of her pier with a fishing pole in her hand. Whenever she would get a nibble, she would shake her pole to urge the fish to "go away."

Pop was a devoted fisherman. He tried all methods, poles and baits in his quest for the best way to catch fish. He even enlisted the help of Grandmother on occasion. In her recipe box, I came across this recipe, written in Pop's hand, for a type of trotline or pole bait. Across the top was scrawled, "Gertrude, double this, please." Now, I'm no fisherman, so this is the only untested recipe in this book. But Pop swore the fish loved it!

Catfish Bait

1 onion
Water
1 cup flour
1 cup yellow cornmeal
½ cup oatmeal
¼ cup Cheese Whiz
1 teaspoon sugar
Cold water

Boil the onion in a large saucepan filled with water until soft, 15 – 20 minutes. While onion is cooking, mix the remaining ingredients, adding enough cold water to thicken and hold the mixture together. Knead until smooth. Roll the dough into tiny balls about the size of small grapes. Remove the onion from the saucepan of water and drop the dough balls in the water. Boil until balls start to float, then take out and put on a plate to cool and harden. This bait will keep for several days and may be freshened by placing a damp cloth on top of the balls. *MAKES: 5 – 6 dozen small balls*

We have most of our rainy weather in the fall or spring. At that time, the water level in the lake will rise and the excess begins to flow over the spillway. When it does, everyone drops what they are doing and heads to the lake to stand mesmerized at the top of the spillway, looking down on the roaring torrent. The fishermen come out in droves, because fishing is excellent in the creek below the spillway. The moving waters attract fish from the larger lake several miles downstream. Dad especially enjoys fishing in these conditions, since it's nearly impossible not to come back to the cabin with a good "mess of fish." Mother gets her special marinade ready while Dad cleans and fillets the fish. After everyone has had a chance to rest a bit and relive the fish stories, it's time for Dad to put them on the grill.

Sam's Grilled Fish

2 pounds fish fillets (bass, crappie, swordfish, shark, halibut, etc.)
½ cup vegetable oil
½ cup sesame seeds
⅓ cup lemon juice
⅓ cup cognac or brandy
3 tablespoons soy sauce
1 teaspoon salt
1 clove garlic, crushed

Place fish in a single layer in a shallow baking dish. Combine remaining ingredients, pour over fish and let stand for 30 minutes, turning once. Remove fish, reserving sauce for basting. Cook on a barbecue grill about 4 inches from moderately hot coals for 4 – 8 minutes. Baste with remaining sauce. Turn and cook for 4 – 8 minutes longer or until fish flakes easily when tested with a fork and sesame seeds have browned. Serve any remaining sauce with fish. *SERVES: 6*

NOTE: If you have thin fillets or a particularly flaky type of fish, you may find a hinged wire basket designed for cooking on the grill to be helpful.

The grilled fish recipe was prepared many times when I was younger. Mother's brother Hal decided that Mother was just throwing her money away buying little bottles of sesame seeds to make the marinade. One day he appeared at Puddin Hill with a twenty pound sack of sesame seeds he had bought at a processing plant somewhere in East Texas. Mother was dumbfounded, but remembered to thank Hal. She put the sack in the freezer and, over the next few years, served lots of grilled fish and gave away lots of sesame seeds. Of course, these days it's just as easy to go to the fish market and bring home a good catch . . . and a little bottle of sesame seeds.

When we head to the lake for the weekend in the summer, I almost always take along ingredients for homemade ice cream. Of course, the peach ice cream is the sentimental favorite for the Fourth of July, but I have found that my family will let me try other ice cream recipes the rest of the summer months. I keep a small ice cream freezer at the lake that is easy to use and clean, so we don't always bring out the big hand-cranked model. There's just nothing like a dish of homemade ice cream on a hot day.

The chocolate ice cream recipe is a variation of one I begged from one of the most knowledgeable chocolate technicians in the country, Malcolm Campbell of Van Leer Chocolate Company. We were sitting on the deck at the lake eating

Nancy Parker's Grapefruit Sorbet one night, when he told me about his special "secret formula." He had never even shared the recipe with his family! I was intrigued and, after hearing Malcolm confess his pleasure in discovering new ice cream recipes, offered to trade him every one I had for just his one chocolate ice cream recipe. He agreed, but made me promise never to give out his exact formula. To better suit the laid back Club Lake lifestyle, I ended up making a few variations on his original recipe anyway. I can still keep my promise and not give out Malcolm's formula — just a very close, very easy version.

Unbelievable Chocolate Ice Cream

1 11½-ounce package milk chocolate chips
1 6-ounce package semi-sweet chocolate chips
1 12-ounce can evaporated milk
3 cups whole milk

In a large heavy-bottomed saucepan, combine both kinds of chocolate chips with evaporated milk. Heat over low heat, stirring occasionally, until chips are melted and mixture is smooth. Add milk and stir to blend thoroughly. Remove from heat and chill at least 4 hours or overnight, stirring occasionally. Freeze and pack according to ice cream maker directions. *MAKES: 1½ quarts or 8 servings*

Cherry Dream Ice Cream

1 15-ounce can sweetened condensed milk
¼ cup lemon juice
1 21-ounce can cherry pie filling
¾ cup (9-ounce can) crushed pineapple, well drained
½ teaspoon almond extract
2 cups half and half

Combine all ingredients, stirring to blend thoroughly. Chill several hours. Pour into the container of an ice cream freezer and freeze according to manufacturer's directions. *MAKES: 2 quarts*

NOTE: You may also make a still-frozen dessert that does not need an ice cream maker by folding 2 cups of whipped cream into the mixture in place of the half and half. Pour into a 9×13 pan and freeze.

Peppermint Ice Cream

1 pound of peppermint candy
4 cups (1 quart) whole milk
2 cups (1 pint) heavy cream, whipped

Soak candy in milk until candy is dissolved (at least 6 hours). Fold in whipped cream and freeze and pack according to ice cream maker directions. SERVES: 8

Occasionally, we do have a "fancy" meal at Club Lake. This means everyone wears shorts or jeans instead of the usual swimsuit. I find I also tend to spend a bit more time on meals during the winter when the weather forces us inside. We enjoy the lake as much then as we do in the summer. Club Lake becomes an unofficial wildlife refuge from November to March. If we are lucky a pair of bald eagles nests in the trees below the spillway. The lake is filled with pelicans and "water turkeys," a variety of cormorant. Walks in the woods are the order of the day, with a hearty meal planned to satisfy the famished hikers.

One meal I particularly enjoy serving always gets rave reviews from friends. It is a simple idea — a roasted turkey stuffed with tamales. I like to serve a green chili-cheddar cheese appetizer and refreshing congealed salad with the meal. Then for dessert, ice cream flecked with bits of Mexican sugar pralines is offered.

Chili Queso Grande

¼ cup butter or margarine
5 eggs
¼ cup flour
½ teaspoon baking powder
½ teaspoon salt
1 4-ounce can diced green chilies (do not drain)
1 cup cottage cheese
2 cups (8-ounces) grated Cheddar cheese

Preheat oven to 350°. Melt butter and pour into a 13×9×2-inch pan. In a large mixing bowl, beat eggs thoroughly. Add flour, baking powder and salt and beat again until smooth. Stir in chilies (juice and all), cottage cheese and Cheddar cheese. Pour into prepared pan. The butter will float to the top, so gently stir it into the egg mixture. Bake at 350° for 40 – 45 minutes, or until knife inserted near the center comes out clean. Cut into squares and serve at once. For appetizer servings, cut into 1½-inch squares, for brunch servings, cut into 3-inch squares.
MAKES: 18 – 24 appetizers or 12 brunch servings

Margarita Mold

2 envelopes unflavored gelatin
½ cup cold water
2½ cups prepared Margarita mixer
1 6-ounce can frozen lemonade concentrate, thawed
½ cup sliced maraschino cherries
½ medium honeydew melon, cut into ½-inch cubes (about 2 cups)
½ cup sour cream
¼ cup mayonnaise
Additional sour cream and cherry halves for garnish

Soften gelatin in cold water. In a small saucepan, heat Margarita mixer to boiling over medium heat. Remove from heat and add softened gelatin, stirring constantly until dissolved. Stir in lemonade concentrate. Divide mixture in half, and chill 1 portion until partially set. Blend cherries and honeydew into partially set mixture. Turn into a 2-quart flat baking dish. Chill until almost set. Add sour cream and mayonnaise to remaining mixture, which has been left at room temperature, and beat with a wire whisk or electric mixer until no lumps remain. Slowly pour sour cream mixture over congealed fruit layer. Chill several hours. Cut into squares and garnish each serving with a dollop of sour cream and a cherry. SERVES: 10 – 12

NOTE: Cantalope may be substituted if honeydew melon is not available.

Tamale-Stuffed Turkey

1 12-pound (or thereabouts) whole turkey, thawed, if frozen
4 14½-ounce cans tamales in chile gravy
½ cup (1 stick) butter or margarine
½ teaspoon cumin
½ teaspoon chili powder

Preheat the oven to 450°. Remove neck and organs from the turkey cavity. Rinse the outside with lemon juice or water. Remove paper shucks from tamales and save them for later use. Stuff as many of the tamales as possible inside the cavity of the turkey. It doesn't matter if they crumble, just press them down to make a compact stuffing. Tie the legs together or truss to close cavity. Place the turkey on a greased rack in a roasting pan, breast side down. Pour 1 cup of water in the bottom of the roasting pan. Rub the skin of the turkey with some of the papers from the tamales to give a light coating of the chili. Put the turkey in the preheated oven and immediately reduce the temperature to 350°. Meanwhile, melt the butter in a saucepan over low heat and stir in the cumin and chili powder. Baste the turkey with the butter mixture after 20 minutes of baking time, continuing to baste every 20 – 30 minutes with the butter mixture and the pan juices. Add water, ½ cup at a time, to the bottom of the pan as needed to prevent the drippings from burning. Roast the turkey for about 4 hours, allowing 20 minutes per pound. To serve, remove the turkey to a platter; let cool 10 minutes then carve. Meanwhile, drain the drippings remaining in the roasting pan into a saucepan and carefully remove as much of the fat that has accumulated as possible. Simmer gently to keep warm. Serve slices of turkey with some of the tamale stuffing. You will find that it has crumbled during the baking process and has a dressing-like consistency. Pass the pan drippings as a sauce. You may also grill or smoke the turkey over a charcoal fire, if desired. It's delicious either way! *SERVES: 8 – 10*

NOTE: I like to crumble the remaining tamale stuffing and layer it with the leftover turkey slices and the sauce for a reheatable casserole.

Praline Ice Cream

5 Mexican sugar pralines (either purchased or homemade)
2 eggs, separated
1 15-ounce can sweetened condensed milk
2 cups half and half
⅓ cup maple-flavored syrup
½ teaspoon maple flavoring
¼ teaspoon salt
1 – 2 cups milk

(See page 236 for a good sugar praline recipe.) Chop pralines in a blender or food processor to make coarse pieces. Set aside. Combine egg yolks with condensed milk, half and half, syrup, flavoring and salt, blending well. Beat egg whites until stiff. Fold into egg yolk mixture. Pour into freezer container of ice cream freezer. Add milk as needed to fill container. Freeze according to ice cream maker instructions for 10 minutes. Add reserved chopped pralines and continue freezing. *MAKES: 1 quart*

The best part of the day at Club Lake is sunset. Whether in the swimsuits of summer or bundled up because there is a little nip in the air, everyone spends a few minutes on the deck as the last colors in the sky are reflected over the lake. The trees form a dramatic silhouette against the brilliant display. On clear evenings, all the colors of the rainbow can be seen as the sky goes from blazing red in the west to the deepening purple of the night sky on the eastern horizon. The silence is punctuated by the occasional cry of a Great Blue Heron, the deep croak of a bullfrog, or the splash of a jumping fish. In the woods, the tiny pinpoint lights of lightning bugs wink on and off.

I've heard Mother make this statement countless times as we've all sat quietly, taking in the magnificent spectacle, "You know, you can go all over the world, but I don't think there is a sunset to be found anywhere that can beat the ones at Club Lake."

I think she's right.

"He was the hero who saved Christmas dinner!"

Chapter Nine

A Puddin Hill Christmas

Christmas is far and away the busiest time of the year for Mary of Puddin Hill. After all, many Texans and other folks around the country think of fruit cakes as an important part of their holiday meal. Over the past few years we have added chocolates, cakes and other confections in order to offer our customers more year-round items. Even so, it's still the Christmas season everyone associates with Puddin Hill.

We've all learned to live with the long hours and high pressure that come with the holiday rush. It's not uncommon in November and December to find some of our employees spending fifteen to sixteen hours in the building each day. They know it takes those hours to accomplish what must be done to get the orders filled by Christmas. There are days when it doesn't seem possible to take another step or lift another box. But then a Christmas carol plays on the radio and reminds everyone that it's the holiday season.

Most people assume that the folks at Puddin Hill don't enjoy the holiday season — perhaps even hate it. That couldn't be further from the truth. We are in a business where we spend most of the year getting ready to play Santa Claus for thousands of people. Everyone loves to get something in the mail, especially if it's something good to eat. The thought that we are making so many folks happy makes the hard work and long hours well worth it.

In spite of all the tasks to be done, there always seems to be lots of energy left over. In fact, we all probably get more done and feel better during the rush of those months than the rest of the year. Mother likes to compare this behavior to a team of old-fashioned fire horses. They stand around, doing very little most of the day, waiting until they are needed to pull the fire wagon. The minute the fire bell sounds and the pressure to perform is on, they snap to attention and are all business, finding fulfillment as they race through the streets to the fire.

One good way all the working wives and mothers keep up the stamina it takes to get through the busy times is with a collection of easy recipes that can be quickly made when they get home or put together by other family members. The following recipes are tasty and quick. They can be a real help to anyone who has to cope with the extra pressures of the holiday season.

Working Girl's Stew

- 1 envelope dry onion soup mix
- 1 10½-ounce can cream of celery soup
- 1 10½-ounce can cream of mushroom soup
- 1 10½-ounce can cream of chicken soup
- 1 8-ounce can mushrooms, stems and pieces, drained
- 1 cup Burgundy wine
- 1 teaspoon Worcestershire sauce
- 1 teaspoon garlic powder
- 3 pounds stew meat, cut into bite-sized pieces
- 2 cups (1 pint) sour cream

Preheat oven to 300°. Combine all ingredients except meat and sour cream in a 3 quart casserole, stirring until well-blended. Add meat. Cover and bake at 300° for 3 hours. Stir in sour cream just before serving. Serve over noodles or rice. SERVES: 6 – 8

Mary's Quick Soups

- 1 10-ounce can vegetable soup
- 1 12-ounce can chili without beans
- 1 soup can of water

OR

- 1 10-ounce can minestrone soup
- 1 6½-ounce can tuna, drained and flaked
- 1 soup can of water

Choose one of the above combinations, combine in medium saucepan and cook on low heat until heated through. SERVES: 4

The Christmas rush begins building slowly in September, peaks in early December, and drops off sharply the week before Christmas. The energy inside each of us took three or four months to build up, and does not go away overnight. When the rush is over for the year, instead of collapsing, we all keep busy enjoying the holidays at full speed. There is a good feeling inside, knowing that we have survived another season. Everyone relaxes, and we get reacquainted with our families once again.

Of course, those dear family members are a principal motivation for wanting to make Christmas special. It still amazes me that Mother and Dad managed to make sure I never felt that I was playing second fiddle to a bunch of fruit cakes. I have memories of some days each season where I rarely saw my parents for more than a few minutes at breakfast. But when Christmas Day came, we were together again, and somehow, Mother and Dad had managed to squeeze in some time to do some Christmas shopping so there would be presents under the tree. For Mike and me, it is very important to try and follow their example, seeing to it that our two boys still think Christmas is a magical time of the year.

Part of that magic comes from celebrating the season with family and friends. The Horton bunch has always been long on tradition, especially at the holidays. But that dedication to tradition does not mean that an inflexible ritual is followed. Everyone is encouraged to add new features to the celebration, which is exactly what Mike and I did several years ago when we found ourselves with nothing to do on the Saturday before Christmas. Robert, our older son, was a tiny baby and we felt sure that we could not get a baby sitter on short notice during the holidays. The best solution was to invite a few friends over and have an impromptu party. Mike realized that if we couldn't find a baby sitter, neither could our friends. So we told them to bring the children, too. I got all the food for the party from the broken or damaged cookies and chocolates we had around Puddin Hill. About forty people showed up. The surprising thing was how much the children enjoyed themselves. For most, it was the only holiday party where they had been included.

What started out to be a way to pass an evening has become one of the best-loved holiday parties in Greenville. Our little gathering has grown up to be a full-fledged open house with as many as two hundred people attending. We still include the children, who come dressed in their new Christmas outfits. It is fun to see babes in arms become toddlers, then grow into young ladies and gentlemen as the years pass. Young adults home from college drop by, and a proud pair of grandparents brings the newest grandchild to show off.

Each year I hear the same comment, "Pud, I don't see how you manage to have this party, prepare all this wonderful food, and work, too. You must be exhausted!" But I'm not. I have everyone fooled only because I have the party during our busiest period. In fact, it has become fairly easy to plan and host the party year after year.

The menu is always pretty much the same. That's because I've collected a group of recipes that can be made ahead and frozen or refrigerated. A few others I use require minimal preparation the day of the party.

Guests are greeted with a cup of punch. For the adults, there is Strawberry Wine Punch, a traditional German recipe given to me by longtime friend and Puddin Hill staff member, Marie Heidmann. It is served on any festive occasion in my family, from weddings to the first day of spring. The children are offered apple cider.

Two tables offer food for everyone to enjoy. The larger table is filled with a variety of appetizers, dips and other finger foods. Several selections are chosen with the children's tastes in mind. The second table, set up in another room, holds an assortment of cookies and desserts. I have found that serving food in two locations makes the guests move around and visit with each other a little more. I also place bowls of holiday candies and roasted nuts around the house.

Menu for Christmas Open House

Strawberry Wine Punch
Apple Cider

Main Table
Spicy Party Treats
Provolone Cheese in Pastry Crust
Mushroom Cheese Spread
Grab Bag Dip
Onion Balls
Hot Shrimp Dip
Hocus Pecos Dip*
Sam Lauderdale's Original Chili Dip*

Platter of Assorted Cold Meats
Sliced Deli Turkey or Smoked Turkey, Nancy Parker's Ham*, Sliced Deli Roast Beef
Mayonnaise, Mustard, Coarse Grain Mustard
Basket of Assorted Breads and Rolls

Swiss and Cheddar Cheese Cubes
Assorted Crackers and Chips for Dips and Spreads

Dessert Table
Puddin Hill Fruit Cake with Whipped Cream
Mary's Brownies*
Marzipan
Chocolate Dessert Spread*
Southern Chocolate Delights*
Texas Big Mouth Cookies*
Assorted Truffles*

*see index for recipe

Strawberry Wine Punch

- 2 16-ounce packages whole frozen strawberries — unsweetened
- 4 liters Rhine wine, or other white wine, chilled
- 1-1½ cups sugar (use more if you like a sweeter punch)
- 2 cups brandy
- 1 2-liter bottle of club soda, chilled

Place strawberries in a large container or bowl. Pour enough of the wine over them to completely cover. Add the sugar and brandy and stir until sugar is dissolved. Allow the strawberries to soak in this mixture for about 4 hours. At serving time, pour the strawberry mixture into a large punch bowl and add remaining wine. Stir, then add club soda to taste — at least half the bottle; more if you wish to make the punch go farther.

This makes about two gallons of punch — enough to serve about 24 people. For a really special occasion, you may substitute champagne for the wine (5 bottles will give you about the same amount of punch).

Spicy Party Treats

- 1 12-ounce package frankfurters
- ¾ cup prepared mustard
- 1 10-ounce jar apple jelly
- 2 tablespoons jalapeño or hot-pepper jelly

Cut each frank into thirds; set aside. Combine mustard and jellies in a large saucepan and heat over low heat, stirring occasionally, until jellies have melted. Add franks and simmer slowly over low heat for 1½ – 2 hours, stirring occasionally. Serve hot, using toothpicks or cocktail forks.
SERVES: 8 – 12

Pud's Provolone Cheese in Pastry Crust

1 package refrigerated crescent rolls
2 1-inch slices Provolone cheese (about 12 ounces each)
1 egg, beaten

Preheat oven to 375°. Open the package of crescent rolls and break in half along the perforated line. Press one half into a ball and knead until smooth. Roll out on a floured surface into a 10-inch circle. Place one slice of Provolone in center of circle and bring dough up around cheese. Press together on top of cheese, making a decorative pattern, if desired. Place on an ungreased baking sheet, and brush top with beaten egg. Repeat with remaining dough and cheese. Bake at 375° for about 20 minutes, or until pastries are browned. When pastries are done, immediately remove each from baking sheet onto 10-inch squares of aluminum foil. Cup the foil around each pastry to prevent the cheese from oozing out. Refrigerate until cooled. (If a pastry breaks open and some of the cheese runs out, don't worry! Simply cut the oozed cheese off with a spatula when you've finished baking it, then wrap the pastry in foil.) Before serving, allow pastries to come to room temperature. Don't serve hot or the cheese will melt. Serve on a cutting board allowing your guests to cut thin slices of the pastry. These freeze beautifully! *SERVES: 12*

Mushroom Cheese Spread

2 8-ounce packages cream cheese, softened
2 cups (8 ounces) grated Cheddar cheese
1 4-ounce can mushrooms, drained and chopped fine
2 tablespoons diced pimento
¼ cup finely chopped onion
2 tablespoons chopped parsley
1 clove garlic, minced
1½ teaspoons Dijon mustard
¼ teaspoon salt

Beat cream cheese until smooth, then add Cheddar cheese and beat until well blended. Stir in remaining ingredients, blending well. Chill mixture until firm enough to handle, then form into one large or two smaller balls. Wrap in plastic wrap and chill several hours. Serve with stoned wheat crackers, Melba toasts or bagel crisps. *MAKES: 1 large or two small cheese balls, serving 18-24*

Grab Bag Dip

2 cups mayonnaise
¼ – ½ cup prepared horseradish
1 teaspoon dry mustard
2 teaspoons fresh lemon juice
½ teaspoon salt

Combine all ingredients and mix thoroughly, adding horseradish to taste. This dip may be served hot or cold. Gently stir in any of the suggested ingredients and serve according to the instructions listed below:

FOR COLD DIP —
Choose at least 5 of the following:
1 4-ounce can button mushrooms, drained
2 cups cherry tomatoes, washed, stemmed and left whole
½ cup whole baby corn, drained
1 cup cooked shrimp
1 cup broccoli flowerettes
½ cup whole pitted black olives, drained
½ cup water chestnuts, drained
1 cup cooked scallops
1 cup Swiss cheese, cut into ¾ inch cubes

Combine dip with selected ingredients and stir until everything is thoroughly coated. Chill several hours or overnight. Serve with cocktail forks, allowing guests to spear treats of their choice.

FOR HOT DIP —
Choose at least 5 of the following:
1 4-ounce can button mushrooms, drained
½ cup whole baby corn, drained
½ cup pickled onions, drained
1 cup cooked shrimp
1 cup cooked meatballs
½ cup whole pitted black olives, drained
1 cup fully cooked smoked sausage, cut in ½ inch slices
1 cup cooked scallops
1 5-ounce package cocktail wieners or sausages

Combine dip with selected ingredients and stir until everything is thoroughly coated. Heat in a heavy-bottomed saucepan over low heat until sauce and ingredients are hot. Serve in a chafing dish with cocktail forks, allowing guests to spear treats of their choice. *SERVES: 12 — either hot or cold*

Onion Balls

1 8-ounce package cream cheese, softened
2 tablespoons chopped parsley
3 tablespoons grated onion
2 jars dried beef

Mash cream cheese, parsley and onion together with a fork until blended. Chill 30 minutes. Place dried beef in a blender or food processor and mince very finely. Form cheese mixture into balls about 1 inch in diameter and roll in dried beef. Chill. *MAKES: 2 dozen*

Hot Shrimp Dip

2 8-ounce packages cream cheese
1 medium onion, chopped
1 medium fresh tomato, peeled and chopped
1 – 2 teaspoons garlic salt (or to taste)
1 4-ounce can chopped green chilies
2 – 3 Torrido peppers, finely minced
2 4¼-ounce cans small shrimp, drained

Melt cream cheese in the top of double boiler set over hot water. Add ingredients in the order listed and heat thoroughly. Serve warm with tortilla or corn chips. May be made a day ahead, omitting the shrimp until ready to serve. *MAKES: 3 cups dip*

NOTE: Torrido peppers are available in the Mexican food or pickle section of supermarkets in the southwest. If you can't find them, you can substitute one or two pickled jalapeño peppers or simply omit them.

Puddin Hill Fruit Cake With Whipped Cream

1 cup whipping cream
2 tablespoons powdered sugar
2 tablespoons brandy, rum or cognac
About 1½ pounds Puddin Hill Fruit Cake, cut into 1-inch cubes

Whip cream, gradually adding powdered sugar and beating until soft peaks form. Stir in liquor, blending thoroughly. Serve in a bowl in the center of a serving tray. Surround with fruit cake squares. Provide picks for guests to spear a piece of cake, then dunk into the whipped cream mixture. *SERVES: 20*

HINT: The best way to cut fruit cake into squares is to freeze it first, then slice 1-inch thick slices. Cut each slice into cubes.

Marzipan

2 3.3-ounce rolls almond paste
2 tablespoons light corn syrup
½ cup marshmallow cream
½ teaspoon almond extract
2½ cups powdered sugar
Food colorings

Combine all ingredients, blending and kneading to form a smooth dough. (You may use a food processor, but you might have to work the last bit of powdered sugar in with your hands.) Divide the dough into small batches and add food coloring as desired. Traditionally, marzipan is formed into small pieces shaped like fruits and vegetables. To give texture and interest, roll the oranges, lemons and strawberries over a small grater. Stick a whole clove in the end of fruits for a stem. Paint a pale green pear with a touch of red food coloring diluted in water to give it a realistic blush. Roll potatoes in cocoa to give them the characteristic texture. With imagination and practice, it's easy to create a beautiful tray of marzipan masterpieces. Store any dough not being worked in a plastic bag to keep it pliable. *MAKES: 4 – 5 dozen candies*

At the end of the evening, after devouring platters of food, everyone leaves our home with hugs, smiles and cries of "Merry Christmas!" I know they are also quite full — full of the holiday spirit and literally stuffed with good food!

The next day, Christmas Eve, is reserved for a family celebration. Mother's brothers and sister and any of their children who are home for the holidays gather at Mother's house for supper. For many years, Mother has made a very special seafood stew for Christmas Eve supper. Knowing that everyone had lots to eat the night before at my house and, in anticipation of the big dinner on Christmas Day, she serves the stew with Sam's Salad (see page 90) and hot rolls. Coffee and a plate of cookies and sweets (often leftovers from our party) are passed around at the end of the meal.

Seafood Stew

2 pounds raw shrimp, peeled and deveined
1 pound scallops
1 pound flaked crabmeat
1 cup white wine
2 cups milk
2½ cups soft bread crumbs
½ cup (1 stick) butter or margarine
5 white onions, finely chopped
2 teaspoons paprika
3 cups cream
3 teaspoons salt
1 teaspoon white pepper
Dash orange bitters

Combine the shrimp, scallops, crabmeat and wine in a saucepan. Bring to boil and cook over low heat for about 10 minutes, stirring every 2 – 3 minutes. Strain, reserving the stock. Combine milk and bread crumbs and set aside to soak. Finely chop the shrimp and scallops. In a large saucepan, melt butter over low heat and sauté onions and paprika for about 15 minutes, stirring frequently. Squeeze the excess milk from the crumbs and discard milk. Add the bread crumbs and reserved stock to the onions mixing well. Add chopped shrimp, chopped scallops, crabmeat, cream, salt and white pepper. Cook over low heat for about 15 minutes. Add a couple of dashes of orange bitters, and serve. SERVES: 12

When Mike and I married, we included his parents in our family celebration, and discovered a whole new Christmas Eve menu. In South Texas, where Mike grew up, a Mexican-style supper of tamales or an enchilada casserole is served in both Hispanic and Anglo homes. The meal ends with a selection of Mexican cookies and candies. One Christmas, Mike's mother, Jo, offered to prepare their traditional supper for everyone. It was such a hit with all the Horton bunch that we now alternate menus. One year we have Seafood Stew, the next we have a South Texas Christmas Eve meal.

South Texas Christmas Eve Supper
Frozen Margaritas for a Crowd
Feliz Navidad Casserole
Jo's Mexican Salad
Pan de Polvo
Besas
Mexican Pralines

*see index for recipe

Feliz Navidad Casserole

12 corn tortillas
1½ pounds ground beef
1 medium onion, chopped
1 4-ounce can chopped green chilies, drained
1 10-ounce can cream of chicken soup
1 10-ounce can cream of mushroom soup
1 10-ounce can red enchilada sauce (mild or hot)
¼ teaspoon salt
⅛ teaspoon pepper
2 cups (8 ounces) Cheddar cheese or Monterey Jack cheese, grated

Preheat oven to 350°. Wrap tortillas in foil and soften in oven (or place between two plates and soften for 30 seconds in microwave). Brown meat and onion in a large skillet or saucepan over medium heat; drain off fat. Add remaining ingredients except cheese and simmer 10 minutes. Pour ⅓ of the sauce into a buttered 13×9-inch baking dish and top with 6 corn tortillas. Repeat layers, then pour the remaining sauce on top. Sprinkle grated cheese evenly over the top. Bake for 20 minutes at 350° until mixture is bubbly and cheese has melted. SERVES: 8

Jo's Mexican Salad

6 cups iceberg lettuce, washed and torn into bite-sized pieces
1 16-ounce can ranch-style beans, drained
2 medium tomatoes, chopped
1/2 cup chopped onion
1 cup (4 ounces) grated Cheddar cheese
2 avocados, peeled and diced
2 cups regular size Fritos
1 – 2 cups bottled Catalina-style dressing

Combine all ingredients in a large salad bowl, tossing gently to coat with dressing. Serve at once. SERVES: 8 – 12

Pan De Polvo

½ cup boiling water
2 teaspoons anise seed
2 cinnamon sticks

3 cups flour
⅓ cup sugar
1 cup shortening

SUGAR TOPPING:
2 cinnamon sticks
¼ cup powdered sugar

½ cup granulated sugar

Pour boiling water over anise seed and cinnamon sticks; let steep 10 minutes to make a strong tea, then strain. Preheat oven to 300°. In a large mixing bowl or the work bowl of a food processor, combine flour and sugar. Work in shortening and mix well. Add about ¼ cup of the anise tea to the flour mixture to make a very stiff dough — be prepared to use your hands to mix it if you are not using a food processor. Add remaining tea — a tablespoon at a time — if necessary. Roll dough to about ¼ inch thickness between two sheets of waxed paper. Remove waxed paper and cut into desired shapes with small cookie cutters. Bake at 300° for 15 – 20 minutes — cookies will not brown. While cookies are baking, prepare sugar topping by pulverizing the cinnamon sticks in the blender (Do Not use a food processor — it won't work) until ground to a powder. Combine with the sugars. Roll the hot cookies in the sugar topping and set aside to cool. *MAKES: 6 dozen small cookies*

Besas

2 ounces unsweetened chocolate
½ cup powdered sugar
1½ teaspoons cinnamon
2 egg whites
¼ teaspoon cream of tartar
¼ cup sugar

Preheat oven to 200°. Line two cookie sheets with aluminum foil; set aside. Break chocolate into chunks. Place chocolate, powdered sugar and cinnamon in the work bowl of a food processor and grind to a fine powder. In a mixing bowl, beat egg whites and cream of tartar with an electric mixer until frothy. Gradually add sugar, beating until stiff peaks form. Fold in chocolate mixture. Drop by rounded teaspoons onto prepared pans. Bake at 200° for 2 hours. Let cool, then remove from foil. *MAKES: 2 – 3 dozen.*

Mexican Pralines

2 cups granulated sugar
1 cup brown sugar, firmly packed
3 tablespoons light corn syrup
1¼ cups evaporated milk or light cream
Pinch salt
1 teaspoon vanilla
3½ cups pecan halves or large pieces

Combine sugars, corn syrup, milk and salt in a saucepan. Bring to a boil and cook over medium high heat until mixture reaches 236° on a candy thermometer (soft ball stage). Remove from heat and add vanilla. Stir in pecans. Immediately drop by spoonfuls onto waxed paper and allow to cool and harden. *MAKES: 3 dozen 2-inch pralines*

Every five years a family reunion is held at Christmas. Everyone plans to be in Greenville for the holidays. In order to satisfy those who have a preference for one menu or the other, Mother and Jo combine both traditions and prepare Seafood Stew and Feliz Navidad Casserole. It's a happy combination of cultures.

Before going home or to late-night church services, a holiday toast of eggnog is offered.

Kentucky Eggnog

6 eggs, separated
2 cups sugar
½ teaspoon vanilla
2 cups bourbon

1 cup rum
1 cup milk
3 cups heavy cream
1 cup cognac

Beat egg yolks until frothy. Add sugar and vanilla, and beat again. Stir in bourbon, rum, milk, cream and cognac. Beat egg whites until stiff and fold into nog mixture. Do not cut milk or cream portions without a corresponding cut in liquor. *SERVES: 8-10*

No matter what time we go to bed on Christmas eve, the excitement of Christmas morning gets everyone up early. (Having young children means no alarm clocks have to be set.) After the presents have been opened, we enjoy a festive breakfast. Because I've prepared the French toast "doctored up" with Grand Marnier the night before, cooking is easy and quick. Fresh fruit completes a meal designed to leave plenty of room for the big feast to come.

Holiday French Toast

1 loaf French bread, cut in 1-inch slices
4 eggs
1 cup milk
¼ cup Grand Marnier
1 teaspoon finely grated orange peel
3 tablespoons sugar
½ teaspoon vanilla
¼ teaspoon salt
4 tablespoons butter or margarine
Powdered sugar
Sweetened sliced strawberries (optional)

Arrange bread slices in single layer in a 13×9×2-inch baking dish. Beat eggs with milk, add Grand Marnier, orange peel, sugar, vanilla and salt. Blend well and pour over bread, turning slices to coat both sides. Cover and refrigerate overnight. Heat butter in a large skillet over medium heat and sauté bread slices until golden brown — 3-4 minutes per side. Sprinkle with powdered sugar. Serve with sweetened sliced strawberries, if desired. *SERVES:* 4

I think most family Christmas dinners are steeped in tradition and the one my family shares is no exception. The menu for the meal has been evolving since Mother was a girl, as has the routine for the afternoon. Everyone gathers for a glass of Dad's eggnog while gifts are exchanged. Dad always makes his simple recipe both "mit" and "mitout" the bourbon. That way, even the youngest child can join the festivities. Then, while the kids are showing off their surprises from Santa, last-minute preparations for the meal are carried out in the kitchen. Each cook in the family has responsibility for a certain dish. Sarah has responsibility for the turkey and dressing, and says it is very important that her directions be followed to the letter.

Whenever possible, everyone is seated at one long table. There are usually several "extras" at the table — relatives of "outlaws" or friends who cannot be with their own families for the holidays. I make chocolate place cards for everyone (see page 181), which serve as table decorations, too.

MENU FOR CHRISTMAS DINNER
Sam's Eggnog

Roast Turkey with Cornbread Dressing
Epicurean Peas
Cranberry Relish
Sweet 'Tata Pone
Grandmother's Parkerhouse Rolls*

Osgood Pie
Fresh Coconut Pie
Harvest Pie*

*see index for recipe

After dinner, Pop used to entertain the kids with the tale of his most memorable Christmas, which happened when he was a boy living on Puddin Hill. One of his grandmother's sisters, Aunt Irene, had come for Christmas dinner, and everyone was very glad to see her. Pop said that she offered to help in the kitchen, and someone sent her out to the porch to fetch water from the cistern. When she leaned over to get the bucket, her false teeth fell to the bottom! It was a real crisis, because Aunt Irene had no way to eat Christmas dinner. Pop's grandfather came to the rescue with some clever thinking. He got a very long stick, stuck it down into the well until it touched the bottom, pulled the stick up and took a reading on the depth. After some discussion with the other men assembled, it was decided that young Hal (Pop) could be lowered into the cistern and still have his head above water. They tied a rope under his armpits and lowered him down into the water. Pop says he felt around with his toes until he found Aunt Irene's teeth, then he went under and picked them up. He was the hero who saved Christmas dinner! We always cheered when he finished.

Sam's Eggnog

½ gallon good quality vanilla ice cream
3 – 4 cups milk
1 – 2 cups bourbon (optional)
Nutmeg

Remove ice cream from freezer and allow to soften. Empty into large bowl and add milk and bourbon. Blend thoroughly with electric mixer. Pour into punch bowl and sprinkle with nutmeg. *SERVES: 12-15*

Roast Turkey

1 10 – 12 pound turkey, thawed if frozen	2 – 3 tablespoons shortening

Preheat oven to 450°. Remove neck, giblets and other parts from turkey cavity. Rinse or wipe turkey to clean, then rub outside skin generously with shortening. Place turkey on a rack in a large roasting pan, breast side down. Pour 2 cups water in the bottom of the roasting pan. Place turkey in oven and immediately reduce heat to 350°. Bake until turkey is done (180° on a meat thermometer or when leg moves easily when wiggled.) Allow 15 – 20 minutes per pound. After the first hour, baste turkey every 10 – 15 minutes with pan drippings. Add more water, if necessary, to the bottom of the roasting pan to keep drippings from burning. When turkey is done, remove from oven and let stand about 10 minutes before carving. Make gravy out of pan drippings and giblets, if desired. *SERVES: 12*

GIBLET GRAVY:

Giblets, liver and neck from turkey	¼ cup flour or cornstarch
2 cups pan drippings from turkey	¼ cup cold water
	3 hard cooked eggs, chopped
1 cup milk or half and half	Salt
	Pepper

While turkey is roasting, boil giblets, liver and neck in enough water to cover until tender, about 15 minutes. Drain, reserving broth, and chop giblets and liver coarsely; set aside. Pour drippings from roasting pan into a measuring cup, skimming off as much fat as possible. Add broth from giblets, if necessary, to measure 2 cups. Pour into saucepan and add milk. Heat over medium heat. Stir flour into water until smooth. Stir dissolved flour into drippings, and simmer until thickened. Add eggs, chopped liver and giblets; salt and pepper to taste. *MAKES: 3 cups*

Sarah's Cornbread Dressing

3 cups Stella's Cornbread Mix (see Page 77)
3 eggs
1½ cups milk
6 tablespoons butter or margarine, melted
10 slices stale white bread, torn into small pieces
2 onions, finely chopped
2 8-ounce cans oysters and liquid
1½ cups chopped pecans
2 cups finely chopped celery
1 teaspoon crushed rosemary
2 teaspoons poultry seasoning
2 teaspoons salt
½ teaspoon pepper
2 cups chicken broth
6 eggs

Prepare cornbread mix and bake according to directions in recipe, using first 4 ingredients. Bake in a greased 13×9-inch pan. Let cool, then crumble. Combine with remaining ingredients in a large bowl. Mix with hands, THEN remember to remove your rings (be sure to check for missing stones). More chicken broth may be needed to moisten the mixture. Spoon mixture into two buttered 13×9-inch baking dishes. Bake at 350° 35 – 40 minutes, until browned and crusty. May be made ahead and refrigerated before baking. Add 5 minutes to the baking time.
SERVES: 12 – 15

Epicurean Peas

4 strips bacon, cut in ½-inch wide strips crosswise
1 tablespoon minced onion
1 tablespoon flour
2 tablespoons butter or margarine
1 17-ounce can English peas, do not drain
1 4-ounce can sliced mushrooms, drained
1 cup half and half
½ teaspoon salt
¼ teaspoon pepper

Fry bacon until crisp. Remove from drippings, drain and reserve. Pour off all but about 1 tablespoon of the drippings and sauté onion until translucent. Sprinkle flour over the onions; stir to blend. Add butter, peas with liquid and mushrooms. Simmer until thickened — about 10 minutes. Add half and half, salt and pepper. Simmer until heated through. Stir in reserved bacon and serve.
SERVES: 6

Cranberry Relish

1 pound fresh cranberries
2 small seedless oranges
1 cup crushed pineapple with juice
1 cup sugar
1 cup chopped pecans
¾ cup finely chopped celery

Chop cranberries and whole oranges in a food processor or blender. Transfer to a bowl and add pineapple and sugar, stirring until sugar is dissolved. Chill. Add pecans and celery just before serving. Good relish with turkey or pork roast. *SERVES: 12*

Sweet 'Tata Pone

4 cups raw, peeled grated sweet potatoes (about 3 large)
1½ cups molasses
3 eggs, beaten well
½ cup milk
2 tablespoons butter or margarine, melted
2 teaspoons ginger (or 1 teaspoon grated orange rind)
2 tablespoons brown sugar
1 teaspoon cinnamon
1 cup pecans

Preheat oven to 350°. Grease a 2-quart flat baking dish; set aside. Put the grated sweet potatoes in a large mixing bowl. Add molasses, eggs, milk, melted butter, ginger (or orange rind) to the grated potatoes, blending well after each addition. Turn into prepared baking dish. Bake 25 minutes at 350°. Combine brown sugar, cinnamon and pecans. Sprinkle over potatoes and bake 20 minutes more. Serve at once. *SERVES: 8 – 12*

Osgood Pie

½ cup (1 stick) butter or margarine
1 cup sugar
1 teaspoon cinnamon
1 teaspoon allspice
2 eggs, separated
1 tablespoon vinegar
1 cup chopped pecans
1 cup dates
1 9-inch unbaked pie crust (deep-dish type if using a commercial crust)

Preheat oven to 325°. Cream butter and sugar until light. Add spices and stir until blended. Add egg yolks, beating well, then add vinegar, pecans and dates. In a separate bowl, beat egg whites until stiff, then fold into pecan-date mixture. Pour into unbaked pie crust and bake at 325° for 40 – 45 minutes. Cool. *SERVES: 8*

Fresh Coconut Pie

4 tablespoons flour
¾ cup sugar
pinch of salt
1½ cups milk
3 eggs, separated
1 tablespoon butter
1½ teaspoons vanilla

1 cup grated fresh coconut (or 1 6-ounce package frozen fresh coconut, thawed)
1 9-inch baked pie shell (deep-dish type if using a commercial crust)
1 cup heavy cream
¼ cup powdered sugar

Combine flour, sugar and salt in the top of a double boiler. Add milk, stirring until smooth. Set mixture over hot water and cook until warm. Beat egg yolks lightly, then stir about ¼ cup of the milk into the egg yolks to warm them; then add warmed yolks to cooked mixture. Cook, stirring constantly, until thickened and smooth. Remove from heat and add butter and vanilla, stirring until butter is melted. Beat egg whites until stiff and fold into custard. Add ½ cup of the coconut. Pour into baked pie crust. Let cool, then chill. At serving time, whip the cream with the powdered sugar until soft peaks form. Spread over pie. Sprinkle with remaining ½ cup coconut. *SERVES: 8*

Quick Pie Crust

6 tablespoons butter or margarine, melted
2 tablespoons powdered sugar

1 cup flour

Preheat oven to 400°. Put all ingredients in bowl and mix thoroughly with a pastry blender. Press out into a 9-inch pie pan in an even layer, crimping edges. Prick evenly with a fork and bake at 400° for 10 minutes, or until browned. This pastry is particularly good with refrigerated or custard-based pies where the crust is cooked first. However, it will work as an unbaked pie crust. *MAKES: 1 9-inch pie crust*

After eating far too much of all that good food, everyone staggers home for a nap or to play the newest game that Santa brought.

In the evening, Mother and Dad visit their friends, Bobbie and Forest Lake, to exchange their traditional gifts. Bobbie always makes a container of her pimiento cheese to give Mother and Dad. In turn, Mother makes liver pâté for Bobbie and Forest. They've been giving each other the same gifts for as long as I can remember. Mother swears no one makes pimiento cheese quite like Bobbie, and Bobbie says something similar about Mother's pâté.

Old-Fashioned Pimiento Cheese

4 cups (1 pound) American grated cheese
1 4-ounce jar diced pimientos, drained
2 tablespoons sugar
¾ cup mayonnaise

Combine all ingredients in a large mixing bowl. Mix with electric mixer or by hand until well blended. Store in a covered container. This will keep several weeks in the refrigerator. Spread on bread, crackers or celery stalks. *MAKES: about 3 cups*

NOTE: For a different taste, blend in 2 tablespoons sweet pickle relish or more to taste.

Mary's Liver Pâté

1 pound chicken livers
1 cup (2 sticks) butter or margarine
1 medium onion, chopped
¼ teaspoon nutmeg
¼ teaspoon ground cloves
¼ teaspoon salt
¼ teaspoon pepper
2 tablespoons dry sherry or vermouth
generous dash of Tabasco
¼ cup prepared mustard
¼ cup mayonnaise

Preheat oven to 350°. Put chicken livers and butter in a baking dish. Bake at 350°. for 40-45 minutes, or until liver is cooked through. Let cool. Put liver, butter and onion in the work bowl of a food processor and process until smooth. Add remaining ingredients except mustard and mayonnaise and process again. Line a 6-cup mold or mixing bowl with plastic wrap, and carefully pour in liver mixture. Cover and chill several hours until firm. To serve, unmold onto a serving plate. Combine mustard and mayonnaise in a small bowl, then spread over pâté. Serve with crackers or melba rounds. *SERVES: 6-8*

The highlight of the evening — perhaps the whole day — is dessert at Bobbie's house. There's no supper . . . no one wants to fill up before Bobbie brings out her holiday masterpiece. Everyone gets a big bowl and helps himself to a slice of fresh coconut cake. Over that goes a spoonful of ambrosia, made with oranges, cherries and more fresh coconut. Finally, creamy boiled custard is poured over the cake and ambrosia. As Dad says, "We founder ourselves on Bobbie's dessert every Christmas." We do, but it's a sweet conclusion to a happy day.

Fresh Coconut Cake

1 box white cake mix
3 eggs
⅓ cup vegetable oil
1¼ cups water
1 envelope Dream Whip topping mix
1 cup cream of coconut

2 16-ounce cans Betty Crocker Creamy Deluxe Sour Cream White Frosting
2 cups fresh grated coconut (or frozen fresh coconut, thawed)

Preheat oven to 350°. Grease and flour 2 8-inch cake pans; set aside. Combine cake mix, eggs, oil and water and beat until moistened. Sprinkle topping mix over batter and blend in. Beat until well-blended and smooth. Pour into prepared pans and bake at 350° for 30 – 35 minutes, or until tester inserted in the center comes out clean. Cool cakes in pans 10 minutes, then turn out onto a rack to cool. When cool, drizzle each layer with ½ cup cream of coconut. Place first layer on serving plate and spread top with frosting. Sprinkle with about ½ cup coconut. Top with remaining layer. Frost top and sides with remaining frosting. Top with remaining coconut. *SERVES: 12 – 16*

Ambrosia

8 oranges
1 cup maraschino cherries, without stems

1 cup fresh coconut (or 1 6-ounce package frozen fresh coconut, thawed)
1 tablespoon rum

Peel and section oranges, remove membranes around each section and remove any seeds. Drain cherries and cut each in half. Combine orange sections, cherries and coconut. Sprinkle rum over the top. Chill thoroughly. Serve as a fruit salad or as a topping for coconut cake. *SERVES: 8*

Old-Fashioned Boiled Custard

4 cups milk
6 egg yolks
Pinch salt
½ cup sugar
1 teaspoon vanilla or ¼ cup sherry

Heat milk in the top of double boiler set over hot water until bubbles form around the edges. Beat egg yolks slightly and stir in salt and sugar. Pour about one cup of the hot milk over egg yolks, mixing thoroughly. Add to milk in double boiler and cook, stirring constantly, until the custard coats the back of a spoon. Remove from heat and add vanilla or sherry. Chill. *MAKES: 1 quart*

NOTE: This recipe also makes a very good French vanilla-type ice cream. When custard is thoroughly chilled, freeze in ice cream maker according to manufacturer's directions.

The rest of the holidays are given over to resting and cleaning up the final details of the holiday business at Puddin Hill. But when New Year's comes, then it's time to celebrate again. Throughout the southern states, there is a tradition that one brings in the New Year by eating black-eyed peas. There are two schools of thought about the proper time to consume the peas. Some say they must be eaten at the stroke of midnight for any good luck to come. Others insist that it doesn't matter when, just so everyone has a few spoonfuls before January First is over. We belong to the second bunch, and have made it a tradition to enjoy our black-eyed peas in a wonderful cornbread and sausage casserole while watching the bowl games. It's a delicious brunch dish, on New Year's Day or any other day of the year. The good luck came in finding such a good recipe.

Black-eyed Pea Cornbread

- 1 pound bulk pork sausage
- 1 onion, chopped
- 1 cup white cornmeal
- ½ cup flour
- 1 teaspoon salt
- ½ teaspoon baking soda
- 2 eggs, slightly beaten
- 1 cup buttermilk
- ½ cup vegetable oil
- 1 4-ounce can chopped green chilies, drained
- ¾ cup cream-style corn
- 2 cups (8 ounces) grated Cheddar cheese
- 1 15-ounce can black-eyed peas, drained

Preheat oven to 350°. Grease a 13×9×2-inch pan. Cook sausage and onion in a large skillet until sausage is browned. Drain and set aside. Combine cornmeal, flour, salt and soda in a large bowl. In another bowl, beat eggs, buttermilk and oil together. Combine with dry ingredients using a few quick strokes — batter does not need to be blended until smooth. Add sausage and onion, chilies, corn, cheese and black-eyed peas. Pour into prepared pan and bake at 350° for 50 – 55 minutes, or until knife inserted in center comes out clean. *SERVES: 8-12*

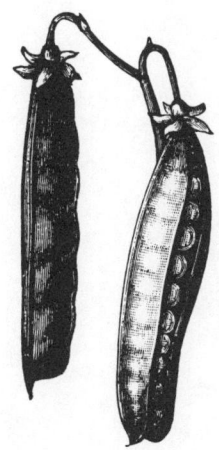

"Pop decided on a different approach."

Chapter Ten

When Company Comes

Entertaining special guests was a particular delight of Grandmother's. She and Pop loved for company to come over, and a day seldom passed when someone wasn't invited to drop by for a visit. The company of good friends or family meant a time of lively conversation, frequently punctuated by one of Pop's witty observances or wry comments. Grandmother had always said that each of her daughters should look first at a man's sense of humor before looking at the contents of his wallet. She maintained that a sense of humor would go lots further in getting through the rough times in life than any amount of money would. And Grandmother set a good example for her daughters and granddaughters to follow. Pop was known as one of the best wits in the area. His friends loved to see what he was going to come up with next in the way of a clever comment or practical joke.

Those quips and stunts have punctuated the family stories I have grown up hearing. The best example of Pop's legendary sense of fun I remember hearing concerns the Hunt County Liars' Contest held every fall for many years. Pop came up with wild tales for two or three years. I'm told the stories went on and on, with lots of exaggerated details, and filled the room with hearty laughter. In each case, no one could top Pop's tall tale, so he was declared the winner. However, after a couple of years of these stories, Pop decided to take a different approach. He got up before the group very quietly, with a "hangdog" sort of look and told the assembled group of fellow liars, "I have never in my entire life ever lied to my dear wife Gertrude, nor have I ever tried to deceive her." Well, there were too many close friends in the audience who knew Pop better. They decided his statement was probably the greatest lie ever told in Hunt County. I understand they immediately closed the contest, declaring Pop the winner. And I'm told that the judges created a Liars' Hall of Fame with Pop the first to be inducted.

But, no matter what he said to the judges, Pop really adored Grandmother, and never tried to pull anything over on her. Of course, he probably knew that she was smart enough to see right through any lies he might try to tell her.

Grandmother had a reputation as one of the most amusing and interesting ladies in Greenville. The parade of visitors through her house ranged from anxious families whose crippled children Grandmother was trying to assist, to the heights of national leadership with Mr. Rayburn and his friends. All found they were made to feel right at home. She could converse on almost any subject, and had that gift for making the person she was talking with feel as if he or she was the only person who mattered at that moment. She wasn't afraid to tackle difficult issues or dispense motherly advice. Grandmother and Pop genuinely loved people and gladly welcomed everyone into their home.

Grandmother felt that anytime company showed up, she ought to be able to offer something to eat. To her, good hospitality meant more than being polite to guests. It also meant being prepared with at least a little something in the pantry to serve to anyone who happened by. Although it might consist of nothing more than a loaf of her delicious apricot bread or a pound cake ready to slice and spread with rose petal butter, something was always ready. She was a wonderful cook, taking real pleasure in serving whatever she had prepared. Grandmother read lots of cookbooks and cooking magazines, keeping up with all the new ideas and trends in food. She loved to try new recipes, and used her guests as well as her family as "tasters." Grandmother also had a gift (Mother says it was a carefully nurtured talent) for making even the simplest food seem like fare fit for royalty. Every dish offered had some particular touch which made it special. Even pizza from the local take-out appeared elegant or extra-special when Grandmother served the beverages in her good crystal glasses. I can remember Mother asking Grandmother why she didn't just use paper cups or at least the everyday glasses. Grandmother replied, "When company comes, it's always a special occasion. Besides, if I don't use and enjoy these pretty things, you and the rest of the family will never appreciate them."

That philosophy has probably done more to influence my own style of entertaining than any etiquette book ever could. When company comes, it IS special. To think enough of someone to want to invite them to come and visit is very important. But it doesn't mean spending hours agonizing over every little detail in an attempt to achieve perfection. Grandmother and Mother have both said that company really doesn't notice whether or not the lamp shades have been dusted or that the last of the Christmas decorations are still tucked under the chair in the corner — and it's April. Most folks are thrilled to be invited anywhere and are busier worrying about themselves than what the house looks like.

But building confidence to entertain easily takes time and practice. Each time another successful meal or party is behind you, it gets a little easier to do the next one. With that in mind, this chapter is written with the idea of sharing some of the more successful menus my family has served over the years. You will find a variety of menus for different occasions. I have tried to blend some of the family classics and some newer recipes into these meals, to show how they can be used together. Of course, it is important to remember that a suggested menu is just that — suggested. It doesn't mean you are locked into only those dishes listed. Each menu should reflect your own personality, taking into account your lifestyle, budget, cooking ability and personal preferences in food. Above all, it should ultimately mean that you can enjoy yourself along with your company.

The first menu shared was one of Grandmother's favorites. She often served an easy chicken and crab casserole flecked with avocado chunks that never failed to receive praise from her guests. The casserole was usually accompanied with a potato dish that was made ahead and allowed to bake for several hours. The freezer supplied wonderful Parkerhouse rolls and a delicious chocolate dessert. The special touch Grandmother added to this meal was in the charming salad she often served. Pear halves, stuffed with a delicious cream cheese and ginger snap mixture, were decorated with food coloring and a leaf garnish to look like real pears. Easy to make, (my two sons often help me make them) they have always been a delight for all ages. All the dishes in this menu were tried-and-true favorites of Grandmother's — and are still popular with Mother and with me.

Grandmother's Favorite Company Supper
(Serves 6-8)
Chicken Crabmeat Rosemary
Big City Scalloped Potatoes
Ginger Pear Salad
Grandmother's Parkerhouse Rolls*
Mosaic Cake

*see index for recipe

Chicken Crabmeat Rosemary

- 2 medium avocados, peeled and diced
- 1 tablespoon lemon juice
- ½ cup (1 stick) butter or margarine
- 2 tablespoons chopped onion
- ½ cup flour
- 1 tablespoon fresh rosemary, chopped (or 1 teaspoon dried rosemary)
- ½ teaspoon salt
- 1 teaspoon paprika
- 2 cups chicken broth
- 2 cups sour cream
- 3 cups cooked, diced chicken
- 2 6-ounce cans crabmeat, drained
- 1 cup soft bread crumbs
- 2 tablespoons butter or margarine, melted

Preheat oven to 350°. Grease a 2-quart flat baking dish. Combine avocados and lemon juice in a small bowl; toss gently and set aside. In a large saucepan, melt butter or margarine over medium heat. Add onion and cook until translucent, about 2 minutes. Stir in flour and cook 2 minutes, stirring constantly. Add seasonings and chicken broth. Reduce heat and simmer until thickened, about 5 minutes. Remove from heat and add sour cream, chicken, crabmeat and reserved avocado. Pour into a prepared dish. Toss bread crumbs and melted butter together and sprinkle over the top. Bake at 350° for 30 minutes until bubbly.
SERVES: 6-8

Big City Scalloped Potatoes

- ½ clove garlic, minced
- 4 medium baking potatoes, peeled and thinly sliced (if small, add one more)
- 2 cups heavy cream
- 3 eggs
- 1 teaspoon salt
- ½ teaspoon pepper
- ¼ teaspoon nutmeg

Preheat oven to 225°. Butter the bottom of an 8-inch square baking pan. Sprinkle with garlic. Layer potatoes in pan evenly and press down firmly. Pan should be about half full. In a small bowl, beat cream and eggs together until smooth. Add salt, pepper and nutmeg. Pour mixture over potatoes, filling pan about ¾ full. Cover with foil and bake at 225° for 3 hours. Remove foil, increase heat to 325°, and bake for another 15 minutes, or until the top is golden brown. Cut into squares and serve hot.
SERVES: 8–12

Mosaic Cake

- 1 envelope unflavored gelatin
- ¼ cup cold water
- 4 ounces unsweetened chocolate
- ½ cup sugar
- ⅛ teaspoon salt
- ¼ cup hot water
- 4 eggs, separated
- ¼ cup amaretto, cream de cacao or white creme de menthe
- ½ cup heavy cream, whipped
- 1 angel food cake cut in ½-inch slices, then in large cubes
- 1 cup pecan pieces, or slivered almonds

Soften gelatin in cold water for 5 minutes. Melt chocolate in the top of a double boiler over hot water. Add sugar, salt and hot water, stirring until sugar is dissolved and mixture blended. Remove from boiling water and add one egg yolk at a time, beating thoroughly after each is added. Stir in gelatin, and replace over boiling water. Cook 2 minutes, stirring constantly. Add liqueur; cool. Beat egg whites until stiff and fold into cooled mixture. Whip heavy cream until soft peaks form and fold into mixture. Line a 13×9×2-inch pan with foil to facilitate serving. Spread half the angel food cake cubes over the foil, packing cubes together closely. Spread half the chocolate mixture over the cake, smoothing to cover evenly. Sprinkle with ½ cup of the nuts. Repeat layers with remaining cake cubes, chocolate mixture and nuts. Cover and freeze or refrigerate for at least 6 hours. (We prefer it frozen.) Fifteen minutes before serving, remove from freezer. Cut into squares and serve. This is an easy dessert to keep on hand in the freezer any time. *SERVES: 12 – 16*

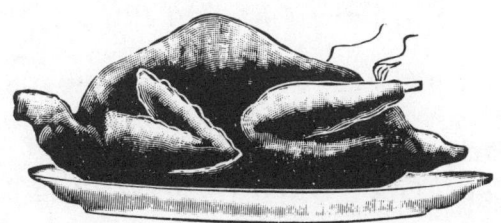

Ginger Pear Salad

½ cup gingersnap crumbs
1 tablespoon heavy cream
1 8-ounce package cream cheese, softened
½ teaspoon ginger
1 teaspoon molasses
2 28-ounce cans pear halves, drained
Red food coloring
Lettuce leaves, cloves and small leaves for garnish

Crush gingersnaps by placing between two sheets of waxed paper and rolling with a rolling pin, or by using a blender or food processor. Combine with cream, cream cheese, ginger and molasses, mixing well. Fill the cavity of each pear half with cheese mixture. Place 2 halves together. Combine a drop or two of red food coloring with water. Brush over large end of pear to give it a blush similar to a fresh, unpeeled pear. Place a lettuce leaf on each serving plate and carefully set pear on lettuce. Stick a leaf in stem end of pear and a clove in the blossom end, if desired, for garnish. SERVES: 6 – 8

The next menu is a casual supper that has a few dishes guaranteed to intrigue any guest. It begins with a tasty appetizer that can be prepared ahead and put in to bake just before the guests arrive. The beef brisket, really quite a simple recipe, tastes as if it had taken hours to make. I have added a rice dish and a green salad with a zesty bacon-horseradish dressing. But the real conversation-grabber of the meal is the baked radish casserole. Everyone will be amazed at how mild the radishes taste, and how truly good they can be when baked. It instantly elevates a simple meal to gourmet status. (If you aren't ready to try baked radishes, then try the Broccoli Pudding or Summer's Bounty Casserole in its place — see the index for the recipes.) The meal ends with Grandmother's Sad Cake, topped with whipped cream or ice cream.

Casual Supper
Serves 8
Southwest Chicken Puffs

Fool 'Em All Beef Brisket
Rice Oregano
Radishes con Queso au Gratin*
Mixed Salad Greens with Bacon-Horseradish Dressing

Sad Cake
*see index for recipe

Southwest Chicken Puffs

1½ cups cooked, finely chopped chicken
⅓ cup toasted, finely chopped almonds
1 cup chicken broth
½ cup vegetable oil
1 tablespoon seasoned salt
⅛ teaspoon celery seed
2 tablespoons chopped fresh parsley
2 teaspoons Worcestershire sauce
¼ teaspoon Tabasco sauce
½ teaspoon cumin
4 cups flour
4 eggs

Mix chicken and almonds together; set aside. In a medium saucepan, combine broth, oil and seasonings and bring to a boil. Reduce heat and add flour, beating rapidly until mixture leaves the sides of the pan and forms a smooth ball. Remove from heat and add eggs one at a time, beating after each addition until mixture is shiny. Stir in chicken and almonds. (Mixture can be refrigerated until needed at this point.) Drop about 2 tablespoons mixture onto a greased baking sheet, spacing about 2 inches apart. Bake at 400° for 15 minutes, or until browned. Serve hot.
MAKES: 3 dozen

HINT: These are great to keep in the freezer for unexpected company. Freeze unbaked puffs on a cookie sheet, then remove from sheet and store in plastic bags until ready to bake. Increase baking time about 5 – 8 minutes for frozen puffs.

Fool 'Em All Beef Brisket

Prepare this the day before you plan to serve it.

4 – 6 pound beef brisket
1 tablespoon garlic salt
1 teaspoon freshly ground pepper
1 green pepper, chopped
1 onion, chopped
1 teaspoon celery salt
5 – 6 whole black peppercorns
1 cup catsup
1 cup water

Preheat oven to 300°. Place brisket in an oblong foil-lined pan, allowing plenty of foil to fold over and seal tightly. Sprinkle brisket on both sides with garlic salt and pepper. In a medium mixing bowl, combine remaining ingredients and pour over meat. Fold foil over and seal. Bake at 300° for 2 – 2½ hours, or until desired degree of doneness is reached. Cool and refrigerate overnight. Slice beef while cold. At serving time, reheat brisket in some of the sauce at 300° for 20 – 25 minutes. Heat remaining sauce in a saucepan and serve as gravy. Makes great sandwiches!
SERVES: 8 – 12 with leftovers

Rice Oregano

2 tablespoons butter or margarine
½ cup sliced fresh mushrooms (or chopped onions)
2 cups raw rice
½ cup (1 stick) butter or margarine, melted
2 cups beef broth
¼ teaspoon oregano

Preheat oven to 375°. Melt butter in a small skillet over medium heat and sauté mushrooms or onions in butter until soft; set aside. Stir rice and remaining butter together. Add broth, oregano, mushrooms or onions. Bake in a 2-quart covered casserole at 375° for 30 – 35 minutes, or until liquid is absorbed and rice is tender. Serve as a side dish with a roast, steaks, or broiled or grilled chicken. SERVES: 8

Bacon-Horseradish Salad Dressing

1 cup mayonnaise
6 slices bacon, cooked crisp and crumbled
¼ cup milk
2 tablespoons prepared horseradish
⅛ teaspoon pepper

Combine all ingredients and stir until well blended. Cover and chill several hours to allow flavors to blend. Serve as a dressing over mixed greens or fresh spinach and mushroom salad. MAKES: 1½ cups

Sad Cake

1½ cups flour
1½ teaspoons baking powder
½ teaspoon salt
2¼ cups brown sugar
4 eggs
1 teaspoon vanilla
1½ cups chopped nuts
Whipped cream for garnish

Preheat oven to 300°. Grease and flour an 11×7-inch pan. Sift flour with baking powder and salt; set aside. Place brown sugar in a large mixing bowl, add eggs one at a time beating well after each addition. Add flour mixture gradually, beating to form a smooth batter. Add vanilla and nuts. Pour into prepared pan. Bake at 300° for 35 – 40 minutes. Let cool in pan. (Cake will fall as it cools.) Cut into squares, and top each serving with a dollop of whipped cream. SERVES: 8

NOTE: To make a chocolate sad cake, reduce flour to 1¼ cups and add ¼ cup cocoa. Continue as instructed above.

Grandmother had a bridge group that got together every week for cards and lunch. I suspect they spent as much time catching up on news and gossip as they did playing bridge. They all loved to cook, and discussing good recipes was probably a major topic of conversation around both the bridge and lunch tables. I know that the bridge club was one of Grandmother's major sources of new recipes, because when I went through her recipe boxes after her death, many of them were jotted down on the backs of bridge tally sheets.

Make-Ahead Luncheon for the Bridge Club
Serves 12
Crabmeat Casserole
Stuffed Tomatoes Rockefeller
Fresh Fruit with Poppy Seed Dressing*
Lemon-On-A-Cloud

*see index for recipe

Crabmeat Casserole

3 6-ounce cans crab meat, drained, reserving liquid
3 4-ounce cans mushrooms, drained, reserving liquid
1 – 1½ cups milk
9 tablespoons butter or margarine
9 tablespoons flour
3 tablespoons dry sherry
3 tablespoons lemon juice
3 hard cooked eggs, chopped
1 2-ounce jar diced pimientos, drained
¾ cup slivered, blanched almonds
½ teaspoon pepper
1½ teaspoons crumbled tarragon
2 tablespoons chopped chives
¾ cup grated Parmesan cheese
8 cups cooked rice or 12 puff pastry shells

Preheat oven to 350°. Grease a 13×9-inch baking dish. Combine reserved liquids in measuring cup, adding enough of the milk to make 3 cups liquid; set aside. Melt butter in a large saucepan over medium heat. Add flour and cook 2 minutes, stirring constantly. Gradually add reserved liquids. Reduce heat and simmer, stirring occasionally, until thickened. Add remaining ingredients — except cheese — stirring well. Pour into prepared dish. Sprinkle with Parmesan cheese and bake at 350° for 25 – 30 minutes until bubbly and golden brown. Serve over rice or in pastry shells. *SERVES: 12*

NOTE: This recipe easily reduces by ⅓ to serve fewer people.

Stuffed Tomatoes Rockefeller

2 10-ounce packages frozen chopped spinach, thawed
1 package chicken-flavor stuffing mix
1¾ cups water
¼ cup butter or margarine
6 eggs
¼ cup finely minced shallots
½ cup grated Parmesan cheese
½ teaspoon garlic salt
½ teaspoon thyme
¼ teaspoon cayenne pepper
1 teaspoon black pepper
¾ cup butter or margarine, melted
12 large tomatoes

Squeeze excess moisture from spinach; set aside. Prepare stuffing mix according to package directions, using water and ¼ cup butter. Beat eggs in a large mixing bowl. Add spinach, stuffing and remaining ingredients, except tomatoes. Stir to blend. Preheat oven to 350°. Butter a 13×9-inch baking dish. Prepare tomatoes by cutting a slice off the top of each tomato and, with a spoon, scraping out the seeds and pulp. Turn upside down to drain out excess liquid. Carefully spoon spinach mixture into each tomato shell, mounding slightly on top. Place in prepared baking dish, sides touching, and bake uncovered at 350° for 20 minutes. Serve immediately. This can be prepared ahead, covered and refrigerated until baking. Add 5 minutes to baking time. *SERVES: 12*

NOTE: I also scoop the spinach mixture out in about ⅓ cup portions, placing them on a greased baking sheet. Bake as directed above. This makes a great buffet dish, especially when topped with cheese sauce. (My sons love these, and call them "spinach volcanoes," making the volcanoes "erupt" by pouring a simple cheese sauce — like melted Cheese Whiz or Velveeta — on top.)

The spinach mixture can also be made into balls about 1 inch in diameter, then baked and served as a hot appetizer.

Lemon-On-A-Cloud

2 cups crushed vanilla or lemon wafers
1 3-ounce package lemon gelatin
1½ cups boiling water
Juice of 3 lemons
Grated rind of 2 lemons
1 teaspoon lemon extract
1 12-ounce can evaporated milk, chilled
½ cup sugar
1 cup heavy cream, whipped
Candied violets or cherries for garnish, if desired

(Be sure evaporated milk is very cold.) Spread an even layer of crushed cookies in the bottom of a 13×9×2-inch dish. Set aside. Combine gelatin and boiling water; stir until gelatin is dissolved. Add lemon juice, rind, and extract. Chill until gelatin is the consistency of egg whites. Whip gelatin with an electric mixer until pale yellow in color. In a separate bowl, whip chilled evaporated milk, gradually adding sugar, until soft peaks form. Fold into gelatin mixture, blending thoroughly. Pour into crumb-lined pan and chill several hours. Garnish each serving with whipped cream and a candied violet or cherry.
SERVES: 12 – 16

Picnics, tailgate meals, or backyard suppers can be events calling for more than hot dogs or fried chicken. I enjoy serving chicken breasts stuffed with a mixture of vegetables and ricotta cheese, a cold beet salad and crunchy bread sticks. And, of course, every picnic needs deviled eggs. My recipe was created after I overheard a conversation two women had about the best deviled eggs they had ever eaten. One said that the best she had tried were made with just a bit of sweetened condensed milk. I was intrigued, but she got away before I could ask her about the recipe. I went home and began experimenting. And, although I'll never know whether or not I'm close to the discussed recipe, my "Devilish Eggs" are always the first thing to disappear.

Picnic or Backyard Supper
Serves 8
Ricotta-Stuffed Chicken Breasts
Devilish Eggs
Marinated Brussels Sprouts*
Pickled Beets
Gone-in-a-Minute Breadsticks*
Grapes with Ginger Creme
Bob's Cookie Jar Gingersnaps*

*see index for recipe

Ricotta-Stuffed Chicken Breasts

- 1½ cups ricotta cheese
- 3 cups finely chopped fresh spinach leaves
- ½ cup finely chopped broccoli
- ½ teaspoon salt
- ¼ teaspoon pepper
- ¼ teaspoon thyme
- ¼ teaspoon tarragon
- 8 chicken breast halves, boned, but with the skin left on
- ¼ cup butter or margarine, melted

Preheat oven to 350°. In a large bowl, combine the ricotta, chopped spinach, chopped broccoli, salt, pepper, thyme and tarragon. (You may use a food processor.) Using a sharp knife, slit the skin of the chicken on one side and, with fingers, lift the skin from the center to form a pocket, leaving three sides still attached. Stuff each breast with about ¼ cup of the ricotta mixture. Fold the sides of the breast underneath (to form a compact pouch). Place the chicken breasts in a shallow baking dish and brush each with melted butter. Bake at 350° for about 45 minutes, or until the top is golden and the stuffing starts to ooze out. Serve hot, or chill and serve as a delightful picnic dish. *SERVES: 8*

Devilish Eggs

- 12 hard cooked eggs, peeled
- ¼ cup mayonnaise
- 2 tablespoons sweetened condensed milk
- 2 teaspoons dry mustard
- ½ teaspoon salt
- 3 – 4 dashes onion juice
- 2 dashes Tabasco
- ⅛ teaspoon white pepper

Cut each egg in half and remove yolk. Set whites aside. Combine yolks with remaining ingredients in a mixing bowl and blend until smooth. Spoon or pipe mixture into egg whites. Cover and chill. *MAKES: 2 dozen*

Pickled Beets

½ cup sugar
¼ cup vinegar
¼ teaspoon cloves
¼ teaspoon allspice
¼ teaspoon cinnamon
⅓ cup thawed orange juice concentrate, undiluted

2 16-ounce cans pickled beets, drained
1 orange, peeled and thinly sliced

Combine sugar, vinegar, spices and orange juice in a small saucepan over medium heat and bring to a boil. Reduce heat and simmer 2 minutes. Pour over beets and sliced orange. Cover and chill several hours or overnight. Serve cold as a side dish with ham, chicken or picnic fare.
SERVES: 8

Grapes With Ginger Creme

4 cups seedless grapes
½ cup brandy
½ cup Cointreau
2 cups sour cream
1 cup heavy cream

¼ cup powdered sugar
1 teaspoon finely minced crystallized ginger
¼ cup brown sugar

Pick grapes off stems and wash and drain well. Place in a shallow dish and pour brandy and Cointreau over them. Marinate at least 2 hours in the refrigerator. At serving time, blend sour cream, heavy cream and powdered sugar together in a mixing bowl. Beat with an electric mixer until light; it will get some volume but will not have the consistency of whipped cream. Stir in ginger, then add grapes and marinade, blending thoroughly. Spoon into serving bowl or dessert glasses. Sprinkle with brown sugar.
SERVES: 8

Company doesn't have to mean a mob of people to be worth the effort of cooking something special. Often having one or two friends over for a nice meal can be just as satisfying as throwing a big party. And the menu can reflect those pleasures by being a bit more special. I have developed three menus for the more intimate times. Each will easily double if you've invited more guests.

The first menu is designed for a real celebration, the kind where, as Pop used to say, you "put the big pot in the little pot and go all out." It's a sumptuous menu beginning with a creamy cheese spread made from Camembert cheese. The dinner proceeds with chicken breasts cooked in a delicate champagne sauce, accented with a wonderful carrot dish and fresh, sautéed asparagus. Add hot bread or rolls and a salad of romaine lettuce topped with a creamy dressing of blue cheese and pureed vegetables. Finish off the evening with a special dessert. I've suggested two — a light sorbet or a sinfully rich cheesecake. Hang up the diet when you serve this meal — but don't wait for a special occasion to enjoy any of the dishes. Each is outstanding by itself!

Celebration Supper
Serves 4
Camembert Cheese Ball with Assorted Crackers
Chicken Breasts in Champagne Sauce
Elegant Carrot Loaf
Sautéed Asparagus with Hollandaise Sauce (optional)
Blue-Green Salad Dressing over Romaine Lettuce
Bread or Rolls
Pear-Mint Sorbet*
OR
Chocolate Amaretto Cheesecake*

*see index for recipe

Camembert Cheese Ball

8 ounces Camembert or Brie cheese
½ - 1 cup dry white wine
¼ cup unsalted butter, softened
½ cup toasted almonds, ground fine

It is best to start this the day before you plan to serve it. Cut all the rind off the cheese, being careful not to cut away too much of the cheese with it. Put cheese in a small bowl and cover with wine. Refrigerate for at least 12 hours. Remove cheese from wine, pat it dry, then beat until smooth. Add the softened butter, beating again until butter is incorporated. Scoop mixture out onto a piece of plastic wrap, and form into a flattened ball (use plastic wrap to help you, because mixture will be very soft.) Chill at least 4 hours. At serving time, remove plastic wrap from cheese and gently roll in ground almonds. Serve with unsalted crackers (like a table water cracker) or wheatmeal crackers. *SERVES: 4-6*

Chicken Breasts In Champagne Sauce

4 chicken breasts, skinned and boned
6 tablespoons butter or margarine
1 tablespoon oil
1 cup champagne
1 teaspoon lemon juice
2 tablespoons heavy cream
½ teaspoon salt
¼ teaspoon pepper
¼ cup chopped parsley
3-4 cups cooked rice

Pound chicken breasts to ¼-inch thickness between sheets of waxed paper or plastic wrap, using a flat-surface pounder or mallet. Melt the butter and oil together in a large skillet over medium heat. Add the chicken breasts and brown on both sides. Cook uncovered for 10 – 15 minutes or until no longer pink inside. Remove chicken to a platter and keep warm. Add the champagne and lemon juice to the drippings in the pan. Bring to a boil and cook until mixture is reduced by half. Remove from heat and add cream; reheat sauce but do not bring to a boil. Add salt and pepper and correct seasoning, if necessary. Pour sauce over chicken breasts and sprinkle with parsley. Serve with rice. (For this dish, I like to cook my rice with chicken broth instead of water.) *SERVES: 4*

Elegant Carrot Loaf

2 pounds carrots, peeled and very thinly sliced
¼ cup butter or margarine
½ teaspoon salt
¼ teaspoon white pepper
6 eggs
2 tablespoons orange juice

Place sliced carrots in a medium saucepan with enough water to cover. Add butter, salt and pepper and bring to a boil. Cook, stirring frequently, until tender, 8 – 10 minutes. Drain, reserving liquid, and set carrots aside. Return liquid to saucepan and simmer over medium heat until liquid is reduced to ½ cup; cool. Preheat oven to 450°. In a large mixing bowl, beat eggs, and orange juice until well-blended. Stir in cooled carrot liquid, then add carrots. Pour mixture into a well-buttered 8-inch square pan. Cover pan with aluminum foil. Place pan in a larger pan with a rim. Carefully pour boiling water into the larger pan to a depth of 1 – 2 inches. Bake at 450° for 45-50 minutes, or until knife inserted in center comes out clean. Remove from water bath and cut into 8 portions. Serve warm, or at room temperature. *SERVES: 8*

Sautéed Asparagus

1 pound asparagus
¼ cup butter or margarine
½ teaspoon seasoned salt
¼ teaspoon pepper

Wash asparagus. To remove woody part of stem, hold each stalk with both hands and bend stalk at the lower end until it breaks; discard woody stems, set tender tops aside. Melt butter in a large skillet over medium heat. Sauté asparagus, rolling stalks gently back and forth, for about 5 minutes, until bright green and tender. Add seasoned salt and pepper, rolling stalks again to coat with seasoning. Remove asparagus to a serving plate. Top with Blender Hollandaise Sauce, if desired, and serve. *SERVES: 4*

Blender Hollandaise Sauce

3 egg yolks
¼ teaspoon salt
Pinch cayenne pepper
2 tablespoons lemon juice
½ cup butter or margarine, melted (kept warm)

Rinse blender or food processor container with hot water to warm; drain thoroughly. Put egg yolks, salt, cayenne and lemon juice in container and blend at medium speed to combine. Open top and with blender running, slowly pour in the melted butter. Blend 30 seconds until sauce is thickened and is a pale lemony yellow color. If you must hold Hollandaise Sauce, it may be kept warm in a thermos. (Before adding sauce, fill thermos with hot water, pour out and dry.)

NOTE: Any remaining sauce may be refrigerated. It will thicken to a nice, mayonnaise-like consistency. Use as a cold spread for ham.

Blue-Green Salad Dressing

½ cup sour cream
¼ cup mayonnaise
2 teaspoons fresh lemon juice
⅛ teaspoon dried tarragon, crumbled
⅛ teaspoon dried dill weed
½ teaspoon salt
1 clove garlic, minced
1 tablespoon minced green onion
⅓ cup finely chopped, fresh spinach
⅓ cup chopped parsley
½ cup crumbled blue cheese

In a small mixing bowl, blend sour cream, mayonnaise, lemon juice, herbs, salt, garlic and onion. Fold in spinach and parsley and crumbled blue cheese. Cover and chill to allow flavors to blend. This salad dressing may be served over any combination of greens and salad vegetables.
MAKES: 1½ cups

NOTE: To make in a food processor or blender, place spinach, parsley, green onion and garlic in processor or blender. Process until finely chopped. Add remaining ingredients and pulse until just blended. Do not over process or you will loose the cheese chunks.

The second menu for four gets everyone in the kitchen while dinner is cooking. There's something comfortable about folks standing around the kitchen, having a good visit while savoring the smells and cheering on the cook. However, if you have a small kitchen or are intimidated by everyone watching you as you work, everything but the sautéed vegetables can be made ahead and kept warm. The vegetables, by the way are wonderful to make in the late summer or early fall, when squash and bell peppers are at their peak. If you can get the red bell peppers, they add both flavor and color to this dish.

Casual Late Summer or Fall Supper
Serves 4
Rum Sausages*
Veal Paprika
Pud's Vegetable Sauté
Sliced Tomatoes with Blue Cheese Vinaigrette
Sawdust Pie

*see index for recipe

Veal Paprika

- 1 pound veal scalloppine (chicken breasts may be substituted)
- ¼ cup flour
- ½ teaspoon salt
- 1 tablespoon butter or margarine
- 2 tablespoons olive oil
- ¼ cup brandy
- 1 tablespoon paprika
- ½ teaspoon freshly ground black pepper
- 1 tablespoon chopped chives
- ½ cup chicken broth
- 1 cup heavy cream
- 1 8-ounce package spinach or egg noodles
- 2 tablespoons butter or margarine
- ¼ cup grated Parmesan cheese

Pound veal to about ¼-inch thickness (if using chicken breasts, skin and bone them, then pound to ¼-inch thickness). Combine flour and salt in a shallow dish and dredge veal pieces, shaking off extra flour. In a large skillet over medium heat, melt butter and olive oil together. Sauté veal 2 – 3 minutes on each side until browned. Remove and keep warm. Add the brandy, paprika and pepper to the drippings in the skillet and simmer until the brandy has evaporated. Add the chives and chicken broth and simmer until reduced by half. Add the cream and simmer again until reduced by half. Cook noodles in boiling water until tender, then drain and toss with remaining butter and Parmesan cheese. Put noodles in a shallow serving dish, place veal slices on top and pour the sauce over all. This may be kept warm, covered, in a 300° oven for up to one hour. *SERVES: 4*

Pud's Vegetable Sauté

- 2 yellow squash
- 2 medium zucchini
- 1 green pepper
- 1 red bell pepper, in season
- 2 tablespoons butter or margarine
- 2 tablespoons olive oil
- 3 green onions and tops, chopped
- ¼ cup grated Parmesan cheese
- ¼ cup sour cream

Cut yellow squash and zucchini into sticks or chunks about ½ × 2 inches. Cut green and red peppers into thin strips. Heat butter and olive oil in a 10-inch skillet over medium heat until butter is melted. Add squash, zucchini, peppers and onions and cook, stirring frequently, until vegetables are tender — about 8 minutes. Remove from heat. Add Parmesan cheese and sour cream, stirring until vegetables are coated. Serve at once. *SERVES: 4-6*

Blue Cheese Vinaigrette

¼ cup white wine vinegar
  or lemon juice
¾ cup vegetable oil
2 cloves garlic, minced
½ teaspoon dry mustard
¼ teaspoon pepper

1 teaspoon salt
3 tablespoons crumbled
  blue cheese
1 tablespoon chopped,
  fresh parsley

Combine all ingredients except blue cheese and parsley in a small mixing bowl and beat with a wire whip until smooth. Stir in blue cheese and parsley. Chill until serving time. Serve over sliced tomatoes or mixed salad greens and finely chopped crunchy vegetables (carrots, green pepper, radishes, celery, etc.) *MAKES: 1 cup*

HINT: According to Madalene Hill, fresh parsley counteracts the strong garlic aftertaste in salad dressings. Use an equal amount of parsley and garlic.

Sawdust Pie

1 9-inch pie crust (deep-
  dish type if using a
  commercial crust)
6 egg whites
1 cup sugar
1 cup coconut

1 cup graham cracker
  crumbs
1 cup pecans
1 cup miniature chocolate
  chips

Preheat oven to 400°. With a fork, prick the sides and bottom of pie crust several times then bake at 400° for 5 minutes. Remove from oven and let cool. Reduce oven heat to 350°. In a large mixing bowl, beat egg whites until frothy, then add sugar slowly and continue beating until egg whites are stiff. Fold in remaining ingredients. Turn into prepared pie crust and bake at 350° for 30 – 35 minutes until lightly browned and set. Cool. *SERVES: 8*

One of Mother's favorite menus is also perfect for sharing with just one or two close friends. She does most of her entertaining at Club Lake, where everyone can sit on the deck and watch the sunset. Mother serves the cheese puffs as an appetizer at that time. Meanwhile, everything else is in the oven, ready to be served when the last rays of the sun have left the sky. The stuffed fish is surprisingly easy to make. It needs nothing more than a dish of baked carrots and a salad. The meal is finished with Mother's cinnamon ice cream served over hot Apple Crumb Betty. No one ever guesses that she started with commercial vanilla ice cream.

Sunset Supper
Serves 4
Cheese Puffs*
Stuffed Sole in Vermouth
Cognac Carrots
Sam's Salad*
Cinnamon Ice Cream
Apple Crumb Betty*

*see index for recipe

Stuffed Sole in Vermouth

¼ cup butter or margarine
1 pound mushrooms, finely chopped
1 clove garlic, minced
¼ cup chopped parsley
½ teaspoon salt
½ teaspoon pepper
4 large sole or flounder fillets (about 8 ounces each)
1 cup soft bread crumbs
½ cup grated Gruyere cheese (or another soft cheese)
¼ cup butter or margarine, melted
About ½ cup dry vermouth

Melt butter in a large skillet over medium heat. Add mushrooms and garlic and cook, stirring frequently, until most of the liquid has evaporated, about 6 – 8 minutes. Remove from heat and stir in chopped parsley, salt and pepper. Preheat oven to 400°. Lightly butter a 13×9-inch baking dish. Cut each fillet in half, crosswise. Place 4 pieces of sole in the bottom of the prepared dish and spoon one-fourth of the mushroom mixture onto each piece. Top with the remaining pieces of fish. Combine bread crumbs and grated cheese and spread over the fish. Drizzle with melted butter. Carefully pour the vermouth down the sides of the dish so that it surrounds the fish; do not pour the vermouth over the fish. Bake at 400° for 20-25 minutes, or until the topping is golden brown and the fish flakes easily when pierced with a fork. Serve at once. *SERVES: 4*

Cognac Carrots

1 pound carrots, peeled and thinly sliced
½ cup (1 stick) butter or margarine, melted
1 tablespoon sugar
2 tablespoons cognac
½ teaspoon salt
¼ cup finely chopped pecans

Preheat oven to 350°. Place sliced carrots in a 2-quart flat baking dish. Combine melted butter, sugar, cognac and salt. Pour over carrots. Cover and bake at 350° for 45 minutes, or until tender but not browned. Sprinkle with chopped pecans. *SERVES: 4*

Cinnamon Ice Cream

½ gallon good quality vanilla ice cream
¼ cup cinnamon

Allow ice cream to stand at room temperature until it has softened. Turn into a large mixing bowl and add cinnamon. Beat with an electric mixer until smooth. Return ice cream to freezer and let stand several hours, or until firm. Serve over hot apple or peach pie or cobbler, or top with chocolate sauce. *SERVES: 8*

Company often means overnight guests. This is especially true over holidays, when a leisurely breakfast can be enjoyed. Mother and Dad love to cook a special breakfast on those occasions. Of course, by the time they get around to even starting it, it could be called brunch! It's a hearty meal, combining the old-fashioned tastes of scrambled eggs and sausage scrapple with the newer tastes of cantaloupe marinated in liqueur and popovers with maple butter.

Mary's Breakfast (or Brunch)
Serves 6 – 8
Sunny Cantaloupe
Sausage Scrapple with Maple Syrup
Scrambled Eggs
Pecan Popovers with Maple Butter

Sunny Cantaloupe

2 medium cantaloupes, peeled and cut in 1" cubes
½ cup orange juice
¼ cup Galliano or Amaretto

Combine all ingredients and chill several hours or overnight. Spoon into bowls or stemmed goblets. Garnish each serving with fresh mint, if desired. SERVES: 6-8

Sausage Scrapple

2½ cups chicken broth, divided
1 cup yellow cornmeal
1 pound bulk pork sausage
1 teaspoon poultry seasoning
¼ teaspoon salt
¼ teaspoon pepper
⅛ teaspoon cayenne
Melted butter or margarine

Place 8½ × 4½ × 2¾-inch loaf pan in refrigerator to chill. In medium bowl, blend 1 cup broth with the cornmeal; set aside. Cook sausage till crumbly and brown. Add the remaining broth and bring to a boil. Slowly stir in cornmeal mixture and seasonings. Reduce heat, cover and simmer about 15 minutes, stirring occasionally until thickened. Spoon into chilled loaf pan. Return to refrigerator and chill for at least 2 hours, or until firm. Slice ½-inch thick and fry in melted butter until brown and crispy on both sides. Serve at breakfast, either plain with eggs on the side or with maple syrup. SERVES: 6-8

NOTE: This can be made the night before, then sliced and fried the next morning.

Pecan Popovers With Maple Butter

POPOVERS:

1 cup flour
¼ cup finely chopped pecans
1 tablespoon butter or margarine, melted
2 eggs
1 cup milk
½ teaspoon salt
1 tablespoon maple syrup

Preheat oven to 450°. Grease and flour a 12-cup muffin tin or popover pan. Put all ingredients in the container of a blender or food processor and blend until smooth. Pour into prepared tin, filling each cup no more than half full. Bake 15 minutes at 450°, then reduce heat to 350° and bake another 25 – 30 minutes, or until popovers are browned. Serve at once with Maple Butter. *MAKES: 1 dozen*

MAPLE BUTTER:

6 tablespoons butter or margarine, softened
6 tablespoons maple or maple-flavored syrup

Combine butter and syrup in a blender or food processor and blend until smooth. Chill. *MAKES: ⅔ cup butter.*

There are occasions when inviting a few friends in for drinks and appetizers is a nice way to entertain, especially if it precedes another event. It can be a simple affair, with one or two appetizers, or a special occasion with an assortment to delight everyone. Grandmother's favorite appetizer was her own creation of chilled boiled shrimp in a Remoulade-style sauce. Mother and I each have our own favorite appetizer recipe, too. Mother likes small turnovers or empañadas, cream cheese pastries with an assortment of savory fillings. I enjoy serving mushroom caps stuffed with crab and crowned with melted cheese. Other favorites to include on an appetizer table are Onion Balls, Grab Bag Dip and Caviar Pie (see index). The best part about an assortment of appetizers as a way to entertain guests is that everyone can get a small taste of lots of different dishes. It's informal and fun, too.

Appetizer Favorites from Three Generations
Shrimp a la Gertrude
Party Turnovers
Crab-Stuffed Mushrooms

Party Turnovers

PASTRY:

2 8-ounce packages cream cheese, softened
1 cup (2 sticks) butter or margarine, softened
2¼ cups flour
½ teaspoon salt

Beat cream cheese and butter together in a food processor or with an electric mixer until well blended. Gradually add flour and salt to form a smooth dough. Divide dough in half and wrap each half in waxed paper. Chill at least 30 minutes. Using one half of the dough at a time, roll out on a floured surface to about ⅛-inch thickness. Cut out circles 2½ – 3-inches in diameter. Fill with one teaspoon of one of the fillings listed below. Fold in half and pinch edges with a fork to seal. Bake on a greased cookie sheet for 15 – 20 minutes at 350° until turnovers are lightly browned. *MAKES: pastry for 8 dozen turnovers*

Fillings (Each will make enough to fill about 4 dozen turnovers.)

1. Cook ½ pound ground beef until browned. Drain off fat and add ½ teaspoon garlic salt, ¼ teaspoon pepper, ½ teaspoon chili powder and ¼ teaspoon cumin. Simmer 5 minutes.

2. Mix 2 cups (8 ounces) grated Monterrey Jack cheese with 1 beaten egg, 1 tablespoon chopped parsley and ⅛ teaspoon garlic salt.

3. Cook 2 strips of bacon until crisp, then drain and crumble them. Mix with 2 cups (8 ounces) grated Cheddar cheese, 1 tablespoon chopped green chilies and 1 tablespoon chopped black olives.

4. Drain 2 4¼-ounce cans of shrimp and chop very fine. Mix with ¼ teaspoon Tabasco sauce, 2 teaspoons lemon juice, 2 tablespoons mayonnaise, 1 tablespoon softened butter and 1 tablespoon dry sherry.

5. Mix 2 cups (8 ounces) grated smoked Gouda cheese, ¼ cup very finely chopped ham, 1 egg, 1 tablespoon chopped black olives and 1 tablespoon chopped parsley until well blended.

HINT: I like to keep an assortment of these on hand in the freezer to pop in the oven when company is coming. Freeze unbaked turnovers on a cookie sheet, then store in plastic bags. Bake as directed, allowing 5 – 8 minutes more baking time.

Shrimp A La Gertrude

2½ pounds cooked, peeled and deveined shrimp
1 cup mayonnaise
2 tablespoons prepared mustard
2 cloves garlic, minced
1 tablespoon vinegar
1 4-ounce bottle of capers, drained and chopped fine
¼ teaspoon salt
¼ cup butter or margarine, melted
3 tablespoons flour

Mix mayonnaise, mustard, garlic, vinegar, capers and salt; set aside. Bring a large pot of water to a boil. Plunge cooked shrimp into water for 2 minutes to heat. Drain thoroughly. Pour shrimp into a large bowl. Quickly add melted butter and flour. Toss with wooden spoons or your hands until all shrimp are well coated. Add mayonnaise mixture and continue tossing. Chill several hours or overnight. Serve with toothpicks or cocktail forks. *SERVES: 10 – 12*

NOTE: If you are using unthawed frozen cooked shrimp, add another minute or two to the time the shrimp is in the boiling water.

Crab-Stuffed Mushrooms

1 pound fresh mushrooms — look for pretty ones with large, well-formed caps
1 6-ounce can crabmeat, drained
1 8-ounce package cream cheese, softened
2 teaspoons garlic salt
2 tablespoons chopped parsley
1 cup (4 ounces) grated Cheddar cheese

Preheat oven to 300°. Clean mushrooms and remove stems. Place caps in an ungreased baking dish with stem side up. Mash crabmeat into cream cheese with a fork until blended. (Do not use a food processor or blender because the mixture will become too runny.) Add garlic salt and chopped parsley and blend. Stuff mixture into mushrooms caps, using about a tablespoonful in each. Sprinkle grated cheese over mushrooms. Bake at 300° for 10 minutes or until cheese has melted. Remove from oven and serve at once. These may be made ahead and refrigerated before baking. (Add about 5 minutes to baking time.) *SERVES: 8 – 12*

Finally, a few words on Grandmother's philosophy about serving her guests. She believed that good food should be an important part of the evening, but not so elaborate as to leave the cook or cooks exhausted. She taught her daughters and granddaughters not to be above getting take-out food when cooking proved to be too much, then serving it on good dishes. She believed in using and enjoying her pretty dishes and serving pieces — not all the time, of course, but often. She was right about the idea that if she didn't use and appreciate them, no one would. "I'd much rather cry about a broken glass because of the memories it held than because it was expensive," she told me many times. "If you don't see these things used and enjoyed, then they will be no more than something to gather dust or to be sold in an estate sale. The value of the sentimental attachment should be a much stronger bond than any real dollar value these pieces might have. The best heirlooms are those that tug on your heart."

"Grandmother, I think you would be proud."

Chapter Eleven

Something Extra

The final chapter of this book is not devoted to recipes. But it is about the art of cooking and entertaining. And about the legacy that I have been fortunate to receive through the recipes and memories of many generations collected and passed on by Grandmother. She had dreams of writing a cookbook of her own some day and acquired recipes and wrote notes with that goal in mind. At one point, in 1962, she served as editor of a cookbook for our church. Her influence on the selection of recipes and style of that volume is evident on every page. It was as close as she ever came to her dream — other projects simply got in the way.

In that church cookbook, *Crestview Culinary Collections*, out of print now for over 20 years, Grandmother set down some of her thoughts about serving food. She believed that equal attention should be given to both the preparation and the presentation of meals. The chapter was titled, "Decorations," but it spelled out far more than just ideas for garnishing.

With some minor editing, I share Gertrude Horton's own words . . .

DECORATIONS OF TABLES AND FOODS
Gertrude Briscoe Horton

Decoration has been a hobby of mine since I first used china berries, bits of leaves and grated brick dust to dress up my mud cakes. If this chapter seems to you to be rather disconnected or sketchy, then you are absolutely correct. It is written with the intention of being hints for the beginners. It is also intended to cover in a few pages, what needs an entire book.

The average hostess fails to cash in on the oldest of tricks in entertaining — that of eye appeal. Taste, then eye appeal is the way some people rate food, but this is debatable. If it does not look good, you might not find out about the taste. They are both important. (And do not save it all for company. Try it on the family!)

Let the dishes be few in number, but excellent in taste and appearance.

For dinners or luncheons, have at least one decorated dish as early in the meal as possible. It lends glamour to the entire party at almost no extra cost. A few minutes more of your time spent on the garnishes and you have a conversation piece for the rest of the party.

BASIC SUPPLIES

Although most of the decorations discussed require nothing more than tools found in an ordinary kitchen, an investment in a few basics for decorating will be repaid ten-fold. Some of the suggested items include: good food coloring, a few decorating tubes, cutters, fluted paper cups, paper lace doilies and two or three special serving pieces.

Colors

I recommend a set of good paste colors instead of the little bottles of liquid coloring. They provide stronger colors and are available in sets of primary colors or separately in any color. (*They can be found at cake decorating supply stores and at most of the larger craft stores.*)

Let me stop right here to drop a word of warning. Eye appeal consists of color first, then arrangement. BE SURE THE COLORS ARE NOT TOO STRONG. The daintier, the better, where food is concerned. Put in much less coloring than you think will be required. Mix well after each addition, then add a tiny bit more each time with a clean toothpick, continuing in this manner until the right shade is reached. Remember, reds, purples and all strong colors tend to deepen after standing a while. It is better to be too light than too dark. Never mix colors by artificial light if they are to be used in natural light.

Decorating Tubes

Select a few basic tubes for piping — the term used to refer to decorating by forcing icing or other mixtures through metal tubes — your decorations onto cakes, cookies, etc. In addition, I'd recommend at least three large pastry tubes and a bag for piping meringues, cookies, whipped cream or mashed potatoes.

Sit down and play with these tubes until you've mastered the technique of piping. (*In Grandmother's day, directions often came with the tubes. If there are none with yours, you might want to purchase a simple instruction book when you buy the tubes.*) The only way to learn is to practice and, since icing ingredients can be expensive, here is a recipe for a cheap practice icing: whip ½ pound vegetable shortening with an electric mixer until light — 4 or 5 minutes. Then, slowly add 1½ cups of sifted cake flour; whip until thoroughly mixed and fluffy. Color as desired and store, tightly covered, in a cool place. Practice on a plate, a piece of glass or waxed paper stuck down at the corners on a bread board. This icing may be used over and over many times — just scrape it off the practice surfaces and return it to the containers until you wish to practice again. Please remember, DON'T EAT THIS ICING.

Cutters

I am referring to the ones that come in sets in a small tin box. There are two sizes — small ones for hors d'oeuvres and garnishes and larger ones for sandwiches, cookies or vegetables.

Fluted Paper Cups

Purchase these in several sizes, from bon-bon cups to those used to line small muffin tins. All are inexpensive and add to the attractiveness of your food. Use them to set off candies and small cookies on your dessert trays, to hold scoops of flavored butters on a buffet table, or to add a special touch to candy or other foods you give as Christmas gifts.

Paper Lace Doilies

Purchase them in several sizes, and in white, gold and silver. I usually prefer white, but the colored ones can be most effective when properly matched or contrasted with the food. Use the larger ones under cakes, to line trays or baskets, or even as placemats on a party table. The smaller ones can be used as coasters, to set off individual servings of desserts, or overlapped to cover a small plate.

Serving Pieces

Shape and color are more important than quality. For instance, a large green pottery leaf and a similar one of green glass are among my pieces used most for informal serving. Both of these are perfect containers for salads. Bread, bread sticks, crackers and chips are equally pleasing to the eye — the cheering green of the dish enhances the golden brown of the bread and chips.

Another favorite is an old-fashioned tall cake stand of pressed glass. The edge of the stand has an openwork border through which ribbon may be run. Besides using it to serve cakes, I find that a fluted mold of any color gelatin with a matching or contrasting ribbon in the border, makes a conversation piece of some note.

Turn the stand upside down, place flowers in the hollow stem, and cookies, sandwiches or slices of cake around the stem. This will serve as a centerpiece for a tea cart or small tea table.

Serving pieces do not have to be conventional trays. I have a mirrored tray that I use quite often. It is an ideal background to enhance the transparent delicacy of individual molded salads or desserts. A garnish of fresh green leaves and whole berries or grapes add a final touch of beauty. (*I had my local glass shop cut me some square and oblong mirrors and polish the edges. I often use several as serving pieces on the same table for a dramatic effect.*)

TRAY DECORATIONS

Trays are probably the most used of all serving pieces. Make your foods even more appetizing by following some of these suggestions for decorating your trays.

Hors d'Oeuvre Tray

Cover tray with two kinds of greens — one kind on the bottom, the other for trim, such as: lettuce on the bottom and English Ivy for trim, lettuce and escarole, lettuce and nasturtium leaves and blossoms, magnolia leaves and parsley, ferns and flowers, etc.

Wash and dry greens and leaves, then wipe with salad oil to make them shine. Allow greens to extend over the edge for a softer look.

Sweet Tray

"Always have a sweet tray" is the advice of a well-known caterer. (*Mother has been a strong advocate of this advice, even offering sweets at cocktail parties. She notes that the sweet trays are the first to be refilled.*)

Cover tray with paper lace doilies, allowing them to extend over the edge, if you like. For your sweet tray, try a torte or thin two-layer cake. Cut the torte ahead of time to make serving easier. Place torte on an old-fashioned cake stand in the center of a large, round tray. Surround the base with cookies, petit fours, candies, crystallized orange peel and mints.

Turkey Tray

Select a tray large enough to hold the turkey, with some extra room for turkey slices. Place large Boston fern leaves down one side and end. Set either the whole or half turkey well to the back of the tray (try to hide where you've sliced off the meat); surround with sliced turkey. To decorate, place large bunches of frosted or plain green and red grapes in the corner where the ferns meet and trail them over the turkey. To make frosted grapes, dip small clusters of grapes into lightly beaten egg white, then sprinkle with granulated sugar. Allow to dry, then gently shake to remove excess sugar.

Sandwich Tray

The way you put your sandwiches on the tray makes it party fare or just food. Center the tray with calla lily sandwiches. Trim the crusts from several slices of fresh white bread, then flatten by rolling each with a rolling pin. Place a 3 – 4-inch long carrot stick diagonally across each flattened bread slice, with one end touching a corner and the other end stopping about two inches short of the opposite corner. Fold the side corners over to make a cone shape, gently pressing to hold them together. Use magnolia leaves or ferns for decorations.

Surround with more sandwiches to be served. Cut each sandwich diagonally into quarters, and stand them on their widest edge so the fillings show. (*This is effective even when serving one sandwich on a plate.*)

DECORATIONS AND GARNISHES FOR FOODS
Eggs

A hard cooked egg has no limit to its possibilities. Tulip Eggs: Make a tulip, using only the white part of the hard-cooked egg. Cut each in half, lengthwise, to form 2 tulips. Make tulip petals by cutting the small ends into points, beginning at the outer edge and cutting three points. The outside petals should be half the size of the center whole petal. Lay on meats or salads with the flat side down. Form the stem and leaves from chives or the tops of young onions. Daisy Eggs: Cut each egg lengthwise into eighths. Press the yolk through a sieve. Make a funnel of waxed paper the size you want the center to be, then drop sieved yolk through the funnel at the place you want your garnish to be located. Radiate the petals from the center, squaring off one end of each petal to make them fit around the center a little better.

Onions

With a little creativity, the lowly onion turns into beautiful and clever garnishes to add that magic touch to your foods.

Onion Lilies: Select nice firm red or white onions, letting the setting and size of the tray determine the size (*finished onions will be at least twice as large in diameter*). Slice onion almost through in half from top to bottom, then into fourths, then eighths, and so on, slicing each section in half until petals are of the desired size. Tie each onion with a cord or cloth to hold its shape, or better still turn each onion upside down in a cup or small bowl. Cover with water tinted to suit your color scheme. Leave several hours or overnight. Rinse well and drain upside down. For a centerpiece, place a large head of chicory or watercress on a mirror. Put the largest onion in the center, flanking it with the smaller ones. Carefully spread the petals to form lilies. You will be surprised how few people recognize these as onions.

Cocktail Onions: Color cocktail onions by draining the liquid from the jar, and replacing it with colored water. Color them purple and use them to form bunches of grapes on cheese balls or a salad mounded on a serving platter. Use either fresh grape leaves or cut leaf shapes from green peppers, marking the veins using the back of a knife. Use toothpicks as necessary to hold the onions in place.

Play Cinderella . . . Invite Two Little White Mice To The Party

Let two little parsnip mice face each other from holes in a block of Swiss cheese. Stand back and wait for the fun to begin. Select parsnips or carrots with nice tapering shapes and good points on the ends. Measure about 4 inches from the pointed end, and cut the remaining section off. Make two small slits about an inch and a half back from the point to hold the ears. Cut two thin rounds crosswise from another parsnip, and insert one into each slit. Use whole cloves for the eyes and black bristles from a brush for the whiskers. Use a pin to pierce 3 holes on each side of the nose and insert the bristles. Tint the nose with brown food coloring, if desired. You may have trouble keeping your mice until the party is over. I once had four get away long before the party ended.

Breakfast Brighteners

A pretty breakfast table starts the day on a cheerful note that brightens the dreariest weather.

Funny Face Pancakes: Cut eyes and mouth jack-o-lantern style out of the top pancake on each stack. Arrange four links of pork sausage over the eyes to form hair. Cut another sausage into short lengths. Place a cut piece into each hole in the pancake to make the eyes, nose, and mouth.

Pancake Shapes: Dip an open-top cookie cutter into oil (*or spray with non-stick spray*) and place on a well-greased griddle. Pour just enough pancake batter into the cookie cutter to cover the griddle surface. Cook until set, them remove the cutter, flip the pancake and continue cooking on the other side. You may have to add a little more liquid to the pancake batter to make sure it is thin enough to spread into the corners of the cookie cutter. Or fill a squeeze bottle with thin pancake batter. Use it to draw shapes and make figures by squeezing the batter right onto the hot griddle.

Cantaloupe Rings: For breakfast, brunch or lunch, slice cantaloupe in rings about 1 to 1½-inch thick. Peel and place on a paper doily on a dessert or salad plate. Fill the center of the ring with a bunch of grapes, blueberries or strawberries. Tuck a grape leaf and a sprig of mint underneath the cantaloupe on the side. Frosted grapes add extra glamour.

Soup

Soup should make a dramatic statement.

Holiday Soups: Make a Christmas tree of very finely chopped parsley. Hold a Christmas tree cookie cutter over the soup and carefully sprinkle parsley inside the cutter to cover the surface of the soup. Lift the cutter carefully, so as not to spoil the shape of the tree. With a little practice you can make many designs. Try paprika hearts for Valentine's Day. These work best on thick cream soups.

Two-Colored Soup: Use canned cream of tomato soup and split pea soup, making each slightly thicker than usual (only add about two-thirds of a soup can of water or milk). Cut both ends from a soup can and place the can in the center of a flat soup bowl. Holding the can securely against the bottom of the bowl, pour the tomato soup around the can, then pour the pea soup inside the can to the same level as the tomato soup. Lift the can gently and you will have a circle of green in the lovely red tomato soup. When they are stirred together, they taste delicious, too. A bit of sour cream may be used to garnish the center of the soup. Add a sliced stuffed olive for a special touch. Many soup combinations may be used: cream of chicken and green pea, cream of broccoli and potato (*even chili and nacho or cheddar cheese soup!*).

Garnishes for Soup: Season popcorn with garlic butter and serve with soup instead of crackers, or sprinkle it over the soup before serving. Float a square crouton with a sprig of parsley or watercress in the soup.

Top the sour cream garnish on soup with tiny hearts cut from cooked beets. Use your imagination to come up with garnishes for other occasions.

Molded Chocolate Leaves

Use real rose leaves or any sturdy smooth leaf as a mold. Leave a short stem on each leaf to use as a handle while coating with chocolate. Put chunks of milk or dark chocolate (*or use compound coating*) in the top of a double boiler set over gently simmering water and stir until partially melted. Remove from heat and stir until smooth. (*Be sure not to let any water get into the chocolate — even a drop or two will cause it to seize up and become unworkable.*) Use a small paint brush to paint the underside of each leaf with a smooth coating of chocolate, stopping just before you reach the edge. Place leaves on a waxed paper lined tray and chill until set. To remove the leaf from the chocolate, insert the point of a paring knife or a toothpick to loosen, then peel the leaf off the chocolate. Return to the refrigerator until time to use. Garnish cakes, ice creams or any dessert with a few chocolate leaves for an elegant touch. Your prestige will rise to new heights when the guests learn these lovely leaves are your creations.

Grandmother's suggestions and tips have been well-used by both family members and lots of cooks in the Greenville area. She always said that it was those little touches that had made her reputation as a great hostess.

As a working woman who loves to entertain, I have found that I have had to take a special approach to planning and hosting any parties that I might have. I usually have several parties a year, from our big Christmas Open House for nearly two hundred guests, down to a dinner party for several couples. It takes lots of organization to plan a party while handling a job, but I have learned some tricks that make party planning easier.

To begin with, I keep pretty thorough records of every party I give. I staple all the information about a particular event together to help keep the clutter down, then file it away. I also add notes or magazine articles with party ideas in them to the file. Then, I can quickly scan through my files for ideas when it's time to plan the next party. It's amazing how much time that step can save, and how much inspiration it can provide. I have discovered that I can't rely on my memory to think of everything, so the files help trigger memories of past mistakes or tips to remember. For the annual events, I make a separate file that I refer to from year to year.

Here are some of the things I think are important to include in my party notes and files, and that I would recommend anyone keep:

1. Guest lists — Include copies of guest lists for every party, even if it's nothing more than a quick jotting down of the names. You can't believe how many times it has saved me the embarrassment of leaving someone off a list for another party. I also keep a master file on index cards that I try to keep updated with everyone's current address.

2. Copies of invitations — I really put lots of effort into clever invitations, feeling that it sets the tone for the whole party. It's also nice to refer back to them to get information on times or the exact wording of an invitation.

3. Menus — I don't believe it's necessary to come up with a completely new menu for every occasion, and there are certainly some events — like Christmas dinner — where I want to make sure that I include everything. When I'm filing everything after the party, I go back over the menu and jot down comments on taste, guests' reactions to the food, and if I had too little or too much of a particular dish. It's so nice not to have to remember each time whether I need to make two or three cheese balls to serve fifty people.

4. Shopping lists — Make a copy of your grocery and decorating needs. These give you a quick and easy starting point when planning your shopping and/or budget.

5. Copies of recipes — Why keep searching through cookbooks or your memory each year? A copy of the standard recipes you use from year to year (your favorite punch recipe, for example) makes quick work of planning. If not an actual copy of the recipe, at least make a note on the menu where the recipe can be found. Here's a thought, too . . . if you are the one generally in charge of holiday dinners, take some time and write down the recipes for all the "traditional" dishes and add them to the file. You'll have them all in one place for both yourself and members of your family.

6. Check lists — Keep lists of your table decorations, flowers, whether or not anyone helped you serve, and other important details. It's easy to keep a running list for each party. As you handle something, take a minute and add it to the list. Then you'll have it there for the future.

7. Comments — Make notes after the party is over about what you would change or forgot to do. Pat yourself on the back, too, by writing down the successful details. It's easy to build the next party on the good points of the past ones.

And here are some tips to make the planning and "get-ready" stages go smoother:

1. Decide in advance what scale this party will be. Ask your-

self what gets the highest priority: the food, decorations, entertainment or just getting together? Focus the greatest amount of your energies on the top item, then spread your time out over the rest.

2. Choose a realistic menu. Don't get in over your head with last-minute preparations (they always take twice as long as you think they will, it seems). You can plan a good blend of make-ahead and last minute dishes if you give it some thought. And remember to garnish the food!

3. Make a "count down" list. Detail what can or needs to be done two weeks before a party, one week before, three days before, and so on to an hour or two before the party begins. You'll be much better organized and not struggling over the last-minute things that have been forgotten.

4. Set your table ahead of the event. If it's a buffet or finger-food table, put the serving pieces out, washed and ready to be filled. Place them on the table just as you would like them to be positioned at party time. Label each piece with a slip of paper indicating which food is to be put in that serving piece. This eliminates guessing and, if you've got others helping you, they don't have to stop you to ask what goes in each dish. This will cut your actual set-up time almost in half!

5. Allow at least one more hour than you think it will take to get everything ready before the party. Then, should you have extra time somewhere, sit down and relax for a minute.

6. Remember, you are part of the festivities, too. There's no use going to the effort of hosting a party if you are not going to enjoy it right along with your guests. And don't spend the evening apologizing for everything! Why make your guests feel that they have been invited to a sub-standard event? People are so thrilled to be invited to a party that they don't notice if tennis shoes are still by the back door or if the soup doesn't have quite enough pepper. If you don't have a good time at your own party, go back and re-evaluate your priorities before planning the next one. No party is ever completely perfect. Believe me, I've had my share of disasters. But confidence comes with having one successful party, then another. And when guests see the hosts enjoying themselves, they'll have a good time, too.

I've been very lucky when it comes to cooking. I've had generations of wonderful examples to guide me along and show me what cooking is really about. I've learned that cooking can be a creative expression as well as providing sustenance for life. What one does to prepare the food can be as satisfying to the soul as the act of eating it can be to the body. Cooking produces meals that can mean family time — when family members gather at the table to share themselves as well as the food they eat. And cooking can be a connection from one generation to another. Lots of practical advice about dealing with more than bread dough came out of my cooking lessons in Grandmother's kitchen. I learned about families, about life, about coping with troubles and about celebrating successes . . . and came out of those sessions with a tray of rolls, too.

Index

We feel that it is important to state that none of the recipes for Mary of Puddin Hill catalog products are included in this book. But you will find many favorites from the menu of the Puddin Hill Store.

A

Acclaimed Flamed Bananas, 91
Alexander a la Forest, 99
Alexandrites, 44
Alfajores, 24
Almond Paste
  Chocolate Amaretto Cheesecake, 173
  Fabulous Party Cake, 176
  Marzipan, 232
  Mocha Almond Paste Frosting, 177
Almond Cookies, Lallie's Lemon, 47
Ambrosia, 245
Ambrosia Hamburger Sauce, 210
Anadama Batter Bread, 40
Anadama Bread, 10
Angel Food Fruit Cake, 102
Appetizers
  Armenian Nachos, 138
  Camembert Cheese Ball, 262
  Caviar Pie, 37
  Cheese Puffs, 70
  Chili Nuts, 61
  Chili Queso Grande, 219
  Crab-Stuffed Mushrooms, 273
  Dips
    Coca-Cola Queso, 191
    Creamy Shrimp Dip, 86
    Dip from the Store Down the Road, 209
    Grab Bag Dip, 230
    Guacamole, 208
    Hocus Pecos Dip, 139
    Hot Shrimp Dip, 231
    Jalapeño Dip, 195
    Mary Faulk Koock's Crab Island Dip, 103
    Sam Lauderdale's Original Chili Dip, 141
  Indian Chicken Balls, 74
  Mary's Cheese Ball, 86
  Mary's Liver Pâté, 244
  Mushroom Cheese Spread, 229
  Onion Balls, 231
  Party Turnovers, 272
  Pico de Gallo, 192
  Pud's Provolone Cheese in Pastry Crust, 229
  Roasted Pecans, 51
  Rum Sausages, 75
  Shrimp a la Gertrude, 273
  Shrimp Piccadillo, 60
  Southwest Chicken Puffs, 255
  Spicy Party Treats, 228
  Zippy Cheese Crackers, 191
Apples
  Apple Crumb Betty, 15
  Eve's Temptation, 134
  Spiced Apples, 150
Apricots
  Apricot Milk Pie, 33
  Apricot Nut Bread, 53
Armenian Nachos, 138
Asparagus, Sautéed, 264

B

Bacon
  Bacon-Horseradish Salad Dressing, 256
  Canadian-Style Bacon and Cheese Soup, 118
Baked Chicken German Style, 157
Baked Chops with Cherries, 30
Baked Eggs, 92
Baked Mustard Potatoes, 197
Balkan Sausage Ragout, 63
Bananas
  Acclaimed Flamed Bananas, 91
  Banana Nut Cake, 85
  Banana-Stuffed French Toast, 204
Barbecue (see also Outdoor Cooking)
  Barbecue Sauce for Chicken, Brisket or Wieners, 213
  Barbecued Steakers, 149
Beans
  Deluxe Limas, 196
  "Has Bean" Chowder, 124
  Green
    Emerald Isle Soup, 125
    Sweet-Sour Beans, 60

Pinto
  Chicken Molé Frijolé, 151
  East Texas Red Bean Gumbo, 126
  Mamie's Red Beans, 96

Beef
Beef or Chicken Teriyaki Marinade, 87
Beef Tea, 49
Corned
  Creamy Reuben Soup, 119
  Reuben Salad, 130
Fool 'Em All Beef Brisket, 255
Ground
  Barbecued Steakers, 149
  Beef Enchiladas, 152
  Cornbread Crepes with Mexican Beef, 70
  Feliz Navidad Casserole, 234
  Goulash!, 124
  Johnnie Bazzeti, 198
  Mad Mary's Chili, 122
  Mamie's Red Beans, 96
  Sam Lauderdale's Original Chili Dip, 141
Roast
  Mamie's Pot Roast, 95
  New Orleans Pot Roast, 108
Steaks
  Beef Steaks in Wine Sauce — and Breakfast the Next Day, 93
  Broiled Steak, 29
  Coca-Cola Fajitas, 192
  Working Girl's Stew, 224
Beets, Pickled, 261
Besas, 236

Beverages
Alcoholic
  Alexander a la Forest, 99
  Frozen Margaritas for a Crowd, 113
  Kentucky Eggnog, 237
  Sam's Eggnog, 239
  Southern Comfort Punch, 98
  Strawberry Wine Punch, 228
Hot Chocolate, 48
Hot Chocolate on Ice, 179
Sam's Eggnog, 239
Serving Tea to a Crowd, 140
Big City Scalloped Potatoes, 252
Biscuits and Syrup, Mama's Split, 17
Black Bottom Pie, 174
Black Chicken, 27
Black-Eyed Pea Cornbread, 247
Black-Eyed Pea Soup, Lucky, 120
Blackberry Cobbler, Pud's, 159
Blender Hollandaise Sauce, 264
Blue Cheese Vinaigrette, 267
Blue-Green Salad Dressing, 265
Blueberry Muffins with Lemon Honey Butter, 206
Bob's Cookie Jar Gingersnaps, 164

Breads
Cornbreads
  Hot Water Cornbread, 10
  Mamie's Jalapeño Cornbread, 97
  Spoon Bread, 9
  Stella's Cornbread Mix, 77
Gone-in-a-Minute Bread Sticks, 211
Mama's Split Biscuits and Syrup, 17
Muffins
  Blueberry Muffins with Lemon Honey Butter, 206
  Date Nut Muffins with Orange Glaze, 54
  Skinny Blender Muffins, 92
Quick Breads
  Apricot Nut Bread, 53
  Cranberry Orange Bread, 54
  Everybody's Favorite Poppy Seed Bread, 160
  Olive Nut Bread, 66
  Whole Wheat Zucchini Bread, 160
Rolls
  Excellent Tea Rolls, 41
  Grandmother's Parkerhouse Rolls, 28
  Pecan Popovers with Maple Butter, 271
  Sourdough Rolls, 67
Salt Rising Bread, 5
Yeast Breads
  Anadama Bread, 10
  Anadama Batter Bread, 40
  Cobblestone Breads, 142
  Golden Dumpling Bread, 39
  Puddin Hill Store (and Stephens College) Whole Wheat Bread, 143
  Sally Lunn Bread, 9
  Sweet Rye Bread, 42

Breakfast and Brunch
Baked Eggs, 92
Banana-Stuffed French Toast, 204
Beef Steaks in Wine Sauce — and Breakfast the Next Day, 93
Blueberry Muffins with Lemon Honey Butter, 206
Chili Queso Grande, 219
Crustless Quiche, 162
Egg in Nest, 48
Funnel Cakes, 69

Golden Dumpling Bread, 39
Graham Cracker Coffee Cake, 205
Grapes in Sour Cream, 205
Holiday French Toast, 238
Mama's Split Biscuits and Syrup, 17
Pecan Popovers with Maple Butter, 271
Pud's Granola, 165
Sausage Scrapple, 270
Skinny Blender Muffins, 92
Sunny Cantaloupe, 270
Terry Horton's Dutch Babies, 68
Two Timin' Potatoes, 32
Breast of Chicken with Oysters, 76
Broccoli Pudding, 31
Broiled Peaches, 31
Broiled Steak, 29
Brussels Sprouts, Marinated, 131
Butter and Egg Cobblestone Bread, 142
Butter, Flavored
  Lemon Honey Butter, Blueberry Muffins with, 206
  Madalene Hill's Herb Butter, 104
  Maple Butter, Pecan Popovers with, 271
  Rose Petal Butter, 25
Buttermilk Pie, 163

C

Cabbage
  Cabbage Slaw with Lemon Dressing, 63
  "Good Cabbage Dish", 13
  Kosher Cabbage, 58

Cake Frostings, Fillings and Toppings
  Ambrosia, 245
  Coffee Buttercream Icing, Coffee Angel Food Cake with, 185
  Lemon Jelly, 34
  Mocha Almond Paste Frosting, 177

Cakes
  Angel Food Fruit Cake, 102
  Banana Nut Cake, 85
  Chocolate Amaretto Cheesecake, 173
  Coca-Cola Cake, 193
  Coffee Angel Food Cake, 185
  Fabulous Party Cake, 176
  Fresh Coconut Cake, 245
  Funnel Cakes, 69
  Graham Cracker Coffee Cake, 205
  Joyce's Birthday Cake, 73
  Just Plain Ol' Cake, 25
  Legacy Fudge Cake, 18
  Mosaic Cake, 253
  Payday Cheesecake, 149
  Perfect Pound Cake, 184
  Puddin Hill Store's Carrot Cake, 135
  Rocky Road Torte, 178
  Sad Cake, 256
  Tomato Juice Cake, 65
California Salad with Honey-Lime Dressing, 89
Camembert Cheese Ball, 262
Canadian-Style Bacon and Cheese Soup, 118

Candy
  Chocolate-Covered Strawberries and Sweet Pickles, 180
  Chocolate Nut Slices, 198
  Chocolate Truffles, 172
  Grandmother's Candied Orange Peel, 52
  Grandmother's Minted Pecans, 51
  Marzipan, 232
  Mexican Pralines, 236
  Southern Chocolate Delights, 170
  Sugar Taffy, 38
  White Chocolate Truffles, 170
Cantaloupe, Sunny, 270

Carrots
  Cognac Carrots, 269
  Elegant Carrot Loaf, 263
  Puddin Hill Store's Carrot Cake, 135

Casseroles
  Baked Chicken German Style, 157
  Black-eyed Pea Cornbread, 247
  Crabmeat Casserole, 257
  Eggplant on Parade, 88
  Feliz Navidad Casserole, 234
  Polenta Casserole, 154
  Summer's Bounty Casserole, 162
  Twenty Four Hour Salad Plus Thirty Minutes at 350°, 201
  Yellow Squash Casserole, 71
Catfish Bait, 215
Caviar Pie, 37
Champagne Sauce, Chicken Breasts with, 263

Cheese
  Camembert Cheese Ball, 262
  Canadian-Style Bacon and Cheese Soup, 118
  Cheese Chowder, 119
  Cheese Enchiladas, 152
  Cheese Puffs, 70
  Cheesy Chicken Lasagna, 196
  Chili Queso Grande, 219
  Cobblestone Bread, Cheese, 142

Coca-Cola Queso, 191
Country Cheese Pie, 109
Crustless Quiche, 162
Hocus Pecos Dip, 139
Jalapeño Dip, 195
Mary's Cheese Ball, 86
Mushroom Cheese Spread, 229
Old Fashioned Pimento Cheese, 244
Pud's Provolone Cheese in Pastry Crust, 229
Ricotta-Stuffed Chicken Breasts, 260
Salad Dressings
  Blue Cheese Vinaigrette, 267
  Blue-Green Salad Dressing, 265
  Parmesan Salad Dressing, 87
Swiss Cheese and Thousand Island Dressing Sandwiches, 188
Zippy Cheese Crackers, 191
Zucchini and Swiss Cheese Soup, 123

Cheesecakes
Chocolate Amaretto Cheesecake, 173
Payday Cheesecake, 149

Cherries
Baked Chops with Cherries, 30
Cherry Dream Ice Cream, 217

Chicken
Baked Chicken German Style, 157
Barbecue Sauce for Chicken, Brisket or Wieners, 213
Black Chicken, 27
Breast of Chicken with Oysters, 76
Cheesy Chicken Lasagna, 196
Chicken a la Chasseur, 30
Chicken Breasts in Champagne Sauce, 263
Chicken Crabmeat Rosemary, 252
Chicken Enchiladas, 152
Chicken Gumbo, 127
Chicken Molé Frijolé, 151
Chicken Teriyaki Marinade, Beef or, 87
Chicken with Mushrooms and Vermouth, 166
Curried Chicken Salad, 66
Fried Chicken, 95
Fried Chicken Salad, 129
Fruited Chicken-Pecan Salad, 131
Grandmother's Jellied Chicken, 12
Herbed Cornbread Ring with Creamed Chicken, 21
Hurry Curry, 89
Imperial Chicken, 77
Indian Chicken Balls, 74
Japanese Chicken Salad, 132
Mexican Chicken with Fruit Sauce, 84
Molded Chicken Salad, 46
Oriental Chicken Salad, 132
Pocket Full O' Sandwich, 128
Ricotta-Stuffed Chicken Breasts, 260
Smothered Chicken, 96
Southwest Chicken Puffs, 255

Chili
Dip from the Store Down the Road, 209
Mad Mary's Chili, 122
Mary's Quick Soups, 224
Sam Lauderdale's Original Chili Dip, 141
Chili Nuts, 61
Chili Queso Grande, 219
Chilled Cream of Shrimp Soup, 75
Chioppino, 156
Chipper Fried Fish, 212

Chocolate
Besas, 236
Black Bottom Pie, 174
Chocolate Amaretto Cheesecake, 173
Chocolate-covered Strawberries and Sweet Pickles, 180
Chocolate Dessert Spread, 171
Chocolate Mint Mystery Cookies, 139
Chocolate Nut Slices, 198
Chocolate Pie, 199
Chocolate Place Cards, 181
Chocolate Truffles, 172
Coca-Cola Cake, 193
Fabulous Party Cake, 176
Fudge Sauce, 183
Hot Chocolate, 48
Hot Chocolate on Ice, 179
Legacy Fudge Cake, 18
Mary's Brownies, 179
McLow's Chocolate Fingers, 44
Mosaic Cake, 253
Rocky Road Torte, 178
Sad Cake, 256
Southern Chocolate Delights, 170
Unbelievable Chocolate Ice Cream, 217
White Chocolate Truffles, 170

Chowders
Cheese Chowder, 119
Confetti Clam Chowder, 121
"Has Bean" Chowder, 124

Cinnamon
  Cinnamon Ice Cream, 269
  Cinnamon Sticks, 17
Chess Pie, Southern, 14
Clam Chowder, Confetti, 121
Cobbler, Pud's Blackberry, 159
Cobblestone Breads, 142

Coca-Cola
  Coca-Cola Cake, 193
  Coca-Cola Fajitas, 192
  Coca-Cola Queso, 191
  Coca-Cola Salad, 193

Coconut
  Fresh Coconut Cake, 245
  Fresh Coconut Pie, 243
Coffee Angel Food Cake, 185
Cognac Carrots, 269
Confetti Clam Chowder, 121

Cookies and Brownies
  Alexandrites, 44
  Alfajores, 24
  Besas, 236
  Bob's Cookie Jar Gingersnaps, 164
  Chocolate Mint Mystery Cookies, 139
  Fruit Cake Bar Cookies with Chocolate Glaze, 100
  Gussied-up Grahams, 72
  Lallie's Lemon Almond Cookies, 47
  Mama Carlisle's Teacakes, 16
  Mary's Brownies, 179
  McLow's Chocolate Fingers, 44
  McLow's Sinkers, 43
  Orange Pecan Cookies, 72
  Orange Slice Cookies, 71
  Pan de Polvo, 235
  Texas Big Mouth Cookies, 169
  Whole Wheat Gems, 140

Corn
  Corn Creole, 46
  Corn Pudding, 12
  Fried Roastin' Ears, 4
  Summer's Bounty Casserole, 162

Cornbread
  Black-eyed Pea Cornbread, 247
  Cornbread Crepes with Mexican Beef, 70
  Herbed Cornbread Ring with Creamed Chicken, 21
  Hot Water Cornbread, 10
  Mamie's Jalapeño Cornbread, 97
  Sarah's Cornbread Dressing, 241
  Spoon Bread, 9
  Stella's Cornbread Mix, 77
Country Cheese Pie, 109

Crab
  Chicken-Crabmeat Rosemary, 252
  Crab-Stuffed Mushrooms, 273
  Crabmeat Casserole, 257
  Crabmeat, Ham and Rice Salad, 76
  Mary Faulk Koock's Crab Island Dip, 103

Cranberries
  Cranberry Orange Bread, 54
  Cranberry Relish, 242
Creamed Chicken, Herbed Cornbread Ring with, 21
Creamy Lemon Fruit Salad, 133
Creamy Pecan Soup, 121
Creamy Reuben Soup, 119
Creamy Shrimp Dip, 86
Crepes, Cornbread with Mexican Beef, 70
Crustless Quiche, 162
Crystallized Rose Petals, 23
Cumberland Sauce for Baked Ham, 75

Curry
  Curried Chicken Salad, 66
  Curried Fruit, 91
  Hurry Curry, 89

D

Date-Nut Muffins with Orange Glaze, 54
Deep-Fried Baby New Potatoes, 158
Delores Plunket's Papitas, 62
Deluxe Limas, 196

Desserts
  Acclaimed Flamed Bananas, 91
  Alexander a la Forest, 99
  Apple Crumb Betty, 15
  Cherry Dream Ice Cream, 217
  Chocolate Dessert Spread, 171
  Cinnamon Ice Cream, 269
  Fruit Cake Ice Cream, 100
  Glory Hallelujah, 99
  Grape Sherbet, 189
  Grapefruit Sorbet, 112
  Grapes in Sour Cream, 205
  Grapes with Ginger Cream, 261
  Heavenly Brulee, 166
  Hot Chocolate on Ice, 179
  Imperial Mousse, 105
  Lemon Jelly, 34
  Lemon-on-a-Cloud, 259
  Peach Ice Cream, 214
  Pear Mint Sorbet, 112
  Peppermint Ice Cream, 218
  Praline Ice Cream, 221

Pud's Blackberry Cobbler, 159
Puddin Hill Fruit Cake with
    Whipped Cream, 232
Strawberries Framboise, 129
Unbelievable Chocolate Ice Cream,
    217
Devilish Eggs, 260
Dip from the Store Down the Road,
    209
Dressing, Sarah's Cornbread, 241
Drunk Fruit Chess Pie, 7
Dutch Babies, Terry Horton's, 68

E

East Texas Red Bean Gumbo, 126
Effervescent Crescent, 128
Eggs
    Baked Eggs, 92
    Crustless Quiche, 162
    Devilish Eggs, 260
    Egg In Nest, 48
    Egg Salad with Green Chilies
        Sandwiches, 187
    Pickled Eggs, 36
Elegant Carrot Loaf, 263
Emerald Isle Soup, 125
Enchiladas, Beef, Chicken or Cheese,
    152
Enchilada Sauce, Green for Beef,
    Chicken or Cheese, 151
Entice-Mint Pie, 136
Epicurean Peas, 241
Essence of Christmas Pie, 101
Eve's Temptation, 134
Everybody's Favorite Poppy Seed
    Bread, 160
Excellent Tea Rolls, 41

F

Fabulous Party Cake, 176
Fajitas, Coca-Cola, 192
Feliz Navidad Casserole, 234
Fish
    Chipper Fried Fish, 212
    Perfect-Every-Time Baked Fish,
        165
    Sam's Grilled Fish, 216
    Stuffed Sole in Vermouth, 268
    Sweet and Sour Baked Fish, 155
Flower and Herb Cooking
    Crystallized Rose Petals, 23
    Grandmother's Mint Syrup, 26
    Just Plain Ol' Cake, 25
    Madalene Hill's Herb Butter, 104
    Rose Petal Butter, 25
Fool 'Em All Beef Brisket, 255

French Onion Soup, 120
French Toast, Banana-Stuffed, 204
Fresh Coconut Cake, 245
Fresh Coconut Pie, 243
Fried Chicken, 95
Fried Chicken Salad, 129
Fried Roastin' Ears, 4
Fried Whole Okra, 68
Frozen Margaritas for a Crowd, 113
Fruit (see also specific fruits)
    Ambrosia, 245
    California Salad with Honey-Lime
        Dressing, 89
    Creamy Lemon Fruit Salad, 133
    Curried Fruit, 91
    Drunk Fruit Chess Pie, 7
    Fruited Chicken-Pecan Salad, 131
    Salad Dressings
        Old Fashioned Fruit Salad
            Dressing, 47
        Puddin Hill Store's Fruit Salad
            Dressing, 133
Fruit Cake
    Angel Food Fruit Cake, 102
    Essence of Christmas Pie, 101
    Fruit Cake Cookies with Chocolate
        Glaze, 100
    Fruit Cake Ice Cream, 100
    Glory Hallelujah, 99
    Puddin Hill Fruit Cake with
        Whipped Cream, 232
Fruited Chicken-Pecan Salad, 131
Fudge Sauce, 183
Funnel Cakes, 69

G

Gazpacho, 123
Ginger
    Bob's Cookie Jar Gingersnaps, 164
    Ginger Pear Salad, 254
    Gingersnap Crust, 175
    Grapes with Ginger Creme, 261
Glory Hallelujah, 99
Golden Dumpling Bread, 39
Gone-in-a-Minute Bread Sticks, 211
"Good Cabbage Dish", 13
Goulash!, 124
Grab Bag Dip, 230
Graham Cracker Coffee Cake, 205
Grandmother's Candied Orange Peel,
    52
Grandmother's Favorite Pie Crust, 35
Grandmother's Jellied Chicken, 12
Grandmother's Mint Syrup, 26
Grandmother's Minted Pecans, 51
Grandmother's Parkerhouse Rolls, 28

Granola, Pud's, 165
Grapefruit Sorbet, 112
Grapes
   Grape Sherbet, 189
   Grapes in Sour Cream, 205
   Grapes with Ginger Cream, 261
Greek Lemon Soup, 45
Green Chilies, Egg Salad with, 187
Green Enchilada Sauce for Beef,
   Chicken or Cheese Enchiladas, 151
Grilled Lamb, 90
Guacamole, 208
Gumbo
   Chicken Gumbo, 127
   East Texas Red Bean Gumbo, 126
Gussied-up Grahams, 72

H

Ham
   Crabmeat, Ham and Rice Salad, 76
   Cumberland Sauce for Baked Ham, 75
   Ham Baked in Milk, 3
   Nancy Parker's Simply Delicious Ham, 110
Harvest Pie, 137
"Has Bean" Chowder, 124
Heavenly Brulee, 166
Herbed Cornbread Ring with Creamed Chicken, 21
Herbs (See Flower and Herb Cooking)
Hocus Pecos Dip, 139
Holiday French Toast, 238
Hollandaise, Blender, 264
Horseradish Salad Dressing, Bacon, 256
Hot Chocolate, 48
Hot Chocolate on Ice, 179
Hot Shrimp Dip, 231
Hot Water Cornbread, 10
"How to Make White Sauce", 14
Hurry Curry, 89

I

Ice Creams and Sherbets
   Cherry Dream Ice Cream, 217
   Cinnamon Ice Cream, 269
   Fruit Cake Ice Cream, 100
   Grape Sherbet, 189
   Grapefruit Sorbet, 112
   Peach Ice Cream, 214
   Pear Mint Sorbet, 112
   Peppermint Ice Cream, 218
   Praline Ice Cream, 221
   Unbelievable Chocolate Ice Cream, 217

Imperial Chicken, 77
Imperial Mousse, 105
Indian Chicken Balls, 74
Italian Cobblestone Bread, 142

J

Jalapeños
   Cobblestone Bread, Jalapeño, 142
   Delores Plunket's Papitas, 62
   Jalapeño Dip, 195
   Mamie's Jalapeño Cornbread, 97
   Pico de Gallo, 192
Japanese Chicken Salad, 132
Jo's Mexican Salad, 234
Johnnie Bazzeti, 198
Joyce's Birthday Cake, 73
Just Plain Ol' Cake, 25

K

Kentucky Eggnog, 237
Kosher Cabbage, 58
Kraut-Stuffed Chops, 157

L

Lallie's Lemon Almond Cookies, 47
Lamb, Grilled, 90
Left-overs
   Beef Steaks in Wine Sauce — and Breakfast the Next Day, 93
   Fruit Cake
      Angel Food Fruit Cake, 102
      Essence of Christmas Pie, 101
      Fruit Cake Bar Cookies with Chocolate Glaze, 100
      Fruit Cake Ice Cream, 100
      Glory Hallelujah, 99
   Gone-in-a-Minute Bread Sticks, 211
   Mary's "Gotta Go" Soup, 104
   Mama's Split Biscuits and Syrup, 17
   Two Timin' Potatoes, 32
Legacy Fudge Cake, 18
Lemon
   Cabbage Slaw with Lemon Dressing, 63
   Creamy Lemon Fruit Salad, 133
   Greek Lemon Soup, 45
   Lallie's Lemon Almond Cookies, 47
   Lemon Jelly, 34
   Lemon Pie, 35
   Lemon-on-a-Cloud, 259
Liver Pâté, Mary's, 244
Lucky Black-Eyed Pea Soup, 120

M

Mad Mary's Chili, 122
Madalene Hill's Herb Butter, 104
Mama Carlisle's Teacakes, 16
Mama's Split Biscuits and Syrup, 17
Mamie's Jalapeño Cornbread, 97
Mamie's Pot Roast, 95
Mamie's Red Beans, 96
Margarita Mold, 219
Margaritas, Frozen, for a Crowd, 113
Marinated Brussels Sprouts, 131
Mary Faulk Koock's Crab Island Dip, 103
Mary's Brownies, 179
Mary's Cheese Ball, 86
Mary's "Gotta Go" Soup, 104
Mary's Liver Pâté, 244
Mary's Quick Soups, 224
Marzipan, 232
McLow's Chocolate Fingers, 44
McLow's Sinkers, 43
Mediterranean Tomatoes, 163
Mexican (See Southwest Cooking)
Mexican Beef, Cornbread Crepes with, 70
Mexican Chicken with Fruit Sauce, 84
Mexican Pralines, 236
Mexican Salad, Jo's, 234
Milk, Ham Baked in, 3
Mint
 Chocolate Mint Mystery Cookies, 139
 Entice-Mint Pie, 136
 Grandmother's Mint Syrup, 26
 Grandmother's Minted Pecans, 51
 Pear Mint Sorbet, 112
 Peppermint Ice Cream, 218
Miracle Pan Preparation, Nancy Parker's, 113
Mocha Almond Paste Frosting, 177
Molded Chicken Salad, 46
Mosaic Cake, 253
Muffins
 Blueberry Muffins with Lemon Honey Butter, 206
 Date-Nut Muffins with Orange Glaze, 54
 Skinny Blender Muffins, 92
 Stella's Cornbread Mix, 77
 Whole Wheat Zucchini Bread, 160
Mushrooms
 Chicken with Mushrooms and Vermouth, 166
 Crab-Stuffed Mushrooms, 273
 Mushroom Cheese Spread, 229
 Pud's Mushroom Soup, 122

N

Nancy Parker's Miracle Pan Preparation, 113
Nancy Parker's Simply Delicious Ham, 110
Nancy Parker's Spaghetti Squash, 111
New Orleans Pot Roast, 108
Nuts, Chili, 61

O

Okra, Fried Whole, 68
Old Fashioned Fruit Salad Dressing, 47
Old Fashioned Pimento Cheese, 244
Old Fashioned Boiled Custard, 246
Olive Nut Bread, 66
Onions
 French Onion Soup, 120
 Onion Balls, 231
Oranges
 Ambrosia, 245
 Cranberry Orange Bread, 54
 Grandmother's Candied Orange Peel, 52
 Orange Pecan Cookies, 72
 Orange Slice Cookies, 71
Oriental Chicken Salad, 132
Osgood Pie, 242
Outdoor Cooking
 Ambrosia Hamburger Sauce, 210
 Barbecue Sauce for Chicken, Brisket or Wieners, 213
 Beef or Chicken Teriyaki Marinade, 87
 Coca-Cola Fajitas, 192
 Grilled Lamb, 90
 Pickled Smoked Turkey, 59
 Sam's Grilled Fish, 216
Oysters, Breast of Chicken with, 76

P

Pan de Polvo, 235
Parmesan Salad Dressing, 87
Party Turnovers, 272
Pasta
 Cheesy Chicken Lasagna, 196
 Pud's Spaghetti Sauce, 153
 Puddin Hill Store's Tortellini Salad, 130
Payday Cheesecake, 149
Peaches
 Broiled Peaches, 31

Peach Ice Cream, 214
Peanut Butter
  Peanut Butter Pie, 136
  Peanut Butter Sauce, 184
Pears
  Ginger Pear Salad, 254
  Pear Mint Sorbet, 112
Peas, Black-eyed
  Black-eyed Pea Cornbread, 247
  Lucky Black-eyed Pea Soup, 120
Peas, Epicurean, 241
Pecans
  Cobblestone Bread, Pecan, 142
  Creamy Pecan Soup, 121
  Fruited Chicken-Pecan Salad, 131
  Grandmother's Minted Pecans, 51
  Mexican Pralines, 236
  Orange Pecan Cookies, 72
  Pecan Paté Sandwiches, 187
  Pecan Popovers with Maple Butter, 271
  Roasted Pecans, 51
Peppermint Ice Cream, 218
Perfect Pound Cake, 184
Perfect-Every-Time Baked Fish, 165
Pickled Beets, 261
Pickled Eggs, 36
Pickled Smoked Turkey, 59
Pico de Gallo, 192
Pies and Pie Crusts
  Apricot Milk Pie, 33
  Black Bottom Pie, 174
  Buttermilk Pie, 163
  Chocolate Pie, 199
  Drunk Fruit Chess Pie, 7
  Entice-Mint Pie, 136
  Essence of Christmas Pie, 101
  Eve's Temptation, 134
  Fresh Coconut Pie, 243
  Harvest Pie, 137
  Lemon Pie, 35
  Osgood Pie, 242
  Peanut Butter Pie, 136
  Pie Crusts
    Gingersnap Crust, 175
    Grandmother's Favorite Pie Crust, 35
    Orange Pie Crust — Apricot Milk Pie, 33
    Quick Pie Crust, 243
  Savory
    Caviar Pie, 37
    Country Cheese Pie, 109
  Sawdust Pie, 267
  Southern Chess Pie, 14
  Vinegar Pie, 15
Pimiento Cheese, Old Fashioned, 244

Pineapple Sandwiches, Pork and, 188
Place Cards, Chocolate, 181
Pocket Full O' Sandwich, 128
Polenta Casserole, 154
Poppy Seed
  Everybody's Favorite Poppy Seed Bread, 160
  Poppy Seed Dressing, 91
Pork
  Baked Chops with Cherries, 30
  Kraut-Stuffed Chops, 157
  Pork and Pineapple Sandwiches, 188
Potatoes
  Baked Mustard Potatoes, 197
  Big City Scalloped Potatoes, 252
  Deep-Fried Baby New Potatoes, 158
  Delores Plunket's Papitas, 62
  Two Timin' Potatoes, 32
Poultry (see Chicken and Turkey)
Praline Ice Cream, 221
Pralines, Mexican, 236
Pud's Blackberry Cobbler, 159
Pud's Granola, 165
Pud's Mushroom Soup, 122
Pud's Provolone Cheese in Pastry Crust, 229
Pud's Spaghetti Sauce, 153
Pud's Vegetable Sauté, 266
Puddin Hill Fruit Cake with Whipped Cream, 232
Puddin Hill Store (and Stephens College) Whole Wheat Bread, 143
Puddin Hill Store's Carrot Cake, 135
Puddin Hill Store's Fruit Salad Dressing, 133
Puddin Hill Store's Tortellini Salad, 130

Q

Quick Pie Crust, 243
Quick Soups, Mary's, 224

R

Radishes con Queso au Gratin, 61
Raisin Sandwiches, 23
Reuben Salad, 130
Rice
  Crabmeat, Ham and Rice Salad, 76
  Rice Oregano, 256
  Texas Rice, 105
  Wild Rice Pilaf Soup, 125
Ricotta-Stuffed Chicken Breasts, 260
Roast Turkey, 240
Roasted Pecans, 51
Rocky Road Torte, 178

Rolls
 Excellent Tea Rolls, 41
 Grandmother's Parkerhouse Rolls, 28
 Sourdough Rolls, 67
Rose Petals
 Crystallized Rose Petals, 23
 Rose Petal Butter, 25
Rum Sausages, 75
Rye Bread, Sweet, 42

S

Sad Cake, 256
Salad Dressings
 Bacon-Horseradish Salad Dressing, 256
 Blue Cheese Vinaigrette, 267
 Blue-Green Salad Dressing, 265
 Honey-Lime Dressing, California Salad with, 89
 Lemon Dressing, Cabbage Slaw with, 63
 Old Fashioned Fruit Salad Dressing, 47
 Parmesan Salad Dressing, 87
 Poppy Seed Dressing, 91
 Puddin Hill Store's Fruit Salad Dressing, 133
Salads
 Cabbage Slaw with Lemon Dressing, 63
 California Salad with Honey-Lime Dressing, 89
 Congealed
  Coca-Cola Salad, 193
  Grandmother's Jellied Chicken, 12
  Margarita Mold, 219
  Molded Chicken Salad, 46
  Spinach Aspic, 197
  Tomato Aspic, 11
 Cranberry Relish, 242
 Creamy Lemon Fruit Salad, 133
 Delores Plunket's Papitas, 62
 Ginger Pear Salad, 254
 Guacamole, 208
 Jo's Mexican Salad, 234
 Main Dish
  Crabmeat, Ham and Rice Salad, 76
  Curried Chicken Salad, 66
  Fried Chicken Salad, 129
  Fruited Chicken-Pecan Salad, 131
  Grandmother's Jellied Chicken, 12
  Japanese Chicken Salad, 132
  Molded Chicken Salad, 46
  Oriental Chicken Salad, 132
  Puddin Hill Store's Tortellini Salad, 130
  Reuben Salad, 130
  Tuna Hula Salad, 133
  Twenty Four Hour Salad Plus Thirty Minutes at 350°, 201
 Marinated Brussels Sprouts, 131
 Mediterranean Tomatoes, 163
 Sam's Salad, 90
 San Diego Salad, 107
 Strawberries Framboise, 129
 Sweet-Sour Beans, 60
Sally Lunn Bread, 9
Salt Rising Bread, 5
Sam Lauderdale's Original Chili Dip, 141
Sam's Eggnog, 239
Sam's Grilled Fish, 216
Sam's Salad, 90
San Diego Salad, 107
Sandwiches
 Effervescent Crescent, 128
 Egg Salad with Green Chilies Sandwiches, 187
 Old Fashioned Pimiento Cheese, 244
 Pecan Paté Sandwiches, 187
 Pocket Full O' Sandwich, 128
 Pork and Pineapple Sandwiches, 188
 Raisin Sandwiches, 23
 Swiss Cheese and Thousand Island Dressing Sandwiches, 188
 Tortilla Maria, 116
Sarah's Cornbread Dressing, 241
Sauces
 Ambrosia Hamburger Sauce, 210
 Barbecue Sauce for Chicken, Brisket or Wieners, 213
 Blender Hollandaise Sauce, 264
 Cumberland Sauce for Baked Ham, 75
 Dessert Sauces
  Fudge Sauce, 183
  Grandmother's Mint Syrup, 26
  Lemon Jelly, 34
  Old Fashioned Boiled Custard, 246
  Peanut Butter Sauce, 184
 Green Enchilada Sauce for Beef, Chicken or Cheese Enchiladas, 151
 "How To Make White Sauce", 14
 Pico de Gallo, 192
 Pud's Spaghetti Sauce, 153

Sauerkraut
  Creamy Reuben Soup, 119
  Kraut-Stuffed Chops, 157
  Reuben Salad, 130
Sausage
  Balkan Sausage Ragout, 63
  Rum Sausages, 75
  Sausage Scrapple, 270
  Spicy Party Treats, 228
Sautéed Asparagus, 264
Sawdust Pie, 267
Scallops Sausalito, 98
Seafood (see also specific fish or shellfish)
  Chioppino, 156
  Seafood Stew, 233
  Serving Tea to a Crowd, 140
Shrimp
  Chilled Cream of Shrimp Soup, 75
  Creamy Shrimp Dip, 86
  Eggplant on Parade, 88
  Hot Shrimp Dip, 231
  Shrimp a la Gertrude, 273
  Shrimp Bisque au Rhum, 187
  Shrimp Picadillo, 60
  Skimpy Shrimp, 49
Side Dishes
  Broiled Peaches, 31
  Curried Fruit, 91
  Devilish Eggs, 260
  Pickled Beets, 261
  Pickled Eggs, 36
  Spiced Apples, 150
Skimpy Shrimp, 49
Skinny Blender Muffins, 92
Smothered Chicken, 96
Snacks
  Cinnamon Sticks, 17
  Funnel Cakes, 69
  Mama's Split Biscuits and Syrup, 17
  Raisin Sandwiches, 23
Soups
  Balkan Sausage Ragout, 63
  Beef Tea, 49
  Canadian-Style Bacon and Cheese Soup, 118
  Cheese Chowder, 119
  Chicken Gumbo, 127
  Chilled Cream of Shrimp Soup, 75
  Chioppino, 156
  Confetti Clam Chowder, 121
  Creamy Pecan Soup, 121
  Creamy Reuben Soup, 119
  East Texas Red Bean Gumbo, 126
  Emerald Isle Soup, 125
  French Onion Soup, 120
  Gazpacho, 123
  Goulash!, 124
  Greek Lemon Soup, 45
  "Has Bean" Chowder, 124
  Lucky Black-Eyed Pea Soup, 120
  Mad Mary's Chili, 122
  Mary's "Gotta Go" Soup, 104
  Mary's Quick Soups, 224
  Pud's Mushroom Soup, 122
  Seafood Stew, 233
  Shrimp Bisque au Rhum, 187
  Wild Rice Pilaf Soup, 125
  Working Girl's Stew, 224
  Zucchini and Swiss Cheese Soup, 123
Sourdough Rolls, 67
Southern Chess Pie, 14
Southern Chocolate Delights, 170
Southern Comfort Punch, 98
Southwest Chicken Puffs, 255
Southwest Cooking
  Beef, Chicken or Cheese Enchiladas, 152
  Besas, 236
  California Salad with Honey-Lime Dressing, 89
  Chicken Molé Frijolé, 151
  Chili Nuts, 61
  Chili Queso Grande, 219
  Coca-Cola Fajitas, 192
  Coca-Cola Queso, 191
  Cornbread Crepes with Mexican Beef, 70
  Creamy Pecan Soup, 121
  Delores Plunket's Papitas, 62
  Dip from the Store Down the Road, 209
  Egg Salad with Green Chilies Sandwiches, 187
  Feliz Navidad Casserole, 234
  Frozen Margaritas for a Crowd, 113
  Gazpacho, 123
  Green Enchilada Sauce for Beef, Chicken or Cheese Enchiladas, 151
  Guacamole, 208
  Hocus Pecos Dip, 139
  Hot Shrimp Dip, 231
  Jalapeño Cobblestone Bread, 142
  Jalapeño Dip, 195
  Jo's Mexican Salad, 234
  Mad Mary's Chili, 122
  Mamie's Jalapeño Cornbread, 97
  Mamie's Red Beans, 96
  Margarita Mold, 219

Mexican Chicken with Fruit Sauce, 84
Mexican Pralines, 236
Pan de Polvo, 235
Pico de Gallo, 192
Praline Ice Cream, 221
Radishes con Queso au Gratin, 61
Sam Lauderdale's Original Chili Dip, 141
Shrimp Picadillo, 60
Southwest Chicken Puffs, 255
Summer's Bounty Casserole, 162
Tamale-Stuffed Turkey, 220
Texas Rice, 105
Tortilla Maria, 116
Zippy Cheese Crackers, 191
Spaghetti Sauce, Pud's, 153
Spaghetti Squash, Nancy Parker's, 111
Spiced Apples, 150
Spicy Party Treats, 228

Spinach
Spinach Aspic, 197
Stuffed Tomatoes Rockefeller, 258
Twenty Four Hour Salad Plus Thirty Minutes at 350°, 201
Spoon Bread, 9

Squash
Nancy Parker's Spaghetti Squash, 111
Pud's Vegetable Sauté, 266
Summer's Bounty Casserole, 162
Yellow Squash Casserole, 71
Zucchini and Swiss Cheese Soup, 123
Zucchini Crisps, 110
Steak, Broiled, 29
Stella's Cornbread Mix, 77

Stews
Balkan Sausage Ragout, 63
Chioppino, 156
Seafood Stew, 233
Working Girl's Stew, 224

Strawberries
Chocolate-Covered Strawberries and Sweet Pickles, 180
Strawberries Framboise, 129
Strawberry Wine Punch, 228
Stuffed Sole in Vermouth, 268
Stuffed Tomatoes Rockefeller, 258
Sugar Taffy, 38
Summer's Bounty Casserole, 162
Sunny Cantaloupe, 270
Sweet and Sour Baked Fish, 155
Sweet Pickles, Chocolate-Covered Strawberries and, 180
Sweet Potatoes

Sweet Potatoes Baked in the Fireplace, 4
Sweet 'Tata Pone, 242
Sweet Rye Bread, 42
Sweet-Sour Beans, 60
Swiss Cheese and Thousand Island Dressing Sandwiches, 188

T

Taffy, Sugar, 38
Tamale-Stuffed Turkey, 220
Tea, Serving to a Crowd, 140
Teacakes, Mama Carlisle's, 16
Teriyaki Marinade, Beef or Chicken, 87
Terry Horton's Dutch Babies, 68
Texas Big Mouth Cookies, 169
Texas Rice, 105
Thousand Island Dressing Sandwiches, Swiss Cheese and, 188

Tomatoes
Gazpacho, 123
Mediterranean Tomatoes, 163
Stuffed Tomatoes Rockefeller, 258
Tomato Aspic, 11
Tomato Juice Cake, 65
Tortellini Salad, Puddin Hill Store's, 130
Tortilla Maria, 116

Truffles
Chocolate Truffles, 172
White Chocolate Truffles, 170
Tuna Hula Salad, 133

Turkey
Pickled Smoked Turkey, 59
Roast Turkey, 240
Tamale-Stuffed Turkey, 220
Twenty-Four Hour Salad Plus Thirty Minutes at 350°, 201
Two-Timin' Potatoes, 32

U

Unbelievable Chocolate Ice Cream, 217

V

Veal Paprika, 266

Vegetables
Baked Mustard Potatoes, 197
Big City Scalloped Potatoes, 252
Broccoli Pudding, 31
Cognac Carrots, 269
Corn Creole, 46
Corn Pudding, 12
Deep-Fried Baby New Potatoes, 158

Delores Plunket's Papitas, 62
Deluxe Limas, 196
Elegant Carrot Loaf, 263
Epicurean Peas, 241
Fried Roastin' Ears, 4
Fried Whole Okra, 68
"Good Cabbage Dish", 13
Kosher Cabbage, 58
Marinated Brussels Sprouts, 131
Mediterranean Tomatoes, 163
Nancy Parker's Spaghetti Squash, 111
Pickled Beets, 261
Pud's Vegetable Sauté, 266
Radishes con Queso au Gratin, 61
Rice Oregano, 256
Sautéed Asparagus, 264
Stuffed Tomatoes Rockefeller, 258
Summer's Bounty Casserole, 162
Sweet Potatoes Baked in the Fireplace, 4
Sweet 'Tata Pone, 242
Sweet-Sour Beans, 60
Texas Rice, 105
Twenty Four Hour Salad Plus Thirty Minutes at 350°, 201
Two Timin' Potatoes, 32
Yellow Squash Casserole, 71

Zucchini Crisps, 110
Vinegar Pie, 15

W

White Chocolate Truffles, 170
"White Sauce, How to Make", 14
Whole Wheat Bread, Puddin Hill Store (and Stephens College). 143
Whole Wheat Gems, 140
Whole Wheat Zucchini Bread, 160
Wild Rice Pilaf Soup, 125
Wine Punch, Strawberry, 228
Working Girl's Stew, 224

Y

Yellow Squash Casserole, 71

Z

Zippy Cheese Crackers, 191

Zucchini
   Pud's Vegetable Sauté, 266
   Summer's Bounty Casserole, 162
   Whole Wheat Zucchini Bread, 160
   Zucchini and Swiss Cheese Soup, 123
   Zucchini Crisps, 110

Notes

Notes